Diction for Singers

2nd Edition

Diction for Singers

A concise reference for English, Italian, Latin, German, French, and Spanish pronunciation

Joan Wall
Robert Caldwell
Sheila Allen
Tracy Gavilanes

Copyright 2012 Robert Caldwell

ISBN 978-1934477700

All Rights Reserved. This book or any part thereof may not be reproduced in any form whatsoever without written permission.

Second Edition
Third Printing Jan, 2012
Printed in the United States of America

Online Interactive Listening Labs are available at
www.dictionforsingers.com for Italian, Latin, German, and French.
Or call 855-Diction (toll-free)
Copies of this book may be ordered from:

Diction for Singers. com
Division of Celumbra
PO Box 421
Redmond, WA 98073

www.dictionforsingers.com

Cover Design: Marti Dees
Interior Design: Robert Caldwell, Cindy Praeuner

Excerpts from the English translations of the Roman Missal Copyright 1973
International Committee in the Liturgy, IMC
English Translations of the Kyrie, Sanctus, Benedictus, and Gloria In Excelcis by the International Consultation on English Texts
All Rights Reserved

Contents

Introduction 1
- How to Use This Book 1
- The International Phonetic Alphabet 2
- Vowels 3
- Vowel Diagram 4
- Consonants 5
- Consonant Chart 6
- What is Good Diction 6
- Good Diction is Understandable 7
- Well-Articulated Speech Sounds 7
- Correctly Pronounced Words 8
- Appropriately Linked Words 8
- Appropriately Emphasized Words 8
- Good Diction is Appropriate
  for the Music and Occasion 10
- Good Diction Does Not Call Attention to Itself . 10
- Typical Diction Problems in Singing 11
- Summary 11

English Diction 13
Special Features of English 14
- Syllabification 14
- Stressing 15
  - Strong and Weak Syllables 16
  - Vowel Sounds of English 16
  - Pure Vowels 17
Special Vowels of English 17
  - The vowel [æ] 18
  - The vowel [ʊ] 18
  - The Paired Vowels [ʌ] and [ə] 18
  - The Paired R-Colored Vowels [ɝ] and [ɚ] . . . 19
Diphthongs 21
  - Muffled Consonants 23
  - Incomplete Closure 23
    - The stop-plosive consonants [p] and [b] 23
    - The stop-plosive consonants [t] and [d] 24
    - The Paired Stop-plosive Consonants [k] and [g] . . . 26
  - Incomplete friction 27
    - The paired fricative consonants [f] and [v] . . 27
    - The paired fricative consonants [θ] and [ð] . . 28
    - The Paired Fricative Consonants [s] and [z] . . 29
    - The Paired Fricative Consonants [ʃ] and [ʒ] . . 30
    - The Fricative Consonant [h] 31

Contents

    Incomplete Nasality. 31
        The Nasal Consonant [m].. 32
        The Nasal Consonant [n]. 32
        The Nasal Consonant [ŋ]. 33
  Retroflex Consonant R. **34**
    The Consonant X 35
  Affricative Consonants **36**
  Articulation of Vowels. **36**
    Vowel Substitutions. 36
  Omissions **40**
    Some Common Omissions 40
  Additions **42**
  Pronunciation Considerations **43**
    Misplaced stress. 43
    Elision 44
    Assimilations 44
        Appropriate Assimilation: 44
        Inappropriate Assimilation.. 45
    Linking 46
  Meaningful Emphasis of Words in Sentences . . **47**
    Choosing which word to emphasize 47
    How to emphasize the important word 48
  Final Note **49**

Italian Diction. 51
Chart of Italian Sounds. 52
Special Features of Italian 56
  Syllabification 56
    Single Consonant Between Vowels 56
    Two Consecutive Consonants 56
    Three Consecutive Consonants 57
    Consecutive Vowels. 57
  Stressing. 58
    Rules for Stressing. 59
  Stress and Meaning 60
  Features of Italian Pronunciation 60
  Double Consonants 60
  Special Doubling. 61
  Long and Short Vowels 61
  The Consonant l 62
  The Consonants d, t, and n 62
  The Stop-Plosive Consonants. 63
  The Italian Vowel a 63
  The Italian Vowels e and o 64
  Flipped and Trilled r. 65

Contents

The Two Italian Glides: [j] and [w]	65
Enya [ɲ] and Elya [ʎ]	66
Apocopation	66
Elision	67
Rules for Pronouncing Consecutive Vowels	68
Diphthongs	68
Glides	69
Triphthongs	70
Two Syllables	71
1. Two Strong Vowels	71
2. Two- or Three-Letter Words	71
3. Polysyllabic Words	72
Additional Comments About Consecutive Vowels	73
Singing Consecutive Vowels	73
Glides	73
Diphthongs	73
[maː i]	74
[sɛː i]	74
Triphthongs	74
Two Syllables	74
Connecting Words in Italian	75

Italian Vowels in Detail 76

a	76
e	78
The letter e in Stressed Syllables	78
The Letter e in Unstressed Syllables	79
i	87
The Letter o in Stressed Syllables	93
The Letter o in Unstressed Syllables	93
o	93
u	99

Italian Consonants in Detail 103

b	103
c	103
d	107
f	107
g	108
h	111
j	112
k	112
l	112
m	113
n	114
p	115
q	116
r	116

Contents

s *118*
t *121*
v *122*
w *123*
x *123*
y *123*
z *123*

Latin Diction 125
Chart of Latin Sounds 126
Special Features of Latin 129
Liturgical Latin 129
Syllabification 129
Single Consonant Between Vowels 129
Two Consecutive Consonants 130
Three Consecutive Consonants 131
Consecutive Vowels 131
Stress 132
Two Syllables 132
More Than Two Syllables 132
Elision 133
Latin Vowels 133
Pronouncing Consecutive Vowels 133
Single Vowel Sound 133
Diphthongs 134
Glides 135
Two Syllables 135

Latin Vowels in Detail 137
a *137*
e *138*
i *139*
o *140*
u *140*
y *141*
b *142*
c *142*

Latin Consonants in Detail 142
d *143*
f *144*
g *144*
h *145*
j *145*
k *145*
l *146*
m *146*
n *146*
p *147*
q *148*
r *148*

Contents

s *149*
t *150*
v *151*
w *151*
x *151*
z *153*

The Ordinary of the Mass 154

German Diction 161
Chart of German Sounds 162
Special Features of German 166
Syllabification 166
Single Consonant between Vowels 166
Multiple Consonants 167
Prefixes and Suffixes 168
Compound Words 170
Stress 170
Foreign Origin 172
Unstressed Syllables 173
Distinctive German Vowels 173
The letter a 174
The letter e 174
The letter o 174
General Rules for
Pronouncing German Vowels 175
Close and Long Vowels 176
Vowels That are Close but not Long: 179
Open and Short Vowels 180
Mixed Vowel Sounds 182
Diphthongs 182
The Diphthong [ae] 183
The Diphthong [ao] 183
The Diphthong [ɔø] 183
Distinctive German Consonants 184
The Consonant ch 184
Ichlaut [ç] 184
Achlaut [x] 184
Ichlaut and Achlaut with
Forward and Back Vowels 185
Dental Consonants D, T, N, and L 185
[d] and [t] 185
[n] 185
[l] 185
Voicing and Unvoicing b, d, g 186
Interpretive Use of Consonants 187
Double Consonants 188

Contents

Glottal Stop 189
    Initial position .189
    Medial Position 189
German Vowels in Detail 191
    a *191*
    e *196*
    i *200*
    o *203*
    u *206*
    y *210*
German Consonants in Detail 211
    b *211*
    c *211*
    d *215*
    f *216*
    g *216*
    h *218*
    j *218*
    k *219*
    l *219*
    m *220*
    n *220*
    p *221*
    q *222*
    r *222*
    s *223*
    t *226*
    v *227*
    w *227*
    x *228*
    z *228*
French Diction 229
  Chart of French Sounds 230
  Special Features of French 236
    Syllabification .236
      Single Consonant Between Vowels 237
      Two Consecutive Consonants 237
      Three Consecutive Consonants 238
      Consecutive Vowels. 238
    Stress 239
    Features of French Pronunciation 241
      The Mixed Vowels 241
    Glides 243
    Nasal Vowels 245
    Final mute e 249
    The Pure Vowels [e] and [o]. 250
    Mute and Aspirate h 250
    The Enya 251

Contents

    Pronounced and Silent Consonants 251
    Liaison and Elision. 256
        Rules for Liaison and Elision. 257
French Vowels in Detail 259
        a 259
        e 264
        o 277
        u 282
        y 284
        b 286
French Consonants in Detail 286
        c 287
        d 289
        f 290
        g 290
        h 292
        j 293
        k 293
        l 294
        m 295
        n 296
        p 296
        q 297
        r 298
        s 299
        t 301
        v 302
        w 302
        x 303
        z 304

Spanish Diction 305
Chart of Spanish Sounds. 306
Special Features of Spanish 309
    Syllabification 309
        Single Consonant Between Vowels 309
        Two Consecutive Consonants 309
        Three Consecutive Consonants 310
        Four Consecutive Consonants. 310
        Two Consecutive Vowels 311
    Features of Spanish Pronunciation. 311
        Breath Phrases. 311
    b, v, d, g: Pronunciation and Word Position . . .312
    Lack of Aspiration in [p], [t], [k] 313
    Assimilation of [s] 314
    Assimilation of [n] 315
    Consonants Sounds Not Found in English 316
    Pure, Simple Vowels. 318

Contents

Strong Vowels .... .319
Diphthongs .... .320
Glides .... .320
Stress .... .321
    Predictable Patterns .... .321
    Syllable Length .... .322
    Lack of Secondary Stress .... .323
    Cognate Words .... .323
    Stress Timing .... .324
Vowel Changes Across Word Boundaries .... .324
Triphthongs .... .326
Dialectal Variations .... .327

Spanish Vowels in Detail .... .329
    a .... .329
    e .... .330
    o .... .333
    u .... .334
    y .... .336

Spanish Consonants in Detail .... .337
    b .... .337
    c .... .338
    d .... .339
    f .... .341
    g .... .341
    h .... .343
    j .... .343
    k .... .343
    l .... .344
    m .... .345
    n .... .345
    p .... .346
    q .... .346
    r .... .347
    s .... .348
    t .... .350
    v .... .350
    w .... .350
    x .... .351
    z .... .351

Introducton

Introduction

Online Interactive Listening Labs

Throughout this text, we offer tables of example words that begin with a number, such as LL05.03.89, representing an online listening lab number. These labs are available at www.dictionforsingers.com for Italian, Latin, French, and German. The labs allow you to interact with a vocal coach, recording and playing back your own voice against the vocal coach's voice. For more information, please log on at www.dictionforsingers.com and click on the *help desk*, write to customerservice@dictionforsingers.com, or call 855-Diction (toll-free).

The following chapters will guide you to pronounce the sounds of English, Italian, Latin, French, German, and Spanish. This book does not presume to be an exhaustive account of the phonology of these languages. Rather it is intended as a concise reference for singers who need to pronounce these languages in their libretti or song text. It is especially suited for use as an undergraduate text in diction classes and offers a solid foundation in pronouncing these languages, as well as future use as a standard reference.

Rules of pronunciation are important to learn—to know when to pronounce close *e* [e] and open *e* [ɛ], for instance—because they will help you quickly recognize patterns in the languages. But the rules themselves are not the *most* important thing to emphasize. It is more important to recognize the patterns of each language, to refine your own speech, and to give attention to its effect on your singing.

Keep in mind that language is dynamic: within a language, even within a single native speaker, there are variations of pronunciation. The pronunciations are sometimes so irregular that even dictionaries disagree on them. The rules should not be considered as rigid truths for pronunciation in all cases, all the time: they are best considered merely as *tools* for recognizing recurring patterns in pronunciation.

How to Use This Book

The book is divided into seven chapters: Introduction, English, Italian, Latin, German, French, and Spanish. The Introduction explains how to use the book and presents the symbols of the International Phonetic Alphabet for vowels and consonants. It defines the characteristics of good diction and introduces typical diction problems.

The English chapter explores the typical diction problems, and gives special considerations for singing in English and sounds unique to English. Since the readers of this book are English speaking singers, the material in the English chapter deals more with articulation than pronunciation of English. In the chapters on the foreign languages, the material focuses on pronunciations in each language.

Each subsequent chapter contains four sections. The first section is a single page overview of what to expect when studying the language.

Introduction

2

The second section is an "at-a-glance" chart of sounds. This chart is most helpful as a reminder of a particular pronunciation, or as a comparison of the sounds of one language with the next. For example, the letters *ai* appear in every language, each with a different pronunciation. In French, *mais* is pronounced [mɛ]; in German, *mai* is pronounced [mae]. These different pronunciations of *ai* are easy to see on these charts. Of course, the chart will not provide all that you need to pronounce the language: it is a reference best used after you have studied the language.

The next section, "Special Features," explains the *general tools* you need to pronounce that language. There are concise rules for how to divide a word into syllables, how to determine the syllabic stress, and how to handle the special features of each language. These tools are condensed, streamlined, and organized to facilitate your learning, and you can keep them at hand to pry apart a spelling and extract its pronunciation. For instance, in the chapter on Spanish diction, under the special feature "Assimilation of *n*," you will learn when to pronounce *n* as *m*. Or, in the chapter on Italian diction, under the special feature "Consecutive Vowels," you will learn how to sing triphthongs when the composer has given you only one note for all three vowel sounds.

The final section is a detailed description of each vowel and consonant (and significant groupings of vowels and consonants) for each language. This section serves as a special resource, almost like a concise encyclopedia of letters and their corresponding sounds. For example, under "The letter *e*" in Italian, you will find a full discussion of how to handle final *e*'s, when and where to pronounce *e* as open [ɛ] or close [e] and the exceptions to those rules, with word examples to practice. Use this section as a special reference, a classroom drill, and a source of more detailed information on each letter.

The International Phonetic Alphabet

To obtain more information about the International Phonetic Alphabet and the formation of individual speech sounds, refer to The International Phonetic Alphabet for Singers *by Joan Wall which is a companion book for* Diction for Singers.

The study of the International Phonetic Alphabet is the study of speech sounds. Or, more precisely, it is the study of the symbols which *represent* speech sounds. A phonetic alphabet is an alphabet in which a *single* sound is represented by a *single* symbol. The International Phonetic Alphabet, or IPA, is such an alphabet.

The study of the IPA is valuable to singers because it permits easy and clear communication about the sounds of language. IPA is used in universities, in voice lessons, in diction classes, in textbooks, and in dictionaries as a common language to communicate pronunciation rules of the languages of opera and art song literature.

Introducton

3

Precise Articulation

Successfully pronouncing a language ultimately requires skillful and flexible—sometimes subtle, almost imperceptible—adjustments of your lips, tongue, jaw, and soft palate in order to produce a particular sound. You will discover that each sound is affected by even the smallest movements of your articulators.

On the next few pages, you will find a vowel diagram and a consonant chart. These charts represent individual speech sounds and illustrate the relationship between the sounds and how they are produced.

A singer ultimately is an artist with words. When you become intimate with the production of individual speech sounds, you develop the tools for a singing diction that will shape language into meaningful and beautiful expressions.

> Note: The paragraphs on vowels and consonants have excerpts from *The International Phonetic Alphabet for Singers*.

Vowels

The sound you identify as a vowel sound is the result of the acoustical properties of your vocal tract (mouth, throat, and nose). Each vowel sound has a specific harmonic structure, governed by the position of your lips, jaw, tongue, and soft palate—articulators that change the size and shape of your vocal tract.

Languages have pure vowels and diphthongs. A vowel is called a *pure vowel* when its sound can be sustained without movement of the articulators or any change in the quality of sound until the air flow ceases. A *diphthong* is made up of two vowel sounds that have a result perceived as a single distinguishable language unit.

The placement of vowels on the Vowel Diagram suggests the position of the tongue when articulating various vowels. Vowels are classified as forward, central, and back; as close, mid, and open; and as rounded or unrounded.

You will encounter terms such as open e, *and* close e, *which refer to the relative space between your tongue and the roof of your mouth when you pronounce a vowel. The space is more open for* open e *than* close e, *for instance.*

A diphthong may include a pure vowel and a glide, as in the word use [juz].

The phrase a more rounded sound *generally refers to the sound made when the lips are more rounded. You will hear the French schwa described as a more rounded schwa than English, for instance.*

Introduction

Vowel Diagram

On the Vowel Diagram, the terms *forward, central,* and *back* vowels refer to whether the high point of the arch of the tongue is forward, central or back in the mouth.

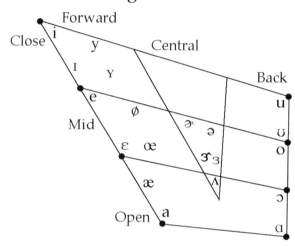

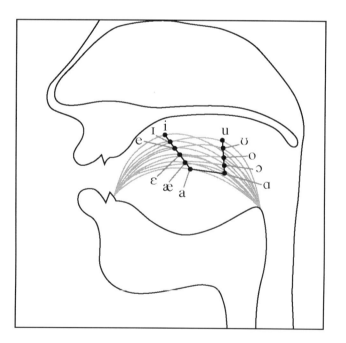

Notice that "forward, central, and back vowels" are language terms and they do not refer to the often used pedagogical terms of "forward and back placement," which refer to specific tone qualities and to the physical location of singing sensations. All vowels can be sung in different tone qualities and with different sensations. For example, a back vowel can be sung with a forward placement of tone.

The terms *close, mid,* and *open* vowels refer to the width of the space between the tongue and the roof of the mouth. The closer the arch of the tongue is to the roof, the more *close* the vowel; the more open the space between the roof of the mouth and tongue and the farther the jaw is dropped, the more *open* the vowel.

Introducton

The terms *rounding* and *unrounding* refer to the position of your lips. Most back vowels use rounded lips, while forward vowels use unrounded lips.

On the Vowel Diagram, neighboring vowels are physically produced similarly. For example, the two vowels [i] and [ɪ], which are next to each other, are produced with minimal differences in the tongue and jaw.

Experiment with the articulation of the two forward vowels [i] and [ɪ] by sustaining an [i] sound and then sliding slowly to [ɪ]. Feel the gradual and tiny movements of your tongue and jaw. The skill of discerning when the [i] has finally opened enough to become [ɪ] is typical of the skills required to successfully learn diction.

Words are made up of syllables; every syllable has a vowel as its core; and syllables are shaped and given meaning by the surrounding consonants. In singing, consonants—not vowels—are the most important element for the communication of the meaning and the expressiveness of a word.

Consonants

A *consonant* is a speech sound that is formed when the articulators interrupt the flow of air through the vocal tract. Precise, well-articulated consonants are necessary to mold language sounds into meaningful words. The study of singing diction centers upon a knowledge of how consonants are articulated.

Consonants are classified according to the place of articulation, the manner of articulation, and the voicing of the consonant. *Place of articulation* refers to the place in the vocal tract where the interruption of the air flow occurs: the lips, teeth, tongue, alveolar ridge, hard palate, soft palate, and glottis. For example, the place of articulation for [p] is at the lips.

Manner of articulation refers to the method of interruption of the air flow, whether by a complete interruption or by a partial interruption in the flow of air. For example, the manner of articulation for [p] is that the air flow is stopped completely before being released suddenly. There are several different manners of articulation: stop-plosive, fricative, nasal, lateral, and glide.

A *stop-plosive* consonant occurs when the air flow is completely prevented from passing through the mouth or nose and then is released suddenly. A *fricative* consonant has the air flow partially interrupted, thus producing a noisy sound. Nasal consonants are those that are produced with air travelling through the nasal passageway. There is

In your vocal studies, you will investigate pure vowel production for good diction, and you will also encounter vowel modification to govern tonal quality and vocal freedom. Vowel modification is the deliberate altering of a vowel sound by slightly opening or closing your mouth, rounding or unrounding your lips, or moving the body of your tongue farther forward or back in your mouth. Learning to use modified vowels is an important and necessary part of your training that takes place in the vocal studio.

Introduction

only one *lateral* consonant in English: the *l* sound as in *lit*; while there are three *glides*: the *r* sound in *red*, the *y* sound in *yet*, and w as in *wear*.

The classification of *voicing* indicates whether the sound has pitch (voiced) or does not have pitch (unvoiced). For example, the consonant sound [g] is voiced, while [k] is unvoiced.

Consonant Chart

	Both Lips		Upper Teeth and Lower Lip		Tongue and Upper Teeth		Tongue and Teeth Ridge		Tongue and Palate		Tongue and Soft Palate		Glottis	
	unv.	v.	unv.	v.	unv.	v.	unv.	v.	unv.	v.	unv.	v.	unv.	v.
Fricative		β	f	v	θ	ð	s	z	ʃ	ç	x	ɣ	h	
Stop-Plosive	p	b					t	d			k	g		
Nasal		m						n ɲ				ŋ		
Lateral								l						
Lateral										ʎ				
Glide		ɥ								r				
Glide	hw	w								j				

Note: Affricatives are a combination of two consonants and are represented by two symbols [tʃ] and [dʒ], or by single symbols [ʧ] and [ʤ].

What is Good Diction

It is possible to confuse good diction with affected speech. In the beginning, precise articulation may sound artificial to you, particularly in your own language of English. However, precise articulation is imperative for the artistry of your performance. The words form the framework for the music and communicate the emotions and thoughts of your songs and arias. Poor speech habits often fail to effectively communicate the meaning and emotional qualities of the words. Sloppy speech may actually distract or even frustrate the audience. Precise diction, rather than being artificial, actually forms the springboard from which you can project your artistry outward to your audience.

Evaluate your singing diction by asking the following:

1) Are the words understandable?

2) Does your diction enhance your performance?

Introducton

Good Diction is Understandable

How many times have you heard American singers singing in English and thought they were singing in a foreign language? Consider how their artistry was diminished, how the lyrics' impact was diluted. Consider why—even though these singers were singing their own language—their words were not understandable.

To sing understandably in any language requires special attention. Keep in mind the following four considerations for understandable language: speech sounds must be well-articulated, words must be correctly pronounced with correct stressing, words must be appropriately linked, and words must be appropriately emphasized for the meaningful flow of the language.

Well-Articulated Speech Sounds

Phonetically, words and sentences are nothing more than a stream of consonants and vowels. In English, you automatically produce a stream of vowels and consonants and your unconscious habits, deletions, and errors automatically stream out as well. In foreign languages, your habits from English linger and often inject themselves into the new language.

As a singer, you need to break down the words of any language into individual consonants and vowels and shape the articulation of each speech sound with precision and energy. Do not unconsciously slur over any sound. Like a loomsmith examining each thread before weaving it into a tapestry, consider the articulation of each sound as essential to the overall impact of your singing.

Primarily, understandable singing requires strong consonants. Otherwise, singing is simply a vocalise without text. Consonants shape the vocal tone from vocalized vowels into vibrant, meaningful, expressive language. Lazy articulation and inattention to diction causes muffled, indistinct words and the beauty and communication of the text is lost.

Understandable singing needs clear vowels. Many singers mis-articulate vowels and diphthongs and their diction becomes muddy and indistinct, instead of teeming with rich, clear, distinct sounds. Mis-articulation habits account for many of the indistinct vowels we hear in singing.

Poor articulation of vowels in singing is often caused by an effort to achieve a more resonant tone. To find their best resonance on a certain pitch, singers will often appropriately modify the articulation of a vowel. Later, on other pitches, where modification is not needed for best resonance, they will inappropriately continue the modified articulation.

Introduction

You may have heard singers who over-modify all of their vowels throughout the range of their voice, causing all of their vowels to sound alike. As a singer, it is imperative that you distinguish between when you are modifying a vowel because of an artistic choice and when you are modifying a vowel because of sloppiness and mis-articulation.

Correctly Pronounced Words

For the words of a language to be understood, you must pronounce them correctly. Pronunciation includes the specific choices of speech sounds and syllabic stresses within a word.

Your study of foreign language diction is structured by this text to help you learn the rules of correct pronunciation of each of the foreign languages. In English, of course, if you have a question about correct pronunciation, you can easily turn to your dictionary.

Correct syllabic stressing is imperative for correct pronunciation and intelligible words. All syllables in a word do not carry the same prominence or importance. There may be a primary stress, a secondary stress, and an unstressed syllable within a single word. Stress is caused by changing some element of sounds: pitch, loudness, timing, and sometimes the vowel. Improper stressing makes a word difficult to understand.

In singing, a challenge arises because your song will have its own stress pattern which may conflict with the stress pattern of a word. You must address this problem if you want your diction to be clearly understood. Learn to create meaningful and dynamic stress and unstressing in your singing.

Different languages use different methods of stressing. This text comments about this important element of diction in the "Special Features" section of each language.

Appropriately Linked Words

In speech, each language has its own method of linking words which must be maintained in singing. Without linking, the language loses its understandability, its flow, and can sound wooden, stilted, and over-articulated. The methods used to connect words are discussed in the "Special Features" sections for each language.

Appropriately Emphasized Words

Understandable diction requires words to have appropriate emphasis for meaningful speech. When a singer articulates syllables and words

Introducton

merely as isolated sounds, without making a connection to ideas, audiences have considerable difficulty understanding the words. This is not only poor interpretation, this is poor diction.

The natural patterns of intensity, inflection, and timing of a language give more importance to certain words and create meaningful speech.

Important words in a language are emphasized by changes in *intensity*. We usually increase loudness for prominent words, although we may do the opposite as when we sing a *subito piano*.

Inflection is the melodic flow in a sentence that creates meaningfulness. In English, you can find the inflection of a sentence by speaking it aloud. Notice your normal spoken inflection. This will be easy for you in English, but as a singer, you must also become sensitive to the patterns of inflection used in other languages.

In your music, of course, the inflection of a sentence is established by the pitches of the melody. Yet, if you first establish the meaningful inflection of the sounds in speech, you can discover that the meanings established by these spoken inflections can easily slip into your singing and the pre-established melody of your song.

Timing in language includes duration and rhythm. The duration of a word often changes with emphasis. Usually the duration of an important word is lengthened. The rhythm of the words in a spoken phrase can be changed to create emphasis. Delaying the pronunciation of an important word, adding small silences, and lengthening the initial consonant of a stressed syllable are ways to emphasize a word.

In music, where duration and rhythm are already established, you can still affect changes in timing. For best understandability, you must maintain the special rhythm of the language even when the musical rhythms do not seem to support it. For example, we know that every eighth note will not carry the same weight: some seem lighter and faster than others. We also use rhythmic devises such as an aggogic accent, pause, tenuto, fermata, rubato, ritardando, and accelerando to stretch or shrink a word or phase.

Use the natural flow of language to emphasize the words in your lyrics. The natural inflections give rise to ideas, meaning, and emotion. Natural inflection can arise only if you know the word-by-word translation of the poem or libretto. A word of caution: do not depend upon a poetic translation or the English words printed in the score under the foreign words. This translation is usually too general and often inaccurate. You must know the *specific* meaning of each word and each sentence.

Read the lyrics aloud as if they are a dramatic monologue, whether the lyrics are in English or in a foreign language. Decide which words

Introduction

should be connected into phrases and which word is most important in each phrase. Emphasize the important word as you read, using the patterns of emphasis appropriate for that language. Emphasize only one important word per phrase. Emphasizing more than one word in a single phrase usually tends to diffuse the meaning.

Sing the song immediately after you have read the lyrics aloud. Transfer the spoken emphasis of the words into your singing.

English and foreign languages use specific patterns of intensity, inflection, and timing to emphasize words. These patterns will be mentioned in each of the chapters.

Good Diction is Appropriate for the Music and Occasion

It is important that your articulations and pronunciations are appropriate for your lyrics, music, and occasion. You will need to know the difference between when you are singing with repetitive personal speech habits and when you are making artistic diction choices. For example, in English, you must know the difference between General American Speech and other non-standard speech patterns, regionalisms, and dialects.

Art songs and opera in English for the national or international stage use *stage diction*—General American Speech—the most accepted prestige dialect in the United States. In concert performances, General American Speech artistically supports the content of the music. If you use non-standard pronunciations, regionalisms, or a dialect while singing this literature, your diction would be inappropriate and would not serve your music.

In other styles of music, however, you may need to use dialect or colloquialisms. The music of Broadway, pop, folk, rock, or jazz will all demand their own diction for stylistic reasons.

Listen to performances by famous singers of each style to determine appropriate diction. Your articulation and pronunciation must enhance the style and content of the poetry, the music, and the occasion, otherwise it will interfere with the performance.

Good Diction Does Not Call Attention to Itself

Your diction is effective when it does not distract the listeners by calling attention to itself. It should unobtrusively support and enhance the music. Diction habits that call attention to themselves include over-articulation, muffled or slurred articulation, mis-pronunciations,

Introducton

regionalisms, and other typical diction problems that you will find discussed in the following section.

Typical Diction Problems in Singing

Singing with good diction requires flexibility—flexibility with your articulators and with your connection to the words, your urges to express your thoughts and emotions. You learn to use your voice in new and different ways to precisely pronounce a word or series of words, particularly in a foreign language, connecting them to the urges to express them in the varied ways demanded by songs and arias. You put your tongue in new positions, protrude your lips until it feels odd, drop your jaw in unexpected places—all while the music pulls you into the larger emotions and musical expressions. The adventure of good diction begins with these new experiences of your articulators and their connection to your artistic expression.

Consequently, the common problems with good diction arise from inflexibility with your articulators, which arise mostly from your speech habits—the ones ingrained in you from childhood and your regional accents. Many of these problems disappear through exploring your articulators, drilling both the full range of movements and combinations and the awareness of the full range of sounds you use. We offer a book that guides you through such a complete process called *The International Phonetic Alphabet for Singers*, the companion title to this book. With enough flexibility, your voice can spring into the continuous shapes to embody the rules of pronunciation.

With requisite flexibility of the articulators, you need to guide your attention to the sounds themselves as part of good diction, noticing specifically where problems are likely to occur. Common problems can be classified under the following headings: muffled consonants, unclear vowels, substitutions, addition and omission of sounds, poor linking of words, and mis-stressing. Since most of these arise from speech habits, you will be guided through these categories as they apply to English. (See English on page 13). They will help you explore your own language habits and develop awareness of the sounds you use. These common problems apply to all languages, so be sure to generalize them, noting the specific solutions for each language as you study its general rules of pronunciation.

Summary

Diction is the playground of the vocal line, so, phrase after phrase, you will apply thousands of distinctions that ultimately shape the sounds, expressions, and intelligibility of your singing. Good diction certainly

Introduction

means greater intelligibility, greater expressiveness, and greater vocal sophistication with your vocal lines. It also means a set of concrete tools you can use with all your work as a vocal artist. Aiming at good diction guides your work at an indispensable level in the multilevel art of singing.

English

English Diction

Phonology is the science of speech sounds.

To study diction, you focus on two aspects of language, articulation and pronunciation. Keeping these two aspects in mind helps you understand and resolve diction problems. With articulation, you focus on shaping individual sounds by moving the articulators. With mis-articulation, you listen for errors in specific speech sounds, which tend to generalize within a person's speech. For example, if you hear a person say *tin* [tɪn] for the word *ten* [tɛn], you hear him misarticulate the phoneme [ɛ]. With your understanding of the International Phonetic Alphabet, you know he is arching his tongue too high and forward for [ɛ]. You will likely hear him make this mis-articulation in similar words (where the letter *e* is followed by a nasal consonant), mis-articulating [ɪ] for [ɛ] in *tempt, when, pen, meant,* and *many*. As another example, you may hear someone articulate [d] at the beginning of *these* (deez) [diz]; in this case, he is misarticulating the *th* [ð]. Again, you would likely hear this error generalize in his speech.

With pronunciation, on the other hand, you focus on selecting sounds and stress among the syllables. With mis-pronunciations, you listen for errors in selecting the appropriate sounds to pronounce a word. Not being habits of the articulators for specific sounds, these errors can typically be resolved by simply consulting a dictionary. A few common mispronunciations (mis-selections of sounds) are:

LL 1.22.01

	incorrect	correct
prescription	[pɚˈskrɪpʃən]	[prəskrɪpʃən]
athletic	[æθəˈlɛtɪk]	[æθlɛtɪk]
walk	[wɔlk]	[wɔk]

Since you already know (subconsciously) a large body of information concerning the individual sounds and sound patterns of English, this chapter is more concerned with articulation than pronunciation. Bearing this in mind, you will not need to learn the phonological system of American English in detail. Rather, you will need to learn the specific issues of articulation that will enhance the musical and artistic expressiveness of your singing.

English
14

Articulation is the process of forming or shaping the individual sounds of a language by the movements of the articulators.

 Special Features of English

In the following sections, you read aloud many sample words that draw your attention to your articulation habits in speech. Since these habits typically transfer into your singing, recognizing them in speech first takes you a long way towards improving your singing diction. With increased sensitivity to your own articulation, you sing with clearer diction, avoid common problems of singing in English, and appreciate how precise articulation results in effective singing diction—all of which helps lead to beautiful singing.

The chapter begins with special topics relevant to singing in English, such as syllabification and strong and weak syllables. It continues with typical articulation problems that interfere with good diction: muffled consonants, unclear vowels, substitutions, omissions, and additions. It provides exercises that focus on each sound and brings into your awareness the problems associated with that sound. Then it points up some pronunciation considerations, such as stressing, elision, assimilation, and linking of words in connected language. The latter part of the chapter discusses the need for meaningful emphasis of words during singing for beautiful and effective diction.

Syllabification

Pronunciation is the selection of sounds and syllabic stress. For example, ea in English can be pronounced in a variety of ways, as in eat, head, preamble. *Selecting the sound to match the spelling is pronunciation.*

While studying this text, we will present articulation rules, which will tell you how to produce a particular sound, and some pronunciation rules, which will tell you which sounds to choose when you look at a spelling.

In songs, we see lyrics usually divided into syllables according to the normal rules for English, but we often speak them differently. We see a consonant as the final sound in a syllable, for instance, but may pronounce it as the initial sound of the next syllable, as in the word *heav-en*, which we pronounce *hea-ven*, putting the consonant *v* with the second syllable.

In the following words, ask yourself whether you pronounce the underlined consonants with the first or second syllable.

LL 1.1.01

heav-en	triump<u>h</u> ant
blu<u>sh</u>-ing	unligh<u>t</u>-ed
flou<u>r</u>-ish	ro<u>s</u>-y

When singing, we must pronounce consonants with the appropriate syllable. In the previous words, we'd have to put them with the second syllable.

English

15

Stressing

Stress is emphasis among the syllables within a word. In any language, stress is critical for correct pronunciations and understandable words. Stress patterns differ significantly across languages, creating the unique nationalistic flavors in songs from different cultures, impacting phrasing and the shape of the melodic line. This is one reason successful translations of lyrics are difficult to achieve.

English speakers usually stress syllables at three levels: primary, secondary and unstressed. Primary syllables carry the strongest stress, secondary syllables, a somewhat lessened stress, and unstressed syllables, the weakest stress.

English speakers usually stress syllables by pronouncing them with increased loudness, raised pitch, and lengthened duration. They unstress syllables by pronouncing the vowel with such a weak intensity and short duration that it actually migrates to another vowel, a neutral schwa [ə] or *ih* [ɪ]. For example, in the word *demon* ['di mən] the unstressed second syllable uses the weak [ə] and not the stressed vowel sound of *oh* [o].

Occasionally an English speaker eliminates an unstressed vowel completely, making the neighboring consonant the core of the syllable, as in the words *little* ['lɪ tl̩] or *Latin* ['læ tn̩]. (The dot under the *l* and *n* indicates the consonant is pronounced as a syllabic *l* or *n*.) When a syllabic consonant is written below a musical note, a singer reinstates the unstressed vowel schwa [ə] and sings the word *little* as ['lɪ təl].

The phenomenon of unstressing is such an important characteristic of English that you must be careful to pronounce the unstressed vowels properly—otherwise the words sound over-articulated and become difficult to understand.

In the following words, pay attention to the underlined unstressed syllables. Observe how you choose to pronounce these vowels with unstressed [ə] or [ɪ].

LL 1.1.02   Read aloud.

pallid	['pæ ləd]	or	['pæ lɪd]
breakfast	['brɛk fəst]	or	['brɛk fɪst]
element	['ɛ lə mənt]	or	['ɛ lɪ mɪnt]
analysis	[ə 'næ lə səs]	or	[ə 'næ lɪ sɪs]
beautiful	['bju tə fəl]	or	['bju tɪ fəl]
lettuce	['lɛ təs]	or	['lɛ tɪs]

The unstressed form of [u] *may become* [ʊ] *in unstressed syllables as in* usual ['ju ʒʊ əl] *or* closure ['kloʊ ʒʊr].

It is not pretentious or artificial to speak distinctly, although it may be unfamiliar at first. Language is music when all the sounds of a word are clearly said. Arthur Lessac likened the individual consonants to different instruments in an orchestra, each one punctuating the stream of vowel sounds with its particular timbre. The analogy is fine — learn to "play" consonants, to sing them artistically, with sensitivity, with expressiveness, with color.

English

16

IPA for Singers *is the companion articulation workbook that will guide you in acquiring these skills with precision.*

Primary stress is indicated in IPA by a diacritical mark ['] before the syllable; secondary stress by a diacritical mark [ˌ] before the syllable, and unstressed by no diacritical mark.

Sometimes the muddiness of a singer's diction—where the vowels all sound alike and the consonants seem all but absent— is due to a well-intended effort to achieve an even tone, a continuous ring in the voice, which is an issue of resonance. However, a consistant resonance can be maintained while you sing a wide range of clear, distinct vowel sounds, and rich, vibrant consonant sounds. As you iron out the wrinkles in your resonance, be careful not to iron out the distinctiveness of the vowels and the richness of the consonants.

Strong and Weak Syllables

English speakers maintain a pattern of strong and weak syllables occuring at fairly regular intervals within sentences. They use secondary stress to help maintain a similar time length between strong stresses.

In the following phrases, observe how the patterns of stress play out. You can identify the primary stress in the underlined vowel; the secondary stress and weak stress by noticing whether the vowel maintains a normal pronunciation or whether it migrates to the neutral [ə] or [ɪ]. For example, in the word *discriminate* [dɪs 'krɪ mə ˌneɪt] you hear primary, secondary, and unstressed syllables.

LL 1.1.03	Read aloud.
The underlined vowels receive primary stress.	
Is space limitless and infinite?	
How do you discriminate the truth of something?	

As a singer, you strive to maintain the natural stress patterns of the language even when the stresses of the music contradict them. When you keep in mind the normal play of the stresses as you sing the melodic line, the meaning and expression in the words have a chance to spring out. You may have heard singers—too focused on tonal quality, perhaps—who neglect the normal stress and rhythm of the words or who give equal, heavy stress on every syllable. As a result, their words are difficult to understand, and the meaning of the text is snuffed out. Instead of the poetry and music fusing together, their diction sounds wooden and they lose the dramatic and artistic believability of the text.

A simple, yet effective method for carrying the stresses and rhythms of the words into the melodic line is to read the poem aloud as a dramatic reading, which will help establish the meaning of the poem, the natural stressing in individual words, and the meaningful emphasis of words within phrases. Immediately after the reading, sing the phrases so that you can transfer the pattern of meaningful stress from speech into song.

Vowel Sounds of English

In chapter I, "Introduction", we define good diction as pronunciation and articulation that produce intelligible words, match the music and occasion, and do not call attention to themselves. We describe the typical problems with good diction: unclear vowels, muffled consonants, substitution of sounds, omission and addition of sounds, and poor stressing within words. Now we look at the individual speech sounds that are special to English. Awareness of them clarifies your diction and helps keep you from carrying them into other languages when singing.

English

17

Pure Vowels

A pure vowel is a sound that can be sustained indefinitely without movement of the articulators. Identifying and producing clear vowel sounds are important skills for good diction. Study the chart of pure English vowels.

The Pure Vowels of English	
Forward Vowels	
[i]	as in *beet*
[ɪ]	as in *bit*
[ɛ]	as in *bet*
[æ]	as in *bat*
Central Vowels	
[ʌ]	as in *bud*
[ə]	as in *about*
[ɝ]	as in *burr*
[ɚ]	as in *butter*
Back Vowels	
[u]	as in *boot*
[ʊ]	as in *book*
[ɔ]	as in *bought*
[ɑ]	as in *box*

This text reflects General American Speech. Kenyon and Knott's A Pronouncing Dictionary of American English *will also distinguish General American Speech pronunciations from regional dialect pronunciations for you.*

Note: The vowel sound bright *ah* [a], which is prominent in other languages, is found in English only in diphthongs [aɪ] as in *might*, and [aʊ] as in *mouse*.

Note: Two other English vowels have a special need in singing: [eɪ] as in *bait*, and [oʊ] as in *boat*. These vowel are consistently pronounced as diphthongs and singers must make specific choices about the timing of singing the two sounds in these diphthongs. See a discussion of diphthongs on page 21.

Special Vowels of English

Of the pure vowels, six are special in English and not found in some other languages we study in this book. Read the words in the following lists to bring these vowel sounds into your awareness.

English

The vowel [æ]:

The vowel sound [æ] is an open forward vowel sound found in such words as *cat*. Sometimes singing this vowel challenges singers because it can spread into an unpleasant, strident sound. Choral directors, for instance, sometimes encourage singers to avoid this vowel sound and substitute bright [a] in its place. However, [æ] is a venerable part of the English language and should be mastered in singing.

LL 1.1.04   Read aloud.

bat
hat
rack
dab
sad
wrap
van
grand
ran

The vowel [ʊ]:

The vowel [ʊ], as in look, good, book, and took is commonly misarticulated by singers. Learn to zero-in precisely on this vowel.

The vowel sound [ʊ] is a neutral vowel found in such words as *book*. While speaking it all the time, American singers are often unaware of [ʊ]. They mistakenly sing [u] instead of [ʊ]. For example, we hear *wood* [wʊd] sung as *wooed* [wud] and *good* [gʊd] sung as [gud]. Practice this vowel to discover its special sound.

LL 1.1.05   Read aloud.

book
could
pull
should
wood
took
stood

The Paired Vowels [ʌ] and [ə]:

The central vowel *uh* [ʌ], as in *bud*, is the most neutral vowel sound in our language. People make this sound when they can't think of what to say. Singers should practice this vowel with vibrant vocal resonance because it can become dull in tone quality.

English

In English, the sound of *uh* [ʌ] occurs only in stressed syllables, while its cousin schwa [ə] occurs in unstressed syllables. The *uh* [ʌ] is usually a more open vowel sound and schwa [ə] a more close vowel sound. While the two vowels have approximately the same sound, the two symbols are used to indicate the important difference in stressing. These two central vowels do not exist at all in the phonological systems of some of the other languages.

In unstressed syllables, any vowel letter can be reduced to schwa [ə]. For example, the letter *o* in *contain* is pronounced [kən 'teɪn], *a* in *central* is ['sɛn trəl], and the first *e* in *pretend* is [prə 'tɛnd].

Read the following words and maintain a consistent resonance in both stressed and unstressed syllables.

Throughout this book, read the examples to bring the point of the exercise into your awareness. Then sing a few of the words. Pick any pitch, any rhythm, and carry the focus of the exercise into an improvised melodic line.

LL 1.1.06   Read aloud.

stressed [ʌ]		unstressed [ə]	
buck	[bʌk]	nickle	['nɪ kəl]
hut	[hʌt]	hammack	['hæ mək]
some	[sʌm]	nasal	['neɪ zəl]
honey	['hʌ nɪ]	problem	['prɑ bləm]
much	[mʌtʃ]	apart	[ə 'pɑrt]

The Paired R-Colored Vowels [ɜ˞] and [ɚ]

The letter *r* is usually pronounced as a brief, gliding consonant sound as in the word *red* [rɛd]. However, when the letter *r* follows a vowel in the same syllable, it often loses its consonant quality and blends with the preceding vowel to become an r-colored vowel sound, as with the letters *ir* in the word *bird*.

Pronounce the r-colored vowel sound with the tip of the tongue retracted and suspended in the center of the mouth. Many English speakers are unaware that this vowel sound exists in our language.

R-colored vowels occur in both stressed and unstressed syllables. In stressed syllables, it is represented by the symbol *ur* [ɜ˞]. Examples are words *bu__rr__*, *mi__rth__*, and *si__r__*. In unstressed syllables, it is represented by the symbol [ɚ], as in *conf__er__*, *moth__er__*, *butt__er__*. The two symbols [ɜ˞] and [ɚ] are similar in sound: they are used to indicate the difference in stressing.

The IPA symbol [ɜ˞] for the r-colored vowel sound in stressed syllables is called by various names: ur, stressed ur, *or* hooked reversed epsilon. *The IPA symbol [ɚ] for the r-colored vowel sound in unstressed syllables is called* unstressed ur *or* hooked schwa.

English

20

The following words can help you become aware of the r-colored vowel sounds in stressed and unstressed syllables.

LL 1.1.07   Read aloud.

Ur [ɜ˞]		Hooked schwa [ɚ]	
in stressed syllables		in unstressed syllables	
fur	[fɜ˞]	ever	[ˈɛ vɚ]
her	[hɜ˞]	scepter	[ˈsɛp tɚ]
sir	[sɜ˞]	sugar	[ˈʃʊ gɚ]
mercy	[ˈmɜ˞ sɪ]	dollar	[ˈdɑ lɚ]
circle	[ˈsɜ˞ kəl]	mirror	[ˈmɪ rɚ]
purple	[ˈpɜ˞ pəl]	humor	[ˈhju mɚ]
dirty	[ˈdɜ˞ tɪ]	pleasure	[ˈplɛ ʒɚ]

The r-colored vowels offer a special challenge in singing. The suspension of the tip of the tongue in the center of the mouth causes a tense vocal production and a tight tone quality that is unpleasant to hear on long, sustained notes. Fortunately, there is a simple two-step solution.

Step One: Simply drop the r-color from your articulation of [ɜ˞] and [ɚ].

You can find the sound by saying the words *mercy* or *bird* with a British or a southern dialect. Just pretend you are Scarlett O'Hara or Rhett Butler in *Gone with the Wind*. When you say the "southern" sound to find r-less *ur* [ɜ], be sure to articulate it with rounded lips. Otherwise, you will be saying *uh* [ʌ] as in *bud* and not r-less *ur* [ɜ] as in *bird*. You also might notice that the sound of r-less *ur* [ɜ] is similar to *ö* [œ] of German.

Step Two: Increase the rounding of your lips slightly just as you release the sound of [ɜ] or [ə].

Notice the IPA for stressed r-less ur [ɜ] does not have the top hook of ur [ɜ˞] and the unstressed symbol is simply schwa [ə].

This lip movement will produce a soft gliding sound that approximates the sound of [r]. Keep the tip of your tongue at the back of your bottom teeth. So you will be singing r-less [ɜ] followed by a soft *r* sound, but not a retroflex *r*. The word *bird* sung in this manner would be transcribed [bɜrd].

These two steps enable the singer to sing the r-colored vowels with freedom of vocalization and with clear diction. An audience will be unaware of the articulation adjustments and they will easily understand your words.

English

Speak and sing the following words using the two step articulation, keeping the tip of your tongue at the back of your bottom teeth when reading and singing the following words. Sustain the stressed and unstressed r-less vowels for two slow counts. Your tongue tip should remain at the back of your bottom teeth.

LL 1.1.08   Sing aloud.

	♩.	♩
dirt	[dɜ -	rt]
earth	[ɜ -	rθ]
learn	[lɜ -	rn]
were	[wɜ -	r]
mirth	[mɜ -	rθ]
worth	[wɜ -	rθ]

LL 1.1.09

	♩.	♩
dollar	['dɑ	lər]
butter	['bʌ	tər]
mirror	['mɪ	rər]

Diphthongs

A *diphthong* is a vowel unit made up of two pure vowels with the acoustic result being perceived as a single unit. There are six diphthongs in English:

LL 1.1.10   Read aloud.

[eɪ]	as in	bay	eight	date	ache
[oʊ]	as in	boat	owe	sew	dough
[aɪ]	as in	high	I	my	lie
[aʊ]	as in	house	bounce	brow	cow
[ɔɪ]	as in	boy	toy	boil	poise
[ju]	as in	use	huge	music	cube

When singing a diphthong under a single note, a singer must decide how much relative duration to give to the two elements of the diphthong. In the following diphthongs, sustain the first vowel with a long duration and then glide to the second vowel just as you release the sound.

English

LL 1.1.11   Sing aloud.

		𝅗𝅮. 𝅘𝅥
[eɪ]	*bait*	[be - - ɪt]
[oʊ]	*boat*	[bo - - ʊt]
[aɪ]	*height*	['ha - - ɪt]
[aʊ]	*house*	['ha - - ʊs]
[ɔɪ]	*boy*	['bɔ - - ɪ]

A common error that many singers make when singing diphthongs is to unknowingly delete the second part of the diphthong. The word *my* [maɪ] becomes *mah* [mɑ]. A diphthong will only be appropriately sung when the second part is articulated. In the song, "Climb Every Mountain" from *The Sound of Music*, for example, you must be sure to fully articulate of [aɪ] in *climb* and [aʊ] in *mountain*.

| Climb every mountain. |
| Till you find your dream. |

For [ju], sing this diphthong differently. Glide quickly past the first sound of [j] and then sing the second vowel for a longer duration.

LL 1.1.12   Sing aloud.

		𝅗𝅮. 𝅘𝅥
[ju]	use	[ju - z]
[ju]	huge	[hju - dʒ]
[ju]	cube	[kju - b]

The use of the diphthong [ju] is in transition in American speech. Following a [d], [n], or [t], both the diphthong and the pure vowel [u] are considered standard pronunciations. In the following words use either [ju] or [u] according to your preference. Consistency is desirable but not mandatory.

LL 1.1.13   Read aloud.

due	tube
dew	tulip
exude	Tuesday
new	numeral
nude	nuclear

English 23

Articulation of Consonants

In the "Introduction" we pointed out the typical diction problems of muffled consonants, substitutions of sounds, and the omissions and addition of sounds. In this section, we investigate individual consonant sounds in English and their special considerations for good singing diction. We discuss precise articulation of consonants and the typical problems that arise with poor singing diction, giving examples of words for you to practice and evaluate your own current habits of articulation.

A consonant is a speech sound produced by stopping or restricting the air flow through the vocal tract by specific movements of the articulators.

The most prevalent problem in singing diction is poor articulation of consonants. Precise consonants—not vowels—are the most important diction element for *intelligibility*. You must learn to sing energized consonants and overcome the tendency to allow your consonants to drop off into indistinct, sluggish, and weak sounds, particularly at the ending of words.

The following exercises will help you become aware of your consonant articulation and the diction concepts that are vital for expressive singing diction.

Muffled Consonants

Muffled, indistinct, and weak consonants result from sluggish articulation. There are three kinds of articulation that lead to muffled consonants: incomplete closure, incomplete friction, and insufficient nasality. We will examine each of these separately. After you have examined your own articulation habits, turn to the words in your songs and evaluate the quality of your consonants in singing. Artistic singing requires more energized consonants than everyday speech.

A stop-plosive consonant is one in which the air flow is completely prevented from passing through the mouth or the nose and then is released suddenly. For full discussion of stop-plosive consonants, see page 26.

Incomplete Closure

The consonants [p b t d k g] are called *stop-plosives*. The name suggests two parts to their articulation. But in reality, there are three parts: first, there is a complete stop (or closure), then a slight build up of air pressure, finally an explosive release of air and sound. When we say a consonant's sound is muffled due to incomplete closure, we mean the articulators are not closed enough to completely stop the air flow and allow for the build up of pressure.

For simplicity, stop-plosive consonants are sometimes called stop consonants.

The following exercises look at each of the stop-plosive consonants.

The stop-plosive consonants [p] and [b].

These paired consonants are produced with the same place and manner of articulation except that [p] is unvoiced; [b] is voiced. For both [p] and

Consonants are called paired consonants when they are produced at the same place in the vocal tract and have the same manner of articulation (such as stop-plosive, fricative, or nasal). The only difference is that one consonant is voiced (has pitch) and the other is unvoiced (does not have pitch.)

[b], close your lips firmly, then feel gentle air pressure build up behind the lips, then release the consonant with a slight burst of air or sound. Be sure that when you close your lips and build up air pressure, there is no excessive tension at the cheeks, lips, or (especially) the throat.

Most people produce clear initial [p] and [b], but often use incomplete closure for the consonants in the medial and final positions. Read the words listed below and evaluate your own articulation. Are you completely closing your lips for the consonants? Can you feel a difference between complete and incomplete closure? Can you feel the slight build up of air behind the lips before you release the air? How different is it to articulate these consonants in the initial, medial, and final positions?

LL 1.1.14   Read aloud.

	[p]	[b]
Initial	peg	beg
	post	boast
Medial	happy	abbey
	puppy	bubble
	rumple	rumble
	helpful	probably
Final	rope	robe
	cap	cab

The stop-plosive consonants [t] **and** [d].

The paired consonants [t] and [d] appear frequently in English words. Speak the word *latter* and then speak *ladder* and feel and hear the difference between the articulation of the unvoiced [t] and the voiced [d].

Be sure the closure is firm for each [t] and [d] consonant in the words listed below. Can you feel the tip of your tongue touch firmly against the teeth ridge for the consonants, particularly in the medial and final positions? Be especially careful to avoid substituting [d] in words with medial [t]. Say *butter*, not *budder*.

LL 1.1.15   Read aloud.

	[t]	[d]
Initial	tie	die
	ton	done

English

Medial	plotting	plodding
	matter	madder
	metal	medal
	center	sender
	latter	ladder
	patted	padded
	shutter	shudder
	little	(not liddle)
	city	(not cidy)
Final	wrote	road
	light	lied

Throughout this book, read the examples to bring the point of the exercise into your awareness. Then sing a few of the words. Pick any pitch, any rhythm, and carry the focus of the exercise into an improvised melodic line.

Practice the words in the first column to articulate a well-formed [t] and transfer that articulation into the words in the second column.

LL 1.1.16   Read aloud.

bit her	bitter
bet her	better
but her	butter
sit he	city
let her	letter
sit he	pretty
lit her	little
it his	it is easy
hit him	hit a ball
what he	what is that
thought high	thought I would

When the final letter *d* follows a voiced consonant, pronounce it as voiced [d]. However, when *d* follows an unvoiced consonant, pronounce it as [t].

LL 1.1.17   Read aloud.

[t]	[d]
clipped	hummed
kicked	sunned
laughed	banged
pronounced	rolled

English

The letter g is occasionally silent as in these common words: diaphragm, sign, resign, phlegm, designer.

The Paired Stop-plosive Consonants [k] and [g].

For [k] and [g], the back of your tongue must firmly press against the soft palate. Observe whether you can feel the back of your tongue touch the soft palate and completely close to stop the flow of air as you say unvoiced [k] and voiced [g]. Feel the build up of air pressure and the subsequent release as you articulate the consonant.

LL 1.1.18   Compare and contrast.

	Initial [k]	[g]
Initial	kit	give
	cane	gain
Medial	racket	ragged
	wicks	wigs
Final	luck	lug
	tack	tag

In some combinations of sounds, singers sometimes use incomplete closure. The following words end with the combinations of consonants [sk], [skt], and [sks]. Be sure to use firm closure on the [k] sound. Do not omit it!

LL 1.1.19   Read aloud.

asked	banks	desks	risks
whisk	disc	husks	tasks

The sound of [k] in these common words must be fully stopped. Feel your articulation.

LL 1.1.20   Read aloud.

acceptable	chicken
aching	accede
talkative	working
succulent	lucky

You have probably heard people fail to completely stop the [g] in words when it should have full closure. Listen for [g] in these words. Feel the closure.

LL 1.1.21   Read aloud.

ignition
cognition
recognize

English

Incomplete friction

A second reason for muffled consonants is incomplete friction while producing fricative consonants [f v θ ð s z ʃ ʒ h]. To produce these consonants, your mouth cavity is narrowed so that the air flow is restricted, except for *h,* where the restriction is at the glottis. If the mouth cavity is not narrowed enough or if the sound is not maintained for enough duration, the consonant will sound indistinct, or will almost sound like a stop.

Read through the following exercises and explore the sounds of these fricative consonants. Learn to savor them, enrich them, draw out the special sound qualities inherent in each: they can add tremendous vibrancy and expressiveness to your diction.

Fricatives are also called continuants *because they can be sustained or continued.*

The paired fricative consonants [f] and [v].

Be sure that you give sufficient duration to the unvoiced [f] and voiced [v] sounds in your singing, particularly when they are in the final position of a word. You will know whether you have sufficient duration when the consonant has a fricative sound and is not a stop. Feel a gentle, buzzy vibration on your lower lip. You will feel a stronger vibration as you articulate the voiced [v] than the unvoiced [f]. Feel and listen for the vibration. In the following exercise, sustain each consonant for four slow counts. Exaggerate the duration of the consonant to explore its fricative sound.

```
1_____2_____3_____4_____
[f]_____
[v]_____
```

LL 1.1.22   Compare and contrast.

	[f]	[v]
Initial	fail	vail
	fat	vat
Medial	refer	reveal
	leafer	lever
	coffer	cover
	after	everyone
	muffler	gravestone
	graphmaker	driveway
Final	half	have
	proof	prove
	safe	save

English

The paired fricative consonants [θ] and [ð].

Pay attention to your articulation of unvoiced *th* [θ] as in *thin* and voiced *th* [ð] as in *there*. Be sure to pronounce the fricative consonants with sufficient duration. Slip the rim of the tongue between the upper and lower front teeth. Neither force the breath nor bite down on the tongue. On the voiced *th* [ð], as in the word *these*, feel a tingling vibration on the tip of your tongue outside of the teeth.

In the following examples sustain each consonant sound for four slow counts.

1 2 3 4
[θ]_____ as in *thin*
[ð]_____ as in *these*

What are your articulation habits with [θ] and [ð]? Do you use sufficient friction? Be sure you give adequate duration the fricative sounds on the following words. Compare and contrast.

	[θ]	[ð]
Initial	think	them
	third	these
Medial	faithful	clothes (not close)
	method	weather
	ethics	rather
	ethereal	loathesome
	birthday	birthed
	northwind	smoothed
Final	loath	loathe
	sheath	sheathe
	bath	bathe

The fricative [ð] must not sound like a stop consonant. Definitely do not substitute a [d] for [ð], as you hear occasionally in dialects. To avoid saying [d], be sure the tip of your tongue slips between your teeth and let the air flow out to produce the fricative sound.

LL 1.1.23   Compare and contrast.

	[d]	[ð]
Initial	dare	there
	day	they
	dine	thine
	dough	though

English

Note: If your tongue feels thick and awkward as you pronounce the fricative [ð], the articulation is probably unfamiliar. Give yourself time and repetition to get the tongue to move smoothly and fluidly.

Be sure to give fricative [ð] sufficient duration after another consonant.

In the sentence, *Can this be so!*, feel the gentle movement of the tip of the tongue as it glides from behind the upper teeth for the [n] to the [ð].

LL 1.1.24 Read aloud.

Can this be so!
Just think.
Fast thinking.
Pick the winner!

Pronounce the *th* with precision in the consonant clusters in the following examples.

Read aloud.

[θ]	[ð]
earth's	soothes
anthem	clothed
fifth	truths
youth's	breathes
anesthetic	mouthed
width	rhythm

The Paired Fricative Consonants [s] and [z].

To avoid muffled diction, articulate the consonants unvoiced [s] and voiced [z] cleanly and clearly.

Compare and contrast [s] and [z] as you complete the following exercises. Sustain each sound for four slow counts in the following example.

LL 1.1.25

1____2____3____4____
[s]_____
[z]_____

Some people misarticulate s and z by mis-placement of the tongue. The result is called a lisp. *Additional attention must be given to these sounds if you have a lisp.*

LL 1.1.26   Compare and contrast.

	[s]	[z]
Initial	sip	zip
	sink	zinc
Medial	lacy	lazy
	misty	music
	pencil	puzzle
Final	pass	pans
	a piece	appease
	this	these

[ts] and [dz] are comprised of two consonants—a stop and a fricative—that combine in some words. Read these words carefully articulating these two sounds.

LL 1.1.27   Compare and contrast.

[ts]	[dz]
bets	beads
artists	bends
cakes	scalds
thefts	holds
limits	demands

The Paired Fricative Consonants [ʃ] and [ʒ].

Avoid muffled diction by articulating unvoiced [ʃ] as in *she* and voiced [ʒ] as in *vision* with sufficient friction and duration. Sustain each sound for four slow counts in the following example.

LL 1.1.28

1	2	3	4
[ʃ]			
[ʒ]			

LL 1.1.29   Read aloud.

	[ʃ]	[ʒ]
Initial	sure	
	sheep	
Medial	assure	azure
	ocean	delusion

There is no initial [ʒ] in English.

English

Final	cash	beige
	mash	mirage
	gosh	garage

The Fricative Consonant [h].

The consonant *h* is an aspirate sound in English. It needs to be heard, but not over-aspirated. Be sure that you use suitable friction and to pronounce *h* clearly in the following phrases.

LL 1.1.30   Read aloud.

	[h]	
Initial	half	behold
	head	hear

LL 1.1.31   Read aloud.

That's his home.
We forgave her.
How could he do it?
I told him.

Speak the following lists of words and observe how *h* is sometimes pronounced, sometimes silent.

LL 1.1.32   Read aloud.

Pronounced h	Silent h
exhale	prohibition
unholy	exhibit
inhuman	exhaust
mishap	exhilarate

Incomplete Nasality

There are three nasal consonants in English: [m], [n], and *ng* [ŋ]. Nasal consonants are defined as those produced with air flowing through the nasal passages. Singers hum on any of the nasal consonants.

When you sing with a well articulated nasal consonant, your diction will be come more understandable and expressive. If you sing these consonants with incomplete duration or nasalization, you will sound muffled, as though you've got a cold in your head, and your diction will suffer.

A special feature of English is that when a nasal consonant is located in a word before another consonant or before a silence (as before a pause at the end of a phrase or sentence), it is pronounced with a longer duration than when it is before a vowel.

The Nasal Consonant [m].

In the following words, each *m* is positioned before a consonant or silence. Take the opportunity to sustain the long [m]. Exaggerate the duration; feel as though you are humming the [m] as you speak. Let the [m] sing out in your speech.

LL 1.1.33   Read aloud.

timber	hem	amplify	come through
farmed	comfort	thimble	I'm leaving
sum	slam	home	climb fast
rumble	hamster	clamped	name four

In speech, *m* is not lengthened before an audible vowel (as in the words *me, marry, clamour*.) Read aloud these words using a brief [m] before a vowel sound. Notice how you develop a different speech rhythm than in the previous list.

LL 1.1.34

may	mock
more	my
missed	man
woman	Amelia

In the following sentence, give long duration to each underlined *m*. Give the lengthened sound to *m* before a consonant sound as in *times* [taɪmz]; the silent *e* in the spelling of *times* does not affect the rhythm of [m]. However, an *m* is not lengthened before the audible vowel (as in the word *me*).

LL 1.1.35   Read aloud.

Sometimes it causes me to tremble, tremble, tremble

(text from "Were You There," a spiritual)

The word *tremmmmble* sung with a long [m] has quite a different rhythm from *treeeeemble* sung with a long vowel. You may notice how lengthening [m] results in a shorter duration of the vowel—a pattern of duration typical of the rhythmical flow of English speech. Maintaining this pattern in songs is important for expressive and intelligible singing diction.

The Nasal Consonant [n].

Notice how you articulate the consonant *n*. Does the tip of your tongue lightly touch the boundary between the teeth ridge and the upper teeth? It should. If it doesn't, notice what it feels like to put it there. Make a gentle humming sound and feel the vibration at the tip of the tongue.

In English, the sound of [n]—like [m]—has longer duration before a consonants or a *silence* than it does before a vowel. Bring the rhythm of this articulation into your awareness by vibrating each underlined [n] fully in the following example.

LL 1.1.36 Read aloud.

concave	infantile	confuse	unprovoked
sound	mention	canyon	unrestrained
accident	conflict	dean	dent
cone	win	spin	plan

Notice the natural rhythm of these words in which *n* is followed by a vowel; the duration of the sound of [n] is quick. When a word has *nn* before a vowel (as in *winner*), say a single brief [n] sound.

LL 1.1.37 Read aloud.

honey	money	many	penny
any	bunny	not	net
sunny	tunnel	winner	loner

The Nasal Consonant [ŋ].

Pronounce the sound of *ng* [ŋ] as in *long* or *sing*. Be sure to use a firm closure between the back of your tongue and the soft palate. Allow the final [ŋ] to vibrate with good duration.

LL 1.1.38 Read aloud.

sing	thing	throng	fling
gong	dung	hung	long
ching	song	ring	king
tongue	range	young	swing

Notice that these words with the sound [ŋ] do not include a [g] sound. *Hang* is [hæŋ] not [hæŋg] and *banging* is [ˈbæŋ ɪŋ], not [ˈbæŋg ɪŋ].

LL 1.1.39 Read aloud.

| banging | singing | flinging | swinging |
| springing | clinging | longing | hanger |

However, there are some words in English that are correctly pronounced with a [g] sound after [ŋ]. When in doubt about the pronunciation, refer to a dictionary.

LL 1.1.40 Read aloud.

| finger | [ˈfɪŋ gər] | stronger | [ˈstrɔŋ gər] |
| language | [ˈlæŋ gwɪʤ] | angle | [ˈæŋ gəl] |

English

single	['sɪŋ gəl]	England	['ɪŋ glənd]
longer	['lɔŋ gər]	linger	['lɪŋ gər]

Some speakers incorrectly use what may be called an *ng* click, that is, they put a [g] or [k] at word boundaries. Listen carefully to your articulation as you read these words aloud. Use firm closure for [ŋ] and move cleanly to the next sound without an *ng* click.

LL 1.1.41   Read aloud.

a long way
hang it up
the thing is
the song is

The following words are correctly pronounced with a [k] sound after *ng* [ŋ].

LL 1.1.42   Read aloud.

bank	[bæŋk]	banker	['bæŋ kər]
Lincoln	['lɪŋ kən]	drunk	[drʌŋk]
wrinkle	['wrɪŋ kəl]	drunkard	['drʌŋ kərd]
think	[θɪŋk]	ankle	['æŋ kəl]

Retroflex Consonant R

The IPA offers a separate symbol for the retroflex r, trilled r, and flipped r. For simplicity in transcribing English and because the consonant r in English is always a retroflex r, this text will use [r] to indicate retroflex r.

The English retroflex *r* does not exist in the other languages presented in this text. Retroflex means turned backward, and in this case, the tip of the tongue is curled up toward the hard palate, backward on itself. The tongue tip is suspended in the center of the mouth, not making contact with any part of the roof of the mouth as it would in other languages where the *r* is flipped or trilled.

When *r* is initial in a word or syllable, it is a brief, gliding consonant sound. Sing it just like you speak it.

Stressed r-less ur is also called reversed epsilon.

Under some circumstances, as when singing in a large hall where intelligibility requires greater energy of consonants, you might choose to pronounce *r* as a flipped or even trilled *r*, usually in words with an initial consonant plus *r* (such as *frothy*).

In the following words give attention to your pronunciation of [r] when initial in word or syllable or following initial consonant in word or syllable.

English

LL 1.1.43   Read aloud.

Initial [r]	Initial Consonants plus [r]	Medial [r] beginning a syllable
red	brought	very
rose	bring	direct
write	shrill	arrive
rich	grew	weary

When the letter *r* is final in a word, you can pronounce the *r* as a schwa [ə] or schwa followed by a soft r [ər] to avoid the sound of the tense retroflex *r*.

Read this list of words with final *r*. Slightly round your lips as you pronounce [ə] or [ər].

LL 1.1.44

dear	par	where	four
tar	bar	bear	mir

At times, when *r* follows a vowel in the same syllable, it joins the vowel to become an r-colored vowel, [ɝ] or [ɚ]. (See page 19 for a full discussion of the r-colored vowel sounds.)

The Consonant X

The letter *x* in English has two pronunciations, unvoiced [ks] and voiced [gz], both of which include a stop-plosive and a fricative sound. The pronunciation depends upon its position in the word and its neighboring letters. If you are unsure about its pronunciation, check a dictionary.

When pronouncing *x*, be sure to give the [k] and [g] full closure.

In the following words pronounce the letter *x* as [ks].

LL 1.1.45   Read aloud.

extra	expect	exhale	expense
excite	experiment	expel	exclaim
fox	box	ax	tax
exit	exodus	exercise	exorable

In these words, pronounce the letter *x* as [gz].

LL 1.1.46   Read aloud.

example	exactly	exhaust	exhilarate
exalt	exotic	exhume	examination

These rules describe how the letter x's pronunciation is dependent upon its position in the word and its neighboring letters. You will meet similar rules later in the book as you study other languages. You will see them written in this pattern: "When this letter is in this position, pronounce it this way; when in that position, pronounce it that way". Each language will have similarities and differences for individual letters and their position in the word. The chart of sounds at the beginning of each chapter will help you keep the languages straight.

English

Affricative Consonants

Affricative consonants combine the articulation of two consonant sounds into a single speech unit. They are also called *combination consonants*. English has two affricatives, both of which are composed of a stop-plosive and a fricative consonant: unvoiced [tʃ] as in *chin* and voiced [dʒ] as in *gin* or *jet*.

When singing, be sure to stop fully before the fricative part of the consonant.

LL 1.1.47   Read aloud.

	[tʃ]	[dʒ]
Initial	chose	jewel
	champ	jam
Medial	matches	angina
	ditches	pidgeon
Final	breech	bridge
	hutch	hedge

Articulation of Vowels

This section continues to explore typical diction challenges in English related to mis-articulation of vowels. The comments and exercises that follow in this section cover a range of common problems with vowels and give a good view of typical problems experienced by many singers.

Vowel Substitutions

Sometimes vowel mis-articulations are simply substitutions of sound which occur by an habitual misuse of one or more of the articulators. For example, if a singer's tongue is habitually too far forward in the mouth for *eh* [ɛ] when it is before [n], *pen* will sound like *pin*, and *den* will sound like *din*. However, that same singer may have little or no difficulty articulating [ɛ] before [d] or [t], as in *bed* or *bet*. Substitutions can be one specific speech sound in an individual's speech, or part of a regional dialect: for instance, Texans may substitute [ɔ] for [a], saying *stawr* for *star*.

Any sequence of sounds may trigger habitual misuse of one or more of the articulators, which results in substitutions. Here are general ways to avoid substituting vowels.

English

1. Listen carefully to the vowel sounds you are speaking or singing.

    Are the vowels you think you are singing really the ones you are singing? Record your singing and listen carefully to your words. Beware of slipping unknowingly to an adjoining vowel on the vowel chart: singing [ɪ] instead of [ɛ], or [u] instead of [ʊ]. (See " Pure Vowels" on page 17.)

2. Notice how the position of a vowel within a word often influences its sound.

    In particular, avoid nasalizing a vowel when it occurs before a nasal consonant.

3. Fully articulate diphthongs.

    Do not substitute pure vowels for diphthongs by eliminating the final glide.

4. Be sensitive to your own speech habits.

    Avoid transferring the habitual patterns of articulations that are part of your casual speech or regional dialect into your singing.

A few common substitution patterns are listed below. They offer an introduction to the many substitutions that American singers use. Read the lists of words aloud to hear your speaking habits and listen carefully to correct any substitution problems. If you identify vowel substitutions in your speech habits, be careful not to use them in your songs.

Singers frequently confuse the articulation of [u] and [ʊ].

When the lips are too lax and unrounded, [u] becomes [ʊ] and *wooed* sound like *would*. When the lips are too tense, [ʊ] becomes [u], and the word *good* becomes *gooed*.

Read aloud.

[u]	[ʊ]
cooed	could
fool	full
who'd	hood
pool	pull

Sing the word *good* with a clear [ʊ] as in: *Good night, my someone; good night, my love.*

English

Another common problem is the substitution of [ɪ], [eɪ], or [æ] for [ɛ].

When the arch of your tongue is too high, [ɛ] migrates to [ɪ] and get sounds like *git*. Also with the tongue too high [ɛ] migrates to [eɪ] and *head* sounds like *haid*. When the arch of the tongue is too low and back, [ɛ] migrates to [æ] and *guess* sounds like *gas*. Read these lists to contrast words with similar vowels and thereby identify your articulation of [ɛ].

LL 1.1.48 Read aloud.

[ɪ]	[ɛ]
pin	pen
tin	ten
him	hem
mint	meant
wind	wend

LL 1.1.49 Read aloud.

[eɪ]	[ɛ]
aid	egg
hate	head
bait	bet
mate	measure
plate	pleasure

LL 1.1.50 Read aloud.

[ɛ]	[æ]
guess	gas
blast	blessed

Many singers substitute [a] with [ɔ].

When the lips are too rounded [a] becomes [ɔ] and *stark* sounds like *stork*. In the following words, use [a] and give special attention to the words with [r] following [a].

LL 1.1.51 Read aloud.

[a]
star
ardor
ark
arm
park
charm

English

palm
calm
pardon

Sometimes singers substitute [ʊ] for [ʌ].

> When the jaw fails to drop and your mouth is too closed, [ʌ] becomes [ʊ] and love [lʌv] sounds like [lʊv].

LL 1.1.52   Read aloud.

[ʌ]	[ʊ]
love	look
stud	stood
hud	hood

Some singers nasalize vowels occurring before a nasal consonant.

> When the soft palate gets lazy and drops before nasal consonants, vowels become nasalized. In the list below, match the non-nasal vowel in the first column with the same vowel before a nasal consonant in the second column. None of the vowels in the second column should have a nasal quality.

LL 1.1.53   Read aloud.

pat	pant
grab	grand
fat	fanned
sad	sand
at	ant
pit	pin
pet	pen
mitt	mint
met	meant
paid	pained
late	lain

Singers sometimes fail to sing the glide in diphthongs.

> Many singers substitute a pure vowel for a diphthong by eliminating the final glide. For example: if you substitute [a] for [aɪ] in *plight* the word becomes *plot*. Listen carefully to words with diphthongs to articulate the final glides [aɪ], [ɔɪ], and [aʊ]. (See page 22 for discussion of [ju]).

English

LL 1.1.54   Read aloud.

pure vowel	diphthong
[a]	[aɪ]
sod	sighed
ma	mine
bah	buy
It's a terrible *plot*	It's a terrible *plight*
He is my *God*	He is my *guide*
She wants a *rod*	She wants a *ride*
[ɔ]	[ɔɪ]
It's a *ball*	It's a *boil*
call	coil
tall	toil
[a]	[aʊ]
pot	power
cop	cower
follow	foul

Omissions

A singer may occasionally omit sounds that should be pronounced in standard speech. Often these omissions are mispronunciations that can be corrected by consulting a dictionary, such as *A Pronouncing Dictionary of American English* (Kenyon and Knott, Merriam Webster).

At other times, however, the omitted sounds are habitual misarticulations, which tend to follow common patterns. The patterns fall into regional dialects and colloquial speech. Omissions might be appropriate in folk songs and other songs that are written for dialects, but are not appropriate in formal poetry and concert literature. Use the following lists of words to investigate your speech habits.

Some Common Omissions

Pronounce [k] in these words using firm closure.

LL 1.1.55   Read aloud.

ask (not ax)	asked (not axed)
disc (not diss)	discs
task	tasks
basked	adjective
act	contact
reject	liked

English

Pronounce [t] and [ts] sounds in these words using firm closure.

LL 1.1.56 Read aloud.

kept (not kep')	tourists (not touriss)
tact (not tac')	tests
texts	lasts

Pronounce final stop-plosive consonants with firm closure.

LL 1.1.57 Read aloud.

clasp (not class)
bulb
bland
Give me your hand (not han')

Pronounce "th" sounds [θ] and [ð] with complete fricative articulation.

LL 1.1.58 Read aloud.

unvoiced [θ]	voiced [ð]
myths (not miss)	writhes
fifths	rhythm
earth's	clothed
depths	breathed

What about these sentences? Do you say all these sounds?

LL 1.1.59 Read aloud.

I'm going to (not Ah'm gonna nor Ah'm a nuh)
Give me (not Gimme)
Help me (not Hep' me)

Pronounce initial consonant sounds. In rapid informal speech, the pronouns *he, him, his, her,* and *them* often those their initial consonant sounds.

LL 1.1.60 Read aloud.

Give it to him. (not Give it to 'im)
Does he know? (not Does 'e know?)
I saw her yesterday. (not I saw 'er yesterday)

Pronounce *have* as [hæv]. When *have* is used as an auxiliary verb in informal language, it is often pronounced [əv].

LL 1.1.61 Read aloud.

I could have gone. (not I could 'uv gone)
We should have told her. (not We should 'uv told 'er)

English

Pronounce the word *of* as [ʌf] or [əf]. When *of* occurs in a prepositional phrase, it is often unstressed and spoken as [ɑ]. Sing it with its full vowel identify.

LL 1.1.62   Read aloud.

cup of coffee (not cuppa coffee)
lots of time (not lots a time)

Additions

Some singers add sounds that should not be there. The following lists include examples. Listen carefully to your speech. Do you add any of these sounds?

Adding [r]: In some dialects, an [r] is added to a vowel that occurs at the end of a syllable, even within a word, or between words.

LL 1.1.63   Read aloud.

wash	not warsh
idea	not idear
piano	not pianer
banana	not bananer
Louisiana and Arkansas	not Louisianar and Arkansas

Adding a syllable: Some singers add a syllable to mispronounce these two common words.

LL 1.1.64   Read aloud.

Correct		With added syllable	
accompanist	[ə ˈkʌm pa nɪst]	ac-com-pa-ni-ist	[ə ˈkʌm pa ni ɪst]
larynx	[ˈlæ rɪŋks]	la-ruh-nicks	[ˈlæ rə nɪŋks]

Adding [schwa]: Sometimes speakers add schwas [ə] preceding an [r] or [l].

LL 1.1.65   Read aloud.

meal	[mil]	not	[ˈmi əl]
sail	[seɪl]	not	[ˈseɪ əl]
fierce	[fɪrs]	not	[ˈfɪ ərs]

Pronouncing silent letters: In these words the letter *l* is silent. Be careful not to add [l].

LL 1.1.66   Read aloud.

walk	[wɔk]	not	[wɔlk]
talk	[tɔk]	not	[tɔlk]

English

calm	[kɑm]	not	[kɑlm]
psalm	[sɑm]	not	[sɑlm]

Adding [j] between words: Do you inadvertently add [j] between words that end and begin with a vowel?

LL 1.1.67   Read aloud.

I am	not I yam

Pronunciation Considerations

Sadly—for our lives would be easier if the opposite were true—English spelling generally does not reflect English pronunciation. The letter *i* may be pronounced in various ways: *might, liter, mitt,* and *nation*. Considerations for pronunciations in this section include syllabic stressing, elision, assimilations, and linking of words in connected speech.

You may not be able to determine preferred, standard pronunciation by looking at a word or just going from your own experience. Your diction may be based on spotty learning, on a regional dialect, and colloquialisms. In order to decide about incorrect or non-standard pronunciations, you must listen to educated speakers or, better yet, consult a dictionary. A useful dictionary for singer is the Merriam-Webster's *A Pronouncing Dictionary of American English* by Kenyon and Knott that gives the IPA transcription for the most standard pronunciation and also some regional pronunciations for each word.

Misplaced stress

In any language, the manner of handling syllabic stress is an element of diction that is critical for correct pronunciation and understandable words. In some languages, stress patterns are regular. In French, for example, stress is put on the syllable at the end of a word or phrase. This regularity makes the rhythmic pattern fairly predictable. In English, on the other hand, the position of primary and secondary stressing and unstressing in words is quite variable.

The most unique element of syllabic stress in English is the phenomenon of unstressing. In an unstressed syllable, speakers weaken the vowel, change it to a neutral sound, and shorten its duration. For a full discussion of stressing and unstressing, see page 15.

Elision

You will find that the pronunciation of certain sounds can be modified by the surrounding sounds when they are linked together. Under several common circumstances, a sound in a word may disappear. This phenomenon of dropping of a sound is called *elision*. We recognize elision in the word *don't* where the vowel *o* in the word *not* disappears.

In conversational speech, an unstressed vowel frequently disappears when it precedes the letter *l* or *n*; the consonant will be sustained and form a syllable without a vowel. When such a syllabic consonant occurs, it is indicated in IPA with a dot under the consonant. For example: the word *middle* is transcribed as ['mɪ dl̩].

When a syllabic consonant occurs under note in the music, you will need to reinstate the unstressed vowel with the sound of schwa [ə]. In the right column in the following example, sing both syllables for the duration of a slow half note.

LL 1.1.68

Read aloud.		Sing aloud in two half notes.	
sudden	['sʌ dn̩]	sud - - den	['sʌ dən]
fiddle	['fɪ dl̩]	fid - - dle	['fɪ dəl]
little	['lɪ tl̩]	lit - - tle	['lɪ təl]

Assimilations

In some instances, a neighboring sound alters a sound, resulting in assimilation. The following words are correctly spoken and sung with assimilation.

Appropriate Assimilation:

When *t* and *u* combine, they produce [tʃu] as in *picture* ['pɪk tʃʊr] or ['pɪk tʃər], not ['pɪk tʊr].

LL 1.1.69   Read aloud.

literature
mature
situation
virtue
fortune
statue

When *d* and *u* combine, they produce [dʒu] as in *education* [ˌɛdʒ u 'keɪ ʃən] or [ˌɛ dʒə 'keɪ ʃən], not [ˌɛd ju 'keɪ ʃən].

LL 1.1.70   Read aloud.

graduation
gradual

English

individual
residual

When *s* and *u* combine, they produce [ʃʊ] as in *tissue* ['tɪ ʃʊ], not ['tɪ sju].

LL 1.1.71 Read aloud.

issue
tissue

Linking words assists legato singing and expressive, understandable diction.

Inappropriate Assimilation.

Although the above assimilations are appropriate, the following assimilations at word boundaries are considered sloppy and inappropriate when singing English. The consonants that are most easily influenced by neighboring sounds are *t, d, s, z,* and *n*. Instances such as the following should be avoided.

When *t* and *y* combine, they produce [tj] as in *last year* [læst jir] not *last cheer*.

LL 1.1.72 Read aloud.

don't you
that you

When *d* and *y* combine, they produce [dj] as in *would you* [wʊd ju] not *would chu*.

LL 1.1.73 Read aloud.

could you
behind you

When *s* and *y* combine, they produce [sj] as in *miss you* [mɪs ju] not *miss shoe*.

LL 1.1.74 Read aloud.

lifts you
bless you

Linking

The previous paragraphs have been concerned with individual sounds. Now we focus on groups of sounds and the way that words are linked for meaningful speech. A characteristic of connected speech is that final word sounds usually carry over to the next syllable of the following word. This linking feature, far from being unacceptable, is recommended.

English

Linking to initial vowels: Link final consonants to initial vowels of the next word.

LL 1.1.75   Read aloud.

| punched it |
| use imagination |

Do not link words if the meaning is obscured. *Tim ate it* should not sound like *Tim mated*.

Repeated consonants: Link repeated consonants across word boundaries. Notice that the doubled consonants lengthen in duration.

LL 1.1.76   Read aloud.

keep pace	hen notes
make candy	good deal
this smile	that time
small lie	Bob builds
big girl	Ben noticed

Related stop-plosives: Link and blend related stop plosives. For example, in the words *drop behind*, the letter *p* is followed by *b*. To link these words, close the air stream but do not explode the *p* as you would in the single word *drop*. Instead, on the closure move to *b* and explode only the second stop-plosive.

LL 1.1.77   Read aloud.

| They began to drop behind in their work. |
| The performance was quite good. |
| It is a great day! |
| We had to go immediately. |

Some consonant combinations must be considered individually by allowing for the particular combination and the expressive needs of the words and music, the tempo, the size of the hall and the needs for projection, and the style of the music. Some sounds might be articulated more or less fully in singing. However, you must be careful that your choice to pronounce both consonants does not result in heavy over-articulation. Much of this will be your personal choice.

These paired words contain consonant combinations that you must consider individually. Speak and sing these words aloud, once in a fast tempo, then in a slow tempo with maximum projection. What are your personal choices?

English

LL 1.1.78 Read and sing aloud.

cast them	not thin	Ned scolded
ask for	grasp my	not fastened

Meaningful Emphasis of Words in Sentences

Just as some syllables have more prominence than others within a word, so also do some words have more prominence than others within a sentence. We give these words extra importance or attention through emphasis. For clarity, we often refer to "stressed" syllables and "emphasized" words.

Choosing which word to emphasize

In the following phrases, explore shifts in emphasis and notice the change in the meaning of the sentence.

LL 1.1.79 Read aloud.

<u>I</u> will not go.	Ellen may go, but I won't.
I <u>will</u> not go.	You can't make me go.
I will <u>not</u> go.	You may think I will go, but I won't.
I will not <u>go</u>.	I won't go, but they can come to me.
You <u>love</u> me? (question)	You love, and don't hate, me?
You love <u>me</u>?	You love me, not Mary? (question)
<u>You</u> love me? (question)	Harry doesn't love me, you do?

When singing songs in English, you should choose one word, and only one, to emphasize within each phrase. Emphasizing too many words in a single phrase will usually diffuse the meaning. The word you choose to emphasize will, of course, affect the meaning of the text.

For example, in the first phrase of *The XXIII Psalm*, by Paul Creston, you could make three different choices, depending upon the meaning you wish to convey. You could choose: "The <u>Lord</u> is my shepherd," or "The Lord is <u>my</u> shepherd," or "The Lord is my <u>shepherd</u>." You would not normally over-emphasize by singing: "The <u>Lord</u> is <u>my</u> <u>shepherd</u>" (unless you wanted to make some type of excessive dramatic impact with that particular phrase.)

How to emphasize the important word

Important words in phrases are emphasized by changes in pitch, intensity, duration, and rhythm. Usually we use higher pitch, greater intensity, and longer duration for prominent words, although the changes could be the exact opposite: lower pitch and decreased intensity, as in a sudden whisper or *subito piano*.

English

Another way we add impact to a word is by emphasizing a single speech sound in a word. Read the word below and lengthen the speech sound that is indicated by the repeated letters. Notice how expressiveness is affected.

LL 1.1.80   Read aloud.

| smash |
| sssssmash |
| smmmash |
| smaaaash |
| smasssssh |

When you are singing a phrase in your song, give greater duration or intensity to the first consonant of the stressed syllable of the word you have chosen to emphasize. This articulation process is a very powerful expressive element of diction.

It is easy to lengthen the duration of a nasal or fricative consonant, since they are continuants. However, to lengthen a stop-plosive, you need to extend the stop portion of the consonant. Lengthen the stop of *p* in the word *powerful* in the example below by giving a longer closure on the consonant.

LL 1.1.81   Read aloud.

| Singing can be powerful. |

Sing the following phrase. We have underlined the first consonants of the stressed syllables of words to emphasize. Give strong emphasis to the underlined consonants and notice how this articulation affects the text. Then, sing a second time and change the words to be emphasized and notice the expressive differences. The text is from a duet from the opera *Hansel and Gretel* by Humperdinck.

LL 1.1.82   Read and sing aloud.

| Brother, come and dance with me, |
| Both my hands I offer thee. |
| Brother, come and dance with me, |
| Both my hands I offer thee. |

Final Note

While studying English diction, errors that are rather subtle, such as singing the work *look* as [luk] instead of [lʊk] are relatively easy to hear because we know the language. As we listen to foreign speakers wrestle with pronouncing our language, their errors leap out at us: we hear articulation and stressing habits that are carried over from their native

English

tongue, creating a distinct accent. In the next chapters the shoe will be on the other foot, and you will like the foreigner, singing sounds without benefit of growing up with the sounds of the language. And you have the added task of singing multiple languages like the natives—without an English accent.

However, unlike a foreigner, you will have the set of guidelines presented in this book to train yourself to articulate the sounds properly. As you learn these guidelines, keep in mind how specific and subtle the differences in sounds can be in English and tune your ears and articulators to that degree of subtlety, and you will acquire fine singing diction in the other languages.

English

Italian

Italian Diction

The dialect of Tuscany, particularly that of Florence, is considered the national standard for Italian diction for stage and singing. The following rules reflect the pronunciations of top level singers.

Italian is often considered a "phonetic" language because each letter of the alphabet is pronounced with a single sound or with few variations. This concept is so widespread that Italian-English dictionaries rarely include the pronunciation of words except for stressed *e* and *o* and voiced or unvoiced *s* and *z*.

Yet it is only partially true that Italian is a "phonetic" language. Although in Italian many letters of the alphabet are pronounced with a single sound, some vowels and consonants can be pronounced in a variety of ways. For instance, you can pronounce Italian vowels (other than *a*) as open or close vowels, or as glides. To choose the correct option, you need to know the stressing of the syllable, the position of the vowel in the word, and the letter that adjoins it. Groups of two and three consecutive vowels also have options, and you need to know whether to pronounce them as diphthongs, glides, triphthongs, or two syllables.

Some consonants in Italian, prominently *c, g, s,* and *z,* also may be pronounced in different ways. Again, the correct pronunciation depends upon the adjoining letters and the position of the consonant in the word.

Since dictionaries frequently do not tell you these variations, you need some general rules to help you make pronunciation choices. The material in "Special Features of Italian" gives you a complete description of how to pronounce the letters you see with the appropriate sounds. You will learn where to divide words and when to pronounce consecutive vowels as diphthongs, glides, triphthongs, or two syllables. You will also learn special articulation and pronunciation features of the language, beginning with how to determine syllabic stress. Then you will find each letter and frequently used combinations of letters listed alphabetically and discussed individually in "Italian Vowels in Detail" and "Italian Consonants in Detail".

Italian

Chart of Italian Sounds

The following chart lists the letters of Italian in alphabetical order. Refer to this chart to quickly check the sound of a spelling. For the special circumstances and exceptions to the spellings that cannot be presented easily in a simple chart, see the discussions of the individual spellings later in this chapter.

Italian Letter and Position in Word		IPA	Example and	IPA	Page
a	a	[a]	amare	[a 'ma re]	76
	ae (two syllables)	[a ɛ]	aereo	[a 'ɛ re o]	77
	ai (diphthong)	[aːi]	mai	[maːi]	77
	ao (two syllables)	[a ɔ]	Paolo	['pa ɔ lo]	78
	au (diphthong)	[aːu]	lauta	['laːu ta]	78
b	b	[b]	batti	['batː ti]	103
	bb	[b]	labbro	['labː bro]	103
c	c before *a, o, u* or a *consonant*	[k]	canta	['kan ta]	103
			classico	['klasː si ko]	103
	cc before *a, o, u*	[kː k]	ecco	['ɛkː ko]	104
	c before *e* or *i*	[ʧ]	certo	['ʧɛr to]	104
	cc before *e* or *i*	[tː ʧ]	Puccini	[putː 'ʧi ni]	105
	ch	[k]	chiama	['kja ma]	106
	cch	[kː k]	occhi	['ɔkː ki]	106
	cqu	[kː k]	acqua	['akː kwa]	106
d	d	[d]	diva	['di va]	107
	dd	[dː d]	addio	[adː 'di o]	107
e	e unstressed	[e]	legale	[le 'ga le]	79
	e unstressed before *l, m, n, r* plus another *consonant*	[ɛ]	bella	['bɛlː la]	81
	e ending a syllable	[e]	pena	['pe na]	81
	e ending a stressed antepenult	[ɛ]	gelida	['ʤɛ li da]	82
	e before *s* plus another *consonant*	[ɛ]	funesto	[fu 'nɛ sto]	82
	e after *i* or *u*	[ɛ]	cielo	['ʧɛ lo]	83
	e before vowel	[ɛ]	sei	[sɛːi]	83
	è or é final	[e]	chè, ché	[ke]	84
	e before consonant in same syllable	[ɛ]	sempre	['sɛm pre]	83
	e before a double consonant*	[e]	stella	['stelː la]	84
	or	[ɛ]	bella	['bɛlː la]	84

Italian

Italian Letter and Position in Word		IPA	Example and IPA		Page
e	e	in suffixes and diminutives*	[e]	Musetta	[mu ˈzetː ta]	84
	ea	(two syllables)	[ɛ a]	idea	[i ˈdɛ a]	85
	ei	(diphthong)	[ɛːi]	lei	[lɛːi]	86
	eo	(two syllables)	[ɛ ɔ]	Orfeo	[ɔr ˈfɛ ɔ]	86
	eu	(diphthong)	[ɛːu]	euro	[ˈɛːu ro]	86
f	f		[f]	fato	[ˈfa to]	107
	ff		[fː f]	affanni	[afː ˈfanː ni]	108
g	g	before *a, o, u* or a *consonant*	[g]	gala	[ˈga la]	108
	gg	before *a, o, u* or a *consonant*	[gː g]	fugga	[ˈfugː ga]	109
	g	before *e* or *i*	[ʤ]	giorni	[ˈʤor ni]	108
	gg	before *e* or *i*	[dː ʤ]	raggio	[ˈradː ʤo]	109
	gh		[g]	ghetta	[ˈgetː ta]	110
	gli		[ʎ]	foglia	[ˈfɔ ʎa]	110
	gl	before *a, o,* or *u*	[gl]	glauca	[ˈglaːu ka]	111
	gn	in the same syllable	[ɲ]	ogni	[ˈo ɲi]	111
	gu		[gw]	guardare	[ˈgwar ˈda re]	111
h	h		silent	ho, chi	[ɔ] [ki]	111
i	i	final or before a consonant	[i]	finiti	[fi ˈni ti]	87
	i	after a vowel	[i]	poi	[pɔːi]	87
	i	after *c, g, sc* and before a *vowel*	silent	giusto	[ˈʤu sto]	88
	ia	(glide)	[ja]	fiamma	[ˈfjamː ma]	89
	ia	(two syllables)	[ˈi a]	Maria	[ma ˈri a]	90
	ie	(glide)	[jɛ]	vieni	[ˈvjɛ ni]	90
	ie	(two syllables)	[ˈi e]	follie	[folː ˈli e]	91
	iei	(triphthong)	[jɛːi]	miei	[mjɛːi]	91
	io	(glide)	[jɔ]	fiocco	[ˈfjɔkː ko]	91
	io	(two syllables)	[ˈi o]	mio	[ˈmi o]	92
	iu	(glide)	[ju]	liuto	[ˈlju to]	92
j	j	used only in older spellings	[j]	gajo	[ˈga jo]	112
k	k	used only in foreign words				
l	l		[l]	libertà	[li bɛr ˈta]	112
	ll		[lːl]	bello	[ˈbɛlː lo]	113

* Can be open [ɛ] or close [e]. Check a dictionary.

Italian

Italian Letter and Position in Word		IPA	Example and	IPA	Page
m	m	[m]	mano	[ˈma no]	113
	mm	[mː m]	gemma	[ˈdʒɛmː ma]	113
n	n	[n]	numero	[ˈnu me ro]	114
	nn	[nː n]	donna	[ˈdɔnː na]	114
	n before *k* or *g*	[ŋ]	bianco	[ˈbjaŋ ko]	115
			sangue	[ˈsaŋ gwe]	115
o	o unstressed	[o]	sospiro	[so ˈspi ro]	93
	o unstressed, before *r* plus another *consonant*	[ɔ]	tornare	[tɔr ˈna re]	94
	o ending a syllable	[o]	sola	[ˈso la]	94
	o ending a stressed antepenult	[ɔ]	opera	[ˈɔ pe ra]	95
	o after *i* or *u*	[ɔ]	piove	[ˈpjɔ ve]	95
	o final and accented	[ɔ]	farò	[fa ˈrɔ]	95
	o before *gli*	[ɔ]	foglio	[ˈfɔ ʎo]	96
	o before a consonant and a glide	[ɔ]	gloria	[ˈglɔ rja]	96
	o before a consonant in same syllable	[ɔ]	forza	[ˈfɔr tsa]	97
	o before *l* followed by *c, f, g, m, p,* or *t*	[o]	dolce	[ˈdol tʃe]	97
	o before *mb, mm, mp*	[o]	ombra	[ˈom bra]	97
	o before single *n* in same syllable	[o]	donde	[ˈdon de]	98
	o before double consonant	[o]	bocca	[ˈbok ka]	98
		[ɔ]	lotto	[ˈlɔtː to]	98
	oa (two syllables)	[ɔ a]	balboa	[bal ˈbɔ a]	98
	oe (two syllables)	[ɔ ɛ]	poesia	[pɔ ɛ ˈzi a]	98
	oi (diphthong)	[ɔːi]	poi	[pɔːi]	99
	oia, oja (two syllables)	[ɔ ja]	gioia	[ˈdʒɔ ja]	99
p	p	[p]	porto	[ˈpɔr to]	115
	pp	[pː p]	drappo	[ˈdrapː po]	115
q	qu	[kw]	qui	[kwi]	116
r	r flipped or trilled	[r]	rado	[ˈra do]	116
	rr	[rː r]	terra	[ˈtɛrː ra]	118
s	s initial in word before a vowel	[s]	sento	[ˈsɛn to]	118
	s initial in word before unvoiced consonant	[s]	sforzando	[sfɔr ˈtsan do]	119
	s initial in syllable after a consonant and before a vowel	[s]	persona	[per ˈso na]	118

Italian

Italian Letter and Position in Word		IPA	Example and	IPA	Page
s	s final	[s]	Radamès	[ra da 'mɛs]	119
	ss	[sː s]	vissi	['visː si]	120
	s between two vowels	[z]	tesoro	[te 'zɔ ro]	119
	s before a voiced consonant	[z]	smanie	['zma nje]	120
	sc before *a, o,* or *u*	[sk]	scolta	['skol ta]	120
	sc before *e* or *i*	[ʃ]	scena	['ʃe na]	120
	sch	[sk]	scherzo	['skɛr tso]	120
t	t	[t]	tanto	['tan to]	121
	tt	[tː t]	batti	['batː ti]	122
u	u before a consonant	[u]	fugare	[fu 'ga re]	99
	u after a vowel	[u]	liuto	['lju to]	99
	ua (glide)	[wa]	quanto	['kwan to]	100
	ua (two syllables)	['u a]	tua	['tu a]	100
	ue (glide)	[wɛ]	guerra	['gwɛrː ra]	100
	ue (two syllables)	['u e]	tue	['tu e]	100
	ui (glide)	[wi]	languire	[laŋ 'gwi re]	101
	ui (two syllables)	['u i]	lui	['lu i]	101
	uo (glide)	[wɔ]	vuole	['vwɔ le]	101
	uo (two syllables)	['u o]	tuo	['tu o]	101
	uie (triphthong)	[wjɛ]	quiete	['kwjɛ te]	102
	uio (two syllables)	['u jɔ]	buio	['bu jɔ]	102
	uoi (triphthong)	[wɔːi]	tuoi	[twɔːi]	102
v	v	[v]	voce	['vo tʃe]	122
	vv	[vː v]	avverso	[avː 'ver so]	122
w x y	*w, x, y* used only in foreign words				
z	z unvoiced	[ts]	zio	['tsi o]	123
	z voiced	[dz]	bronzo	['brɔn dzo]	123
	zz unvoiced	[tː ts]	nozze	['nɔtː tse]	123
	zz voiced	[dː dz]	bizzaro	[bidː 'dza ro]	123

Italian

Special Features of Italian

Syllabification

You will need to divide a word into syllables before you can determine the pronunciation of the letters in a word. The following rules tell you how to divide a word into syllables. First notice whether the word contains a single consonant between vowels, two consecutive consonants, three consecutive consonants, or two or more consecutive vowels. Then, depending upon what you see, follow the rules below.

Single Consonant Between Vowels

When a syllable ends with a vowel, it is called an open *syllable.*

When a single consonant stands between vowels, put the consonant with the second vowel.

LL 2.2.83

no-me	['no me]
a-mo-re	[a 'mo re]
fa-re	['fa re]
fi-ni-ti	[fi 'ni ti]

Two Consecutive Consonants

When a syllable ends with a consonant, it is called a closed *syllable.*

When a consonant is doubled, separate the two consonants.

LL 2.2.84

don-na	['dɔn: na]
bab-bo	['bab: bo]
tut-ti	['tut: ti]
col-la	['kɔl: la]

When there are two consecutive consonants with the same sound (doubled phonetic consonants), separate the two consonants.

LL 2.2.85

c-q:	ac-qua	['ak: kwa]
g-gh:	ag-ghin-da-re	[ag: gin 'da re]
c-ch:	oc-chi	['ɔk: ki]

When *l, m, n,* or *r* precedes another consonant, separate the two consonants:

LL 2.2.86

vol-to	['vɔl to]
tem-po	['tɛm po]

| ven-to | ['vɛn to] |
| Par-ma | ['par ma] |

Note: For a memory "tickler" you can remember this rule as the "lemoner plus another consonant" rule (because the consonants *l, m, n,* and *r* are used in the word *lemoner*).

Otherwise, put two consonants, including the digraphs *ch* [k], *gli* [ʎ], and *gn* [ɲ], with the syllable that follows.

A digraph is a combination of two or more letters that represent a single sound.

LL 2.2.87

fi-glio	['fi ʎo]
la-scia	['la ʃa]
so-gno	['so ɲo]
ci-fra	['tʃi fra]
mi-sto	['mi sto]
ve-nu-sta	[ve 'nu sta]
re-cla-ma	[re 'kla ma]
du-ches-sa	[du 'kesː sa]

Three Consecutive Consonants

In a cluster of three consonants, separate the first consonant from the other two unless the first consonant is an *s*.

LL 2.2.88

men-tre	['men tre]
bar-chet-ta	[bar 'ketː ta]
al-tro	['al tro]
sem-pre	['sɛm pre]

If the first consonant is an *s*, cluster all three consonants in the same syllable.

LL 2.2.89

e-stre-mo	[e 'stre mo]
ma-sche-ra	['ma ske ra]
mo-stra	['mo stra]
di-scre-zio-ne	[di skre 'tsjo ne]

Consecutive Vowels

When two or three vowels are consecutive, they usually form diphthongs, glides, or triphthongs. Put them into a single syllable.

Italian

The [ː] after a vowel indicates that the vowel should be given greater duration. It does not indicate the end of a syllable.

LL 2.2.90

Diphthongs	
mai	[maːi]
sei	[sɛːi]
poi	[pɔːi]
dei	[deːi]

LL 2.2.91

Glides	
chio-ma	[ˈkjɔ ma]
fie-rez-za	[fje ˈretː tsa]
qua	[kwa]
suo-no	[ˈswɔ no]

The rules that indicate whether consecutive vowels are to be pronounced as glides, diphthongs, or two syllables are found on pages 68-71.

LL 2.2.92

Triphthongs	
suoi	[swɔːi]
tuoi	[twɔːi]
miei	[mjɛːi]
lan-guia-te	[laŋ ˈgwja te]

In Italian, the vowels *a*, *e*, and *o* are considered strong vowels. When two strong vowels are consecutive, they usually form two syllables.

LL 2.2.93

ide-a	[i ˈdɛ a]
po-eta	[po ˈɛ ta]

When a stressed *i* or *u* precedes a final vowel without an accent mark, the two vowels form two syllables.

LL 2.2.94

mi-o	[ˈmi o]
tu-o	[ˈtu o]
po-li-zi-a	[po li ˈtsi a]
a-go-ni-a	[a go ˈni a]

Stressing

In Italian, you usually give primary stress to the next-to-last syllable, but you will find that any syllable may be stressed.

Italian

An accent mark over a final vowel tells you to stress the last syllable.

LL 2.2.95

perchè	[pɛr ˈke]
libertà	[li bɛr ˈta]

Word stress presents a challenge because there are no consistent rules to tell you when to stress the third-to-last or the fourth-to-last syllable. Listen to the musical stress of the melodic line and let it guide you into pronouncing the syllables with the appropriate stress. You may also need to refer to a dictionary. To help you with words that receive primary stress on the third- or fourth-to-last syllable in this book, we have underlined the stressed vowel.

LL 2.2.96

<u>o</u>pera	[ˈɔ pe ra]
S<u>a</u>bato	[ˈsa ba to]

In IPA transcriptions, primary stress is indicated by a diacritical mark [ˈ] above and before the stressed syllable.

The syllable that receives the primary stress in a word is referred to as the tonic syllable.

The last syllable is called the final syllable, *the next-to-last syllable of a word is called the* penultimate, *and the third-to-last is the* antepenultimate.

Rules for Stressing

In most Italian words, give the primary stress to the next-to-last syllable.

LL 2.2.97

Ro-ma	[ˈro ma]
vac-ca	[ˈvakː ka]
mes-sa	[ˈmesː sa]
con-ten-to	[kon ˈtɛn to]

When there is an accent mark over the final syllable, give it primary stress.

LL 2.2.98

mor-rò	[morː ˈrɔ]
ser-vi-tù	[sɛr vi ˈtu]
sal-te-rà	[sal te ˈra]
per-chè	[pɛr ˈke]

In some Italian words, the third-to-last syllable receives primary stress.

LL 2.2.99

g<u>e</u>-li-da	[ˈdʒe li da]
<u>e</u>c-co-la	[ˈɛkː ko la]

Italian

p<u>a</u>l-pi-to	['pal pi to]
p<u>o</u>-ve-ro	['pɔ ve ro]

In a few words, the fourth-to-last syllable receives the primary stress. Again, when you see a vowel underlined in this book, stress that syllable.

LL 2.2.100

f<u>a</u>b-bri-ca-no	['fabː bri ka no]

Stress and Meaning

Be careful to pronounce words with appropriate syllabic stress. By changing a word's stress pattern, you may also change its meaning.

LL 2.2.101

p<u>e</u>rdono	['pɛr do no]	means *they lose*
perd<u>o</u>no	[per 'do no]	means *pardon*
m<u>e</u>ta	['me ta]	means *goal*
met<u>à</u>	[me 'ta]	means *half*

An accent mark in a monosyllabic word often indicates a change in the word's meaning. An accent mark does not indicate a change in pronunciation (as it would in French).

LL 2.2.102

With grave accent			Without grave accent		
è	[ɛ]	means *is*	e	[e]	means *and*
chè	[ke]	means *because*	che	[ke]	means *that, who*
sì	[si]	means *yes*	si	[si]	means *himself*
dà	[da]	means *he gives*	da	[da]	means *from*

There are two diacritical marks in Italian: the acute accent ['] and the grave accent [`]. You will see the grave accent more frequently.

Features of Italian Pronunciation

Once you have learned to divide Italian words into syllables and determine syllabic stress, you can begin to work with the sounds of Italian.

Double Consonants

In IPA transcriptions, a colon [ː] after a consonant indicates that the sound should be prolonged. To emphasize further the importance of a double consonant's long sound, you will see the consonant symbol written a second time. For example, you will see bello *transcribed as* ['bɛlː lo].

In Italian, double consonants add a special rhythmic quality to the language. Speak or sing double consonants with a longer *duration* than a single consonant. You can hear this prolonged sound in English when one word ends with the same consonant that begins the next word, as in *tall‿lasses, even‿now, hog‿games,* and *life‿force.* Notice how you linger on the consonants when saying these words.

Italian

Read the following pairs of Italian words aloud to contrast the pronunciation of single and double consonants. Notice how changing the duration of the consonants affects the meanings of the words.

LL 2.2.103

[m]	m'ama	['ma ma]	means *loves me*
[mː m]	mamma	['mamː ma]	means *mother*
[l]	bela	['bɛ la]	means *it bleats*
[lː l]	bella	['bɛlː la]	means *beautiful*
[n]	ano	['a no]	means *anus*
[nː n]	anno	['anː no]	means *year*
[t]	note	['nɔ te]	means *notes*
[tː t]	notte	['nɔtː te]	means *night*
[k]	eco	['ɛ ko]	means *echo*
[kː k]	ecco	['ɛkː ko]	means *here*
[tʃ]	face	['fa tʃe]	means *torch*
[tː tʃ]	facce	['fatː tʃe]	means *faces*

However, when pronouncing a double consonant, do not repeat the consonant sound, merely lengthen it.

Special Doubling

When a monosyllabic word ends with a vowel and is followed by a word that begins with a consonant, pronounce the initial consonant in the second word as a double consonant.

LL 2.2.104

a Roma	[arː 'ro ma]
è bene	[ɛbː 'be ne]
chi sa	[kisː 'sa]

Long and Short Vowels

In Italian, vowels in stressed syllables are pronounced with either a long or short duration. Give longer duration to a vowel that is before a single consonant than to a vowel that is before two or more consonants.

Read the following words aloud. Prolong the vowels indicated by (¯), and shorten the vowels indicated by (˘).

LL 2.2.105

Long Vowels		Short Vowels	
fāme	['fa me]	fătto	['fatː to]
cāra	['ka ra]	căccia	['katː tʃa]
vēro	['ve ro]	vĕste	['vɛ ste]

Lengthening the vowel may help you avoid pronouncing single consonants as double consonants.

Italian

prēga	['pre ga]	piăzza	[pjat: tsa]
sōle	['so le]	sŏmma	['sɔm: ma]
rōsa	['rɔ za]	rŏtta	['rɔt: ta]
vōce	['vo tʃe]	vŏlgo	['vɔl go]
pūma	['pu ma]	pŭnto	['pun to]
tūta	['tu ta]	tŭtta	['tut: ta]

Note: The duration of a vowel does not always correlate to its open or close pronunciation. For example, the close [o] can be pronounced long or short.

LL 2.2.106

vōce	['vo tʃe]
vŏlgo	['vɔl go]

For more information on open and close sounds, see "The Italian Vowels e and o" on page 64.

The Consonant l

Italians always pronounce the consonant *l* as a "clear", dental sound, with the tip of the tongue touching the back of the upper front teeth. You can find a clear *l* in the English words *leap, lit, let, lot, late*. However, English more often uses a "dark" *l* with the tip of the tongue touching the alveolar ridge, as in the words *full, help, wall, fell, truly*.

Be sure to always use the clear *l* in Italian, as in these words:

LL 2.2.107

diletto	[di 'lɛt: to]
lira	['li ra]
idolo	['i do lo]
sol	[sol]
gloria	['glɔ rja].

The Consonants d, t, and n

In Italian the consonants *d, t,* and *n* are dental consonants. That is, they are articulated with the tip of the tongue touching the back of the upper front teeth.

In contrast, English speakers form the consonants *d, t,* and *n* with the tip of the tongue touching the alveolar ridge, as in *dungeon, total, not*.

Learn to articulate *d, t,* and *n* dentally in Italian words such as the following:

LL 2.2.108

dunque	[ˈduŋ kwe]
tema	[ˈte ma]
natale	[na ˈta le]

The Stop-Plosive Consonants

In English, you pronounce the stop-plosive consonants (*b, p, d, t, g,* and *k*) by stopping the flow of air through your mouth and nose and then releasing the air plosively. Pronounce the English words *tote* and *team* and notice your articulation of the stop-plosive sound [t]. The tip of your tongue lifts to touch your alveolar ridge to stop the flow of air through your mouth. Feel the air pressure build up and then explosively release with an aspirate or fricative sound.

In Italian, the stop-plosive consonants are articulated with less aspiration than in English. We call these Italian consonants "dry" consonants to describe this reduced aspiration.

Return to your articulation of [t]. This time pronounce [t] as an Italian dental, dry, stop-plosive consonant. Put the tip of your tongue at the back of your upper front teeth instead of your alveolar ridge. During the stop portion of the articulation, give less build-up of air pressure. Then release the sound with minimal aspiration.

Repeat the sound [t] several times:

LL 2.2.109

[t]	[t]	[t]	[t]	[t]

Then read aloud these words using a dental, dry [t]:

LL 2.2.110

totale	[to ˈta le]
tira	[ˈti ra]
attento	[atː ˈtɛn to]
attico	[ˈatː ti ko]

In Italian, remember to articulate all the stop-plosive consonants in this manner, minimizing plosiveness and aspiration.

The Italian Vowel a

In Italian, the vowel *a* sound is similar to the *ah* in *father*. However, you will find that different books use different IPA transcriptions for this

Italian

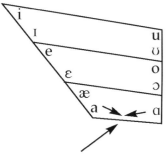

Vowel Diagram

You may find it useful to think of the Italian a as though it is between bright ah and dark ah. This, however, is a subtle point.

sound. Some use the bright [a] (the vowel that Bostoners use when they say, "*pahk the cahr*") and others use dark [ɑ] (as in *father*).

In his *Descriptive Italian Grammar*, the Italian grammarian Robert A. Hall writes: "The low vowel *a* is indifferent as to front or back tongue position," which indicates that the letter *a* can be pronounced either as [a] or [ɑ].

This book transcribes the letter *a* as [a]. We suggest that you think of Italian *a* as being a clear, bright sound located between [a] and [ɑ] on the vowel diagram.

There are two major cautions for American singers concerning the letter *a*. First, you must be careful not to use the neutral sound of [ə] as in *about* or [ʌ] in *bud*. These sounds do not exist in Italian. For example, never use [ə] in the following words:

LL 2.2.111

bella	[ˈbɛl: la]	is not	[ˈbɛl: lə]
pizza	[ˈpit: tsa]	is not	[ˈpit: tsə]
Amarilli	[a ma ˈril: li]	is not	[a mə ˈril: li]
tessitura	[tes: si ˈtu ra]	is not	[tes: si ˈtu rə]

Second, in some American accents, the sounds of *ah* [a] and *aw* [ɔ] are poorly distinguished. You must be careful to keep the sound of Italian *ah* [a] clear and bright, not rounded toward the vowel *aw* [ɔ].

The Italian Vowels e and o

In Italian, the vowels *e* and *o* have close and open pronunciations. The letter *e* is pronounced as close [e] (as in *chaotic*) or open [ɛ] (as in *bed*). The letter *o* is pronounced as close [o] (as in *obey*) or open [ɔ] (as in *bought*). The rules for when to use close and open vowels in the pronunciation of these letters are presented in "The letter e" and "The letter o" later in this chapter.

In Italian, close *e* [e] and *o* [o] are pure vowels and must never be pronounced with the English diphthongal [eɪ], as in *bait*, and [oʊ], as in *boat*. American singers must master the pure, close sounds of these vowels to avoid singing with a heavy accent. *International Phonetic Alphabet for Singers*, a manual that teaches the sounds and symbols of the IPA, offers the following exercises to help you distinguish [e] and [o] from the diphthongs [eɪ] and [oʊ].

> "Speak the word *aim* aloud in slow motion while noticing what your tongue does. Just before the *m* of *aim*, you should be able to feel the front part of your tongue move forward

Italian

and up from [e] to [ɪ]. Listen to the vowel change. This gliding tongue movement produces the diphthong.

"To isolate the pure [e] sound, try speaking the word *hay* aloud in slow motion without moving the tongue to [ɪ]. The word will sound incomplete, strange, and unfamiliar to most Americans. If you do not make a gliding movement with the tongue, you will be producing a pure [e].

"Speak the word *hoe* aloud in slow motion to notice the movement of your lips and tongue. You should be able to tell that your lips become more rounded as the sound progresses from [o] to [ʊ]. The back of the tongue also moves upward from [o]. You may be less conscious of this movement, because it is so slight. It is easily seen in x-ray images.

"To isolate the pure [o] sound, try speaking the word *hoe* in slow motion *without* moving the lips or tongue. The words will sound incomplete and strange to an American. Without the gliding movement, you will produce a pure [o]."

Flipped and Trilled r

The Italian *r* is either a flipped or trilled tongue point *r*; it is never the retroflex *r* of American English.

When Italians pronounce the flipped *r*, it sounds very much like a British pronunciation of *r* in words like *very* (*veddy*) or *merry* (*meddy*). Practicing the flipped *r* will help you achieve a trilled *r*, which is so essential for good Italian diction.

Speak the following words using a British accent for the flipped *r* words. Notice that the tip of your tongue quickly flips against your alveolar ridge.

LL 2.2.112

Flipped *r* (between vowels)			Trilled *r*		
caro	[ˈka ro]	meaning *dear*	carro	[ˈkarː ro]	meaning *cart*
furore	[fu ˈro re]	meaning *rage*	ferro	[ˈferː ro]	meaning *iron*
Figaro	[ˈfi ga ro]		Ferrando	[ferː ˈran do]	

The Two Italian Glides: [j] and [w]

The glides [j] and [w] are already familiar to you as an English speaker. The symbol [j], named *yot* [jɔt], represents the sound of *y* in *you*.

A close *vowel is one that has a smaller space between the high part of the arch of the tongue and the roof of the mouth. An* open *vowel is one that has a larger space than the close vowel.*

In this text the tongue point Italian r is represented by the IPA symbol [r]. The IPA symbol for the flipped r is [ɾ], and [r̄] for the trilled r , however, for simplicity, this chapter will use the symbol [r] to indicate both flipped and trilled r. Rules for flipped and trilled r are presented on pages 116 and 118.

Italian

Produce it by moving your tongue to the position for [i] as in *beet*, then quickly shifting to the vowel that follows, as in *yes* [jɛs] or *yet* [jɛt].

The symbol [w] represents the sound of *w* in *went*, *wine*, or *wear*. Produce it by rounding your lips as if to say [u] in *boot*, then quickly shifting to the vowel that follows, as in *we* [wi].

Enya [ɲ] and Elya [ʎ]

As an English speaker, you have two new consonant sounds to learn in Italian: the consonants *enya* [ɲ] and *elya* [ʎ].

Enya [ɲ], as in the Italian word *ogni* ['o ɲi], does not exist in English, but you can find a similar sound in the *ni* of the word *onion* ['ʌnjən]. Notice that to pronounce the [nj] in *onion*, you make two articulatory movements: you lift the tip of your tongue to touch your alveolar ridge for [n], then lower it to touch the back of your bottom front teeth for [j]. To pronounce the *enya* [ɲ], by contrast, you use only one articulatory movement.

The alveolar ridge is also called the teeth ridge.

Make the sound of *enya* [ɲ] by slightly parting your lips, putting the tip of your tongue behind your bottom front teeth, and arching your tongue upward so that the high arch of your tongue touches your alveolar ridge and the back of your upper front teeth. Add voice and you will hear the nasal, palatal consonant sound *enya* [ɲ]. Although the enya sounds something like [n], it is made with the blade of your tongue, not the tip, touching your alveolar ridge.

Elya [ʎ], as found in *foglia* ['fɔ ʎa], is another sound that does not exist in English. However, you can find a similar sound in *million* ['mɪ ljən]. Notice again how you must make two articulatory tongue movements to say [lj]: you place the tip of your tongue on your alveolar ridge for the consonant [l] and then move it to the back of your bottom front teeth for the glide [j]. By contrast, to say *elya* [ʎ], you use only a single tongue action.

Produce the sound of *elya* [ʎ] by slightly parting your lips, putting the tip of your tongue behind your bottom front teeth, and arching your tongue so that the arch touches the front of your hard palate. Add voice and let the air exit over the sides of your tongue. You will hear a sound something like an [l], only you make it with the blade of your tongue, not the tip, against the boundary between your alveolar ridge and hard palate.

Apocopation

You will find that, except for a few monosyllabic words, most Italian words end with a vowel. Therefore, when a word ends in a consonant, immediately consider whether it has been apocopated—that is, whether the word has been shortened by dropping the final vowel or syllable.

LL 2.2.112 A

sole becomes *sol*
cantare becomes *cantar*
siamo becomes *siam*
partiamo becomes *partian*
fatale becomes *fatal*
viene becomes *vien*

An apostrophe is only used when an entire syllable has been apocopated.

LL 2.2.112 B

poco becomes *po'*
guarda becomes *gua'*

Notice that in an apocopated word, a closed syllable can be created where there had been an open syllable. Although this affects the syllabification of the word, it does not change the original open or close sound of the vowel.

LL 2.2.113

potere	[po 'te re]	becomes	*poter*	[po 'ter]
piacere	[pja 'tʃe re]	becomes	*piacer*	[pja 'tʃer]
padrone	[pa 'dro ne]	becomes	*padron*	[pa 'dron]
core	['kɔ re]	becomes	*cor*	[kɔr]

Elision

To link words together smoothly, you may hear an Italian speaker drop the final vowel of a word before an initial vowel of the next word. Omitting a vowel in this way is called *elision*. The elided vowel is indicated by an apostrophe between the words.

LL 2.2.114

quella aria	becomes	*quell'aria*	[kwelː 'la rja]
bello uomo	becomes	*bell'uomo*	[belː 'lwɔ mo]
una altra parte	becomes	*un'altra parte*	[u 'nal tra 'par te]
mi amate	becomes	*m'amate*	[ma 'ma te]
lo amico	becomes	*l'amico*	[la 'mi ko]
vi aspetto	becomes	*v'aspetto*	[va 'spetː to]
dove è Ernesto	becomes	*dov' è Ernesto*	['do ve ɛr 'ne sto]

Italian

Rules for Pronouncing Consecutive Vowels

Consecutive vowels form either a diphthong, a glide, a triphthong, or two syllables.

Diphthongs

In IPA transcriptions, a colon [ː] after a vowel indicates the lengthening of the vowel sound. The symbol [ː] can be used within a syllable or between syllables.

A *diphthong* is composed of two consecutive vowels uttered in a single impulse of breath to form one syllable. Because each Italian diphthong includes one strong vowel (*a, e,* or *o*) followed by one weak vowel (*i* or *u*), Italian diphthongs are easy to recognize.

You can find diphthongs in English in such words as *my* [maɪ], *boy* [bɔɪ] or *gown* [gaʊn]. Notice that as you pronounce these words, you prolong the first vowel longer than the second vowel.

The same timing holds true in Italian diphthongs; that is, you pronounce the first vowel longer and the second one shorter. Pronounce the Italian words *mai* [maːi], *poi* [pɔːi], or *gaudio* ['gaːu djo] and notice the similarities to the diphthongs in *my, boy,* and *gown*. Unlike English diphthongs, however, pronounce the second vowel of an Italian diphthong with a pure, distinct quality of [i] or [u]. The second vowel should neither resemble a glide nor open to [ɪ] or [ʊ].

Read these words aloud to become familiar with the sounds of Italian diphthongs.

Diphthongs with *i* as the second vowel:

LL 2.2.115

ai	[aːi]	mai	[maːi]	
ei	[eːi]	pei	[peːi]	(less frequent)
ei	[ɛːi]	sei	[sɛːi]	
oi	[oːi]	voi	[voːi]	(less frequent)
oi	[ɔːi]	poi	[pɔːi]	

The sound of [j], called yot [jɔt], is similar to a very brief [i] as in beet. *And [w] is similar to a very brief [u] as in* boot.

Diphthongs with *u* as the second vowel:

LL 2.2.116

eu	[eːu]	Euridice	[eːu ri 'di tʃe]
eu	[ɛːu]	euro	['ɛːu ro]
au	[aːu]	cauto	['kaːu to]

Note: The *eu* and *au* diphthongs occur less frequently than other diphthongs.

Italian

Glides

Like diphthongs, *glides* are composed of two consecutive vowels uttered in a single impulse of breath to form one syllable. A glide includes one weak vowel (*i* or *u*) followed by another vowel, as in *più* [pju] and *qui* [kwi]. Notice that in a glide, the first vowel *i* is pronounced [j] and the first vowel *u* is pronounced [w]. Glides can be heard in the English words *pew* [pju] and *queen* [kwin].

Unlike a diphthong, the first vowel in a glide is short and the second vowel is long.

Read the following vowel combinations aloud to become familiar with the sounds of Italian glides.

LL 2.2.117

Glides with i [j] first				
ia	[ja]	chia-ma-re	[kja 'ma re]	
ie	[je]	fie-rez-za	[fje 'retː tsa]	
ie	[jɛ]	vie-ni	['vjɛ ni]	
io	[jo]	piom-bo	['pjom bo]	(less frequent)
io	[jɔ]	chio-do	['kjɔ do]	
iu	[ju]	fiu-me	['fju me]	

The term glide *may be used to refer either to the specific speech sounds* [j] *and* [w] *or to refer to a vowel combination that includes a* [j] *or* [w].

LL 2.2.118

Glides with u [w] first				
ua	[wa]	quan-do	['kwan do]	
ue	[we]	que-sto	['kwe sto]	(less frequent)
ue	[wɛ]	guer-ra	['gwɛrː ra]	
ui	[wi]	qui	[kwi]	
uo	[wo]	quo-ta-li-zio	[kwo ta 'li tsjɔ]	(less frequent)
uo	[wɔ]	uo-mo	['wɔ mo]	

The glides [j] *and* [w] *are sometimes called semi-vowels or semi-consonants.*

When *i* or *u* is followed by another vowel, the letter combination is usually pronounced as a glide.

LL 2.2.119

più	[pju]
può	[pwɔ]
Liù	[lju]
qua	[kwa]
odiò	[o 'djɔ]
segue	['se gwe]
aria	['a rja]

Italian

uomo	['wɔ mo]
chiuso	['kju zo]
dileguò	[di le 'gwɔ]

This rule for silent i is an important one to keep in mind.
Giovanni [dʒo 'vanː ni], for instance, is never pronounced [dʒio 'vanː ni].

Three exceptions do not conform to this rule:

1. When *i* comes after *c, g,* or *sc*, and is followed by *a, e, o,* or *u*, the *i* is silent. This is the only instance when a vowel is silent in Italian. (See "i" on page 87.)

   LL 2.2.120

ciò	[tʃɔ]
già	[dʒa]
cielo	['tʃɛ lo]
sciolto	['ʃɔl to]

2. When a *stressed i* or *stressed u* is followed by a final vowel without an accent mark, the result is two syllables. (See "Two Syllables" on page 71.)

   LL 2.2.121

mio	['mi o]
lui	['lu i]
io	['i o]
sue	['su e]
malia	[ma 'li a]
polizia	[po li 'tsi a]

3. When a *stressed i* is followed by the third person plural verb ending *-ano*, the result is two syllables. (See "Two Syllables" on page 71.)

   LL 2.2.122

siano	['si a no]
fiano	['fi a no]

Triphthongs

A *triphthong* is composed of three consecutive vowels uttered in a single impulse of breath to form one syllable, as in *tuoi* [twɔːi] or *quieto* ['kwjɛ to].

1. A triphthong usually consists of a glide ([j] or [w]) and a diphthong.

   LL 2.2.123

miei	[mjɛːi]
ri-nun-ziai	[ri nun 'tsjaːi]

Italian

suoi	[swɔːi]
tuoi	[twɔːi]

2. Sometimes a triphthong consists of two glides and one vowel.

LL 2.2.124

quie-to	['kwjɛ to]
se-guia-te	[se 'gwja te]
lan-guia-te	[lan 'gwja te]
a-iuo-la	[a 'jwɔ la]

Two Syllables

Two consecutive vowels form two separate syllables in the following spellings.

1. Two Strong Vowels

Pronounce two consecutive strong vowels (*a*, *e*, or *o*) as two syllables. The vowels *e* and *o* are usually pronounced [ɛ] and [ɔ], but not always. To determine which vowel to stress, observe the general rules for word stressing. (See "Stressing" on page 58.) Usually the second to last syllable of the word receives the stress as in *eroe* [e 'rɔ ɛ] and *poeta* [po 'ɛ ta]. When two strong consecutive vowels occur in an unstressed position in a word, the vowels are given equal duration as in *paesano* [pa ɛ 'za no].

LL 2.2.125   Read aloud.

ae	[a ɛ]	ca-en-do	[ka 'ɛn do]
	[a ɛ]	pa-e-sa-no	[pa ɛ 'za no]
ao	[a ɔ]	a-or-ta	[a 'ɔr ta]
ea	[ɛ a]	i-de-a	[i 'dɛ a]
eo	[ɛ ɔ]	Or-fe-o	[ɔr 'fɛ ɔ]
oa	[ɔ a]	bal-bo-a	[bal 'bɔ a]
	[ɔ a]	so-a-ve	[sɔ 'a ve]
oe	[ɔ ɛ]	e-ro-e	[e 'rɔ ɛ]
	[o ɛ]	po-e-ta	[po 'ɛ ta]

2. Two- or Three-Letter Words

In two- or three-letter words, when *i* or *u* is followed by a final vowel *without* an accent mark, the *i* or *u* is stressed and the two vowels constitute two separate syllables.

If the final vowel has an accent mark, for example, più, the two vowels become a glide, making a single syllable [pju].

LL 2.2.126 Read aloud these words of two or three letters as two syllables.

mio	['mi o]
lui	['lu i]
io	['i o]
tua	['tu a]
sia	['si a]
due	['du e]
zio	['tsi o]
sue	['su e]
tuo	['tu o]

When you sing these words, prolong the first vowel and shorten the second vowel as you would a diphthong. However, the second vowel has even more strength and may even be sung on a separate note when notated as such by the composer.

3. Polysyllabic Words

In a polysyllabic word the only certain clue to pronouncing a weak vowel (*i* or *u*) followed by a final vowel is an accent mark over the final vowel. In that case, pronounce the final vowels as a glide as in *dileguò* [di le 'gwɔ] or *odiò* [o 'djɔ].

If there is no accent mark, you must know which syllable is stressed before you can determine the pronunciation. If the stress is on the weak vowel, pronounce the vowels as two syllables, as in *sinfonia* [sin fo 'ni a] and *malia* [ma 'li a]. If the stress is on an earlier syllable, pronounce the final vowels as a glide, as in *statua* ['sta twa] and *Italia* [i 'ta lja].

To identify this irregular stressing, notice how the word is set metrically in the melody, or consult a dictionary.

Pronounce the final two vowels in these polysyllabic words as two syllables.

LL 2.2.127

signoria	[si ɲo 'ri a]
polizia	[po li 'tsi a]
poesia	[pɔ ɛ 'zi a]
agonia	[a go 'ni a]
natio	[na 'ti o]

Additional Comments About Consecutive Vowels

Vocal pedagogues disagree about how to classify the normally weak *i* and *u* when they receive the primary stress of the word and are followed by a final vowel with no accent mark. Some pedagogues classify these consecutive vowels as two separate syllables, while others classify them as diphthongs.

However, the question of how to classify these consecutive vowels is of less consequence than how to sing them. According to Agard and Di Pietro, "It must be kept in mind that these observations of the vowels forming two syllables are made on the basis of modern spoken language. In poetry, opera librettos, and other artistic uses of the language, any sequence of two (or more) vowels may constitute a single syllable peak." This is important because you may see only one note given to the two-syllable consecutive vowels, as described in the next section.

Singing Consecutive Vowels

In music, composers frequently write consecutive vowels under a single note. You must decide the relative duration of the two vowels. Your goal is to link the vowels smoothly while maintaining distinct pronunciations of glides, diphthongs, triphthongs, and two syllables.

Glides

When the vowel combination forms a glide, you will have no difficulty with the timing. The quick, gliding movement of the semi-vowel [j] or [w] guides the pronunciation so that the second vowel has the longer duration.

Example from "*Danza, danza fanciulla gentile*" (Durante)

al   suo -   no
       [swɔ _____]

Diphthongs

When a vowel combination is a diphthong, however, you must prolong the first vowel and shorten the second vowel and the proportion of timing becomes significant. The timing is influenced by the melody and may vary slightly from one performer to the next. See the examples below to observe some appropriate choices.

Italian

Example from *"Il mio bel foco"* (Marcello)

che giam - mai   s'e - stin - gue - rà

[ma: i]

Example from *"Se tu m'ami"* (Pergolesi)

sei   sog-get- to

[sɛ: i]

Triphthongs

Example from *Vergin, tutto amor* (Durante)

suo   duol   suoi   tri-sti   ac - cen-ti

[swɔ: i]

When the vowel combination is a triphthong, timing presents a similar challenge. Usually divide the duration of the vowels evenly.

Two Syllables

When you sing consecutive vowels that constitute two syllables, you may also need to make a timing decision. When the composer provides two notes, there is no difficulty with timing; you sing one vowel on each note.

Example from *"Pur dicesti, o bocca bella"* (Lotti)

di   sua   fa - cel - la

['su a]

il   mio   pia - cer

['mi o]

Frequently, the two syllables are written beneath a single note. You can make the first vowel longer, or you can divide the two syllables equally.

When giving longer duration to one of the vowels, be sure to follow the rules of stressing for "Two Syllables" on page 71.

Connecting Words in Italian

In singing, several vowels at word boundaries are sometimes assigned to a single note. To determine the appropriate timing for these vowels, you need to know the translation of the text. The meaning of the words indicates which vowel or syllable to stress. For example, the vowels of nouns and verbs receive stronger stress and longer duration than vowels of articles and prepositions. If there is a question about stress, simply time the vowels equally. In the following example, the important words would be the verb "is" and the noun "love".

Example from "*Amarilli*" (Caccini)

è il   mio a - mo - re
<u>is</u> [the] my   <u>love</u>

['ɛ il 'mi o a 'mo re]

Italian

Italian Vowels in Detail

Italian has only seven vowel sounds represented by five letters, as shown here:

LL 2.3.01

a	[a]		
e	[e]	or	[ɛ]
i	[i]		
o	[o]	or	[ɔ]
u	[u]		

Note: The letters *a*, *e*, and *o* are strong vowels; *i* and *u* are weak vowels. The weak vowels *i* and *u* in certain vowel combinations may be pronounced as glides [j] and [w]. (See "Glides" on page 69.)

The letter a

In Italian, the letter *a* is always pronounced as [a], never anything else. This is true when the letter is by itself in a syllable or combined with a glide, diphthong, triphthong, or another strong vowel. Also, unlike the letters *e* and *o*, the pronunciation of *a* is unaffected by whether it occurs in a stressed or unstressed syllable.

Caution: When *a* is in an unstressed position, be careful to pronounce it as [a] and not as *schwa* [ə], as you would in English.

LL 2.3.2   Compare and contrast.

	English	Italian
papa	['pa pə]	['pa pa]
pizza	['pitː tsə]	['pitː tsa]
terracotta	[tɛ rə 'ka tə]	[terː ra 'kɔtː ta]
pasta	['pa stə]	['pa sta]

The single letter a

Pronounce the single letter *a* as [a].

LL 2.3.3   Read aloud.

sal-ve	['sal ve]
amare	[a 'ma re]
Amarilli	[a ma 'rilː li]
affanni	[afː 'fanː ni]

Italian

The letter a in consecutive vowel groups

ae

Pronounce *ae* as the two syllables [a ɛ]. (When two strong vowels appear together, they constitute two syllables.)

LL 2.3.4 Read aloud.

paesano	[pa ɛ 'za no]
aereo	[a 'ɛ rɛ o]

ai

Pronounce *ai* as the diphthong [aːi].

LL 2.3.5 Read aloud.

mai	[maːi]
traino	['traːi no]
vedrai	[ve 'draːi]
l'amai	[la 'maːi]
andrai	[an 'draːi]
dai	[daːi]

aio, aiu, aiuo

Pronounce *a* as a separate syllable followed by a glide or a triphthong.

LL 2.3.6 Read aloud.

aiuto	[a 'ju to]
aiuola	[a 'jwɔ la]
guaio	['gwa jɔ]
fumaiolo	[fu ma 'jɔ lo]

ao

Pronounce *ao* as the two syllables [a ɔ]. (When strong vowels appear together, they constitute two syllables.)

LL 2.3.7   Read aloud.

Paolo	['pa ɔ lo]
pilao	[pi 'la ɔ]

au

Pronounce *au* as the diphthong [aːu].

LL 2.3.8   Read aloud.

pausa	['paːu za]
lauta	['laːu ta]
causa	['kaːu za]
rauco	['raːu ko]
autore	[aːu 'to re]
audace	[aːu 'da tʃe]

Note: The first vowel of the diphthong *au* is usually elongated. One common exception is in the word *paura* [pauː ra], where the second vowel is elongated.

The letter e

In Italian, the letter *e* has two pronunciations: close [e] as in *chaotic* and open [ɛ] as in *bet*. It is important to note that the Italian [e] is a pure vowel sound, never diphthongal [eɪ] as in the English word *bay* [beɪ]. Be especially careful to use pure [e] and not [eɪ].

To determine the pronunciation of the letter *e*, you must first decide whether it occurs in a stressed or unstressed syllable (see "Stressing" on page 58). The letter *e* in a stressed syllable is referred to as *stressed e*, and in an unstressed syllable, as *unstressed e*.

The letter e in Stressed Syllables

If you determine that the syllable is stressed, you need to choose between [e] and [ɛ]; stressed *e* has no other pronunciations. Not only is your choice significant for correct pronunciation, but it can also determine the meaning of the word. Compare the words in the list below.

LL 2.3.9   Read aloud.

venti	['ven ti]	means *twenty*
	['vɛn ti]	means *winds*
legge	['led: dʒe]	means *law*
	['lɛd: dʒe]	means he *reads*
mezzo	['met: tso]	means *over-ripe*
	['mɛd: dzo]	means *medium* (mezzo-soprano)

The pronunciation rules for stressed *e* begin on page 81. They provide reliable guidelines for choosing between [ɛ] and [e]. However, because there are many words that are exceptions to rules in Italian, it is wise to keep a dictionary handy at all times.

Note: In some dictionaries, pronunciation of stressed *e* is indicated by an acute accent *é*, for [e] and a grave accent *è*, for [ɛ].

The Letter e in Unstressed Syllables

If you determine that the *e* is in an unstressed syllable, pronounce it as close [e], except when it comes before *l, m, n,* or *r* plus another *consonant*. However, using [e] or [ɛ] for unstressed *e* does not influence the meaning of the word, as it might for stressed *e*. Consider what phonetician Claude Wise writes: "The difference between [e] and [ɛ] is significant only in stressed syllables. Elsewhere (in unstressed syllables), the vowel sound may vary over a continuous range from [e] to [ɛ], with a statistical predominance of the more open types before nasals, laterals, or trills."

Ultimately, whether to sing unstressed *e* as [e] or [ɛ] is a matter of personal aesthetics, and you will encounter varying opinions among vocal pedagogues. For many years, vocal pedagogues have directed singers to pronounce unstressed *e* as [ɛ] in all syllables that follow the stressed syllable, perhaps in an effort to avoid any of the following problems of singing [e] in unstressed syllables:

- American singers often tend to sing a diphthongal [eɪ] rather than a pure [e]. With this diphthong, *dove, amore,* and *cantare* would sound like ['do veɪ], [a 'mo reɪ], and [can 'ta reɪ]. The resulting English accent is unpleasant, and is particularly noticeable because so many Italian words end with unstressed *e*.

- In English, unstressed *e* is usually a *schwa* [ə] and almost never [e]. (The words *vacation* and *chaotic* are notable exceptions.) The [e] sound is usually found only in stressed syllables, so an American

Italian

singer may tend to overstress an unstressed syllable in Italian when pronouncing it as [e]. *Dove, amore,* and *cantare* would tend to sound like [do 've], [a mo 're], and [can ta 're], which is incorrect stress.

- A third notion—that close [e] is less conducive to singing with a resonant tone—sometimes prompts the choice of [ɛ] for unstressed *e*.

Our choice is to sing unstressed *e* as close [e] and the IPA transcriptions in this book follow this convention. This sound follows spoken Italian, where unstressed *e* is always [e] except before *l, m, n,* or *r* plus another *consonant*, and singing [e] adds authenticity to the pronunciation. Many top pedagogues have become interested in matching the spoken language. In Coffin's *Phonetic Readings of Songs and Arias*, for example, unstressed *e* is transcribed as close [e]. It is certainly possible for American singers to overcome their own speech habits of overemphasizing [e] or turning it into a diphthong. As for facilitating singing, the dynamics of vowel modification will include more choices than just [e], so choosing open [ɛ] over closed [e] is not valuable as a general rule for unstressed *e*.

Use this discussion to make your personal choice whether to sing open [ɛ] or close [e] for unstressed *e*. Then, become aware of your choice and keep it consistent throughout your singing.

Pronounce the words in the following columns to increase your awareness of the two choices for pronouncing unstressed *e*. Pronounce a word in the first column using close [e]. Then pronounce the same word in the second column using an open [ɛ]. Listen and feel the difference.

Note: As mentioned previously, you must use a consistent pronunciation for unstressed *e*. The following words are offered simply as an awareness exercise.

LL 2.3.10   Read aloud to compare and contrast.

timore	[ti 'mo re]	timore	[ti 'mo rɛ]
m<u>a</u>re	['ma re]	m<u>a</u>re	['ma rɛ]
<u>o</u>pera	['ɔ pe ra]	<u>o</u>pera	['ɔ pɛ ra]
conf<u>o</u>ndere	[kon 'fon de re]	conf<u>o</u>ndere	[kon 'fon de rɛ]
m<u>a</u>schera	['ma ske ra]	m<u>a</u>schera	['ma skɛ ra]
fosse	['fɔsː se]	fosse	['fɔsː sɛ]
luce	['lu tʃe]	luce	['lu tʃɛ]

Italian

The single letter e unstressed

Usually pronounce unstressed *e* as [e]. (See "The Letter e in Unstressed Syllables" on page 79.) In the following words, pronounce each unstressed *e* as close [e].

LL 2.3.11   Read aloud.

legato	[le ˈga to]
beccare	[bekː ˈka re]
amore	[a ˈmo re]
Befana	[be ˈfa na]
credere	[ˈkre de re]
arme	[ˈar me]
madre	[ˈma dre]
arretrarsi	[arː re ˈtrar si]
venire	[ve ˈni re]
regale	[re ˈga le]
legale	[le ˈga le]
fedele	[fe ˈde le]

When unstressed *e* is followed by *l, m, n, r* and another *consonant*, usually pronounce it as [ɛ].

LL 2.3.12   Read aloud.

beltade	[bɛl ˈta de]
gentile	[dʒɛn ˈti le]
tempesta	[tɛm ˈpe sta]
versare	[vɛr ˈsa re]
entrare	[ɛn ˈtra re]
mercè	[mɛr ˈtʃe]

Note: For a memory "tickler," you can remember this rule as the "lemoner plus another consonant" rule (because the consonants *l, m, n,* and *r* are used in the word *lemoner*).

The single letter e stressed

When the letter *e* ends a stressed syllable, usually pronounce it as [e].

LL 2.3.13   Read aloud.

pe-na	[ˈpe na]
se-gno	[ˈse ɲo]

Italian

pre-sa	['pre za]	
se-ra	['se ra]	
stre-ga	['stre ga]	
e-gli	['e ʎi]	
che	[ke]	
e	[e]	meaning *and*

These common words do not follow the normal rule. Pronounce them with [ɛ].

LL 2.3.14   Read aloud.

bene	['bɛ ne]
breve	['brɛ ve]
speme	['spɛ me]
crudele	[kru 'dɛ le]
spero	['spɛ ro]
prego	['prɛ go]

Here are three important exceptions.

1. When *e* ends a stressed antepenult (third-to-last) syllable, pronounce it as [ɛ].

    LL 2.3.15   Read aloud.

te-ne-ro	['tɛ ne ro]
me-di-co	['mɛ di ko]
ge-li-da	['dʒɛ li da]
e-ti-co	['ɛ ti ko]

    Note: Rely upon the metric stress of the melodic line to help you determine when to give primary stress to the third-to-last syllable.

2. When *stressed e* ends a syllable before an *s* plus another *consonant*, pronounce it as [ɛ].

    LL 2.3.16   Read aloud.

fu-ne-sto	[fu 'nɛ sto]
tem-pe-sta	[tɛm 'pɛ sta]
pre-sto	['prɛ sto]
fe-sta	['fɛ sta]

    Exception: The common word *questo* ['kwe sto] is pronounced with [e].

3. When *stressed e* ends a syllable after *i* or *u*, usually pronounce it as [ɛ].

LL 2.3.17 Read aloud.

cie-lo	['tʃɛ lo]
que-ru-lo	['kwɛ ru lo]
pie-no	['pjɛ no]
mie-le	['mjɛ le]

Note: When the vowel *e* follows the glide [j] or [w], it is usually pronounced as [ɛ], but sometimes it is pronounced as [e]:

LL 2.3.18 Read aloud.

quelle	['kwelː le]

When stressed *e* is before a vowel (as in a diphthong or two syllables), pronounce it as [ɛ]. (See page 85).

LL 2.3.19 Read aloud.

Diphthongs		Two syllables	
lei	[lɛːi]	idea	[i 'dɛ a]
sei	[sɛːi]	reo	['rɛ o]

Note: See the musical examples that illustrate how to sing consecutive vowels on pages 73 through 75.

When stressed *e* is followed by a consonant in the same syllable, usually pronounce it as [ɛ].

LL 2.3.20 Read aloud.

sempre	['sɛm pre]	
certo	['tʃɛr to]	
verso	['vɛr so]	
pendere	['pɛn de re]	
venti	['vɛn ti]	meaning *winds*

Exceptions: Pronounce these common words with [e].

LL 2.3.21 Read aloud.

verde	['ver de]	
Verdi	['ver di]	
venti	['ven ti]	meaning *twenty*

Italian

When stressed *e* is followed by a double consonant, check a dictionary. Sometimes it is pronounced as [ɛ], sometimes [e].

LL 2.3.22   Compare and contrast.

stella	['stel: la]
ecco	['ɛk: ko]
ella	['el: la]
presso	['prɛs: so]
secco	['sek: ko]
bella	['bɛl: la]

When *é* or *è* is final, pronounce it as [e].

Note: A grave or acute accent over a final *e* does not affect its pronunciation.

LL 2.3.23   Read aloud.

chè, ché	[ke]	meaning *because* or *why*
perchè, perché	[per 'ke]	meaning *because* or *why*
mercè, mercé	[mer 'tʃe]	meaning *thanks*
sè, sé	[se]	meaning *him, himself*

Exception: Notice the difference in pronunciation and meaning in these two common words:

LL 2.3.24

| e | [e] | means *and* | è | [ɛ] | means *is* |

See also the discussion of *ie* on page 90.

è - grave
é - acute

The letter e in suffixes and diminutives

In Italian, many words have endings that include a stressed *e*. These are sometimes pronounced [e] and sometimes [ɛ]. To determine the correct pronunciation, check a dictionary.

Note: Since many Italian dictionaries do not use IPA transcriptions, you will need to rely upon other marks. Most dictionaries indicate close and open pronunciations by an accent mark over the stressed vowel: an acute accent (é) for [e] and a grave accent (è) for [ɛ].

In these stressed-e endings, *e* is usually [e]: *emmo, esco, essa, esti, evole, ezza, mente, etto, etta, etti, ette.*

Italian

Note: Gender changes on final vowels (such as *-etto/-etta*) do not affect the pronunciation of *e*.

LL 2.3.25   Read aloud.

Musetta (*-etta*)	[mu ˈzet: ta]
Masetto (*-etto*)	[ma ˈzet: to]
violette (*-ette*)	[vjɔ ˈlet: te]
contessa (*-essa*)	[kon ˈtes: sa]
principessa (*-essa*)	[prin tʃi ˈpes: sa]
monumento (*-mento*)	[mo nu ˈmen to]
vagamento (*-mento*)	[va ga ˈmen to]
piac*e*vole (*-evole*)	[pja ˈtʃe vo le]
brezza (*-ezza*)	[ˈbred: dza]
bellezza (*-ezza*)	[bel: ˈlet: tsa]
avemmo (*-emmo*)	[a ˈvem: mo]
promesso (*-esso*)	[pro ˈmes: so]

Notice that in these words *-etto* is pronounced as [ɛ].

LL 2.3.26   Read aloud.

aspetto	[a ˈspɛt: to]
letto	[ˈlɛt: to]
diletto	[di ˈlɛt: to]
petto	[ˈpɛt: to]
oggetto	[od: ˈdʒɛt: to]
rispetto	[ri ˈspɛt: to]

In these stressed-*e* endings the *e* is usually [ɛ]: *ero, ello,* and *ente.*

LL 2.3.27   Read aloud.

mistero (*-ero*)	[mi ˈstɛ ro]
altero (*-ero*)	[al ˈtɛ ro]
cappella (*-ella*)	[kap: ˈpɛl: la]
dolente (*-ente*)	[do ˈlɛn te]

The letter e in consecutive vowel groups

ea

Pronounce *ea* as the two syllables [e a]. (When two strong vowels appear together, they constitute two syllables.)

See general rules for consecutive vowels on page 68.

Italian

LL 2.3.28 Read aloud.

ide-a	[i 'dɛ a]
e-to-pe-a	[e to 'pɛ a]
stri-de-a	[stri 'dɛ a]
di-scio-glie-a	[di ʃo 'ʎɛ a]

Exceptions: Pronounce these common words with [e]:

LL 2.3.29

tacea	[ta 'tʃe a]
credea	[kre 'de a]

ei

Pronounce *ei* as the diphthong [ɛːi].

LL 2.3.30 Read aloud.

lei	[lɛːi]
sei	[sɛːi]
costei	[ko 'stɛːi]
bei	[bɛːi]
potrei	[po 'trɛːi]
vorrei	[vorː 'rɛːi]

Exception: Pronounce *pei*, a contraction of *per* and *i*, as [peːi], with a close [e].

eo

Pronounce *eo* as the two syllables [ɛ ɔ]. (Again, when two strong vowels appear together, they constitute two syllables.)

LL 2.3.31 Read aloud.

re-o	['rɛ ɔ]
Orfeo	[ɔr 'fɛ ɔ]
creola	['krɛ ɔ la]
leopardo	[le ɔ 'par do]

eu

Usually pronounce *eu* as the diphthong [ɛːu]. This diphthong is used infrequently in Italian and is occasionally pronounced [eːu]. If in doubt, pronounce it [ɛːu] in a stressed syllable and [eːu] in an unstressed syllable.

LL 2.3.32   Compare and contrast.

euro	[ˈɛːu ro]
Euridice	[eːu ri ˈdi tʃe]
pseudo	[ˈpsɛːu do]
eufonia	[eːu ˈfɔ nja]

The letter i

The letter *i* as a single vowel in a syllable is always pronounced as [i]. When *i* is combined with another vowel in a syllable, you need to decide whether it is pronounced as [i] or [j], or whether it is silent. See the rules below.

Caution: In English, unstressed *i* is often pronounced as [ɪ] as in the word *hit*. Do not carry this practice into Italian. The letter *i* is never pronounced as [ɪ] in Italian.

LL 2.3.33   Compare and contrast.

impero	[im ˈpe ro]	not	[ɪm ˈpe ro]

The single letter i

When *i* is final or occurs before a consonant, pronounce it as [i].

LL 2.3.34   Read aloud.

di	[di]
destino	[de ˈsti no]
capire	[ka ˈpi re]
il	[il]
finiti	[fi ˈni ti]
litigare	[li ti ˈga re]

When *i* occurs after a vowel, pronounce it as [i].

An *i* after a vowel forms a diphthong. Pronounce *i* as [i], giving it shorter duration than the preceding vowel.

LL 2.3.35   Read aloud.

noi	[noːi]
bei	[beːi]
mai	[maːi]
voi	[voːi]

Italian

sei	[seːi]
sai	[saːi]
poi	[pɔːi]
lei	[leːi]
laida	[ˈlaːi da]

When *i* occurs after *c, g,* or *sc* and before *a, e, o,* or *u*, it is silent.

Note: The silent *i* functions as a diacritical mark to soften the pronunciations of *c, g,* and *sc*.

LL 2.3.36   Read aloud.

baciare	[ba ˈtʃa re]
sciala	[ˈʃa la]
cielo	[ˈtʃɛ lo]
sciolto	[ˈʃol to]
ciò	[tʃɔ]
sciuppo	[ˈʃupː po]
fanciulla	[fan ˈtʃulː la]
lasciare	[ˈla ˈʃa re]
già	[dʒa]
gioco	[ˈdʒɔ ko]
giusto	[ˈdʒu sto]
vagheggiar	[va ɡedː ˈdʒar]

Exception: In a few words, the letter combination *ia* occurs at the end of a word, after *c* or *g*. In these words, the *i* is not silent, but forms an accented penultimate syllable.

LL 2.3.37   Read aloud.

Lucia	[lu ˈtʃi a]
nostalgia	[no stal ˈdʒi a]

There is no rule for determining this syllabic stress; you must rely on the metric stress of the melodic line or consult a dictionary. (See page 72.)

Italian

The letter i in consecutive vowel groups

ia

When *ia* is in the interior of a word and does not follow *c*, *g*, or *sc*, pronounce *ia* as the glide [ja].

LL 2.3.38   Read aloud.

fiamma	['fjam: ma]
piaga	['pja ga]
piante	['pjan te]
sembiante	[sɛm 'bjan te]
bianca	['bjaŋ ka]
schiava	['skja va]
andiam	[an 'djam]

See general rules for consecutive vowels on page 68.

When *ia* is unstressed and final in a word and does not follow *c*, *g*, or *sc*, pronounce the *ia* as the glide [ja].

LL 2.3.39   Read aloud.

gloria	['glɔ rja]
Italia	[i 'ta lja]
storia	['stɔ rja]
vittoria	[vit: 'tɔ rja]
aria	['a rja]
infamia	[in 'fa mja]
vicchia	['vik: kja]

When *ia* is in a three-letter word that has no accent mark, pronounce *ia* as two syllables ['i a].

LL 2.3.40   Read aloud.

mia	['mi a]
pia	['pi a]
via	['vi a]
fia	['fi a]

Italian

In a polysyllabic word, when *i* is stressed and followed by final *a* and there is no accent mark, pronounce *ia* as two syllables ['i a].

LL 2.3.41   Read aloud.

grafia	[gra 'fi a]
Maria	[ma 'ri a]
follia	[fol: 'li a]
gelosia	[dʒe lo 'zi a]

Also pronounce *ia* as two syllables in words where stressed *i* precedes *-ano* in the third personal plural verb ending.

LL 2.3.42   Read aloud.

siano	['si a no]
fiano	['fi a no]

ie

When *ie* is in an interior of a word or a final stressed syllable with an accent mark, and does not follow *c*, *g*, or *sc*, usually pronounce it as [jɛ].

LL 2.3.43   Read aloud.

barbiere	[bar 'bjɛ re]
pieno	['pjɛ no]
chiesa	['kjɛ za]
piè	['pjɛ]
chiedo	['kjɛ do]
vieni	['vjɛ ni]
tiene	['tjɛ ne]
obbediente	[ob: be 'djɛn te]

Exceptions: Pronounce *ie* in these common words as [je].

LL 2.3.44   Read aloud.

liete	['lje te]
insieme	[in 'sje me]
pietà	[pje 'ta]
siete	['sje te]

Italian

When *ie* occurs in an interior or final unstressed syllable of a word, pronounce it as [je].

LL 2.3.45 Read aloud.

fierezza	[fje ˈretː tsa]
smanie	[ˈzma nje]

Pronounce *ie* as the two syllables [ˈi e] when it is in three-letter words, without an accent.

LL 2.3.46 Read aloud.

mie	[ˈmi e]

In a polysyllabic word, when *i* is stressed, followed by a final *e*, and there is no accent mark, pronounce *ie* as two syllables [ˈi e].

LL 2.3.47 Read aloud.

follie	[folː ˈli e]

iei

Pronounce *iei* as the triphthong [jɛːi]. (A triphthong is a sequence of three vowel sounds that occur in the same syllable, usually composed of a glide and a diphthong.)

LL 2.3.48 Read aloud.

miei	[mjɛːi]

io

When *io* is in the interior of a word or a final stressed syllable with an accent mark, and does not follow *c*, *g*, or *sc*, usually pronounce it as [jɔ].

LL 2.3.49 Read aloud.

chiodo	[ˈkjɔ do]
fiocco	[ˈfjɔkː ko]
ansioso	[an ˈsjɔ zo]
pioggia	[ˈpjɔdː dʒa]
viola	[ˈvjɔ la]
Violetta	[ˈvjɔ ˈletː ta]

Exception: Pronounce *io* in these common words as [jo].

LL 2.3.50

fiore	[ˈfjo re]
passione	[pasː ˈsjo ne]

Italian

When *io* is unstressed and final in a word, pronounce it as [jɔ].

LL 2.3.51　　Read aloud.

rim<u>e</u>dio	[ri ˈmɛ djɔ]
sil<u>e</u>nzio	[si ˈlɛn tsjɔ]
C<u>a</u>nio	[ˈka njɔ]
v<u>e</u>cchio	[ˈvɛkː kjɔ]

Note: Final -*glio* is [ʎo]. (See "The Letter "g" on page 108.)

Pronounce *io* as the two syllables [ˈi o] when it is in two- or three-letter words without an accent mark.

LL 2.3.52　　Read aloud.

<u>io</u>	[ˈi o]
m<u>io</u>	[ˈmi o]
d<u>io</u>	[ˈdi o]

In a polysyllabic word, when *i* is stressed and followed by final *o* without an accent mark, pronounce *io* as the two syllable [ˈi o].

LL 2.3.53　　Read aloud.

add<u>io</u>	[adː ˈdi o]
colp<u>io</u>	[kol ˈpi o]
nat<u>io</u>	[na ˈti o]
des<u>io</u>	[de ˈzi o]

iu

When *iu* is in the interior of a word or in a final stressed syllable with an accent mark, and does not follow *c, g,* or *sc*, pronounce it as the glide [ju].

LL 2.3.54　　Read aloud.

Liù	[lju]
piuma	[ˈpju ma]
più	[pju]
schiuda	[ˈskju da]
liuto	[ˈlju to]
piuttosto	[pjutː ˈtɔ sto]

Italian

The letter O

Pronounce the Italian *o* in one of two ways: close [o] as in the English word *obey*, and open [ɔ], as the *aw* sound in *awe*.

> Caution: Be careful to sing pure [o] in Italian and never use diphthongal [oʊ] as you would in the English word *bone*.

To determine the pronunciation of the letter *o*, you must first determine whether it occurs in a stressed or unstressed syllable. The letter *o* in a stressed syllable is referred to as *stressed o*, in an unstressed syllable, *unstressed o*.

The Letter o in Stressed Syllables

If you determine that the syllable is stressed (see "Stressing" on page 58), you will need to make a choice between [o] or [ɔ]: stressed *o* has no other pronunciations. Unlike the letter *e*, your choice rarely affects the meaning of the word. See the rules beginning on page 94 for how to determine whether to pronounce stressed *o* as [o] or [ɔ].

> Note: These rules cannot cover all words. Rely upon your memory of often repeated words, or consult a dictionary.

The Letter o in Unstressed Syllables

If you determine that the letter *o* is in an unstressed syllable, then pronounce it as [o], except when it precedes *r* and another *consonant*. Some vocal pedagogues, however, direct singers to pronounce every unstressed *o* that follows a stressed syllable as [ɔ]. (See "The letter o unstressed" on page 94.) The letters *e* and *o* have similar characteristics. Use that discussion to make your personal choice whether to sing open [ɔ] or close [o] for unstressed *o*. Then, become aware of your choice and keep it consistent throughout your singing.

Pronounce the words in the following columns to increase your awareness of the two choices for pronouncing unstressed *o*. Pronounce a word in the first column using close [o]. Then pronounce the same word in the second column using open [ɔ]. Listen and feel the difference.

> Note: In Italian, as mentioned previously, you must use a consistent pronunciation for unstressed *o*. The following words are offered simply as an awareness exercise.

LL 2.3.55   Compare and contrast.

certo	['tʃer to]	certo	['tʃer tɔ]
parlo	['par lo]	parlo	['par lɔ]

Italian

perdono	['pɛr do no]	perdono	['pɛr dɔ nɔ]
primo	['pri mo]	primo	['pri mɔ]
almeno	[al 'me no]	almeno	[al 'me nɔ]
grido	['gri do]	grido	['gri dɔ]

The letter o unstressed

Usually pronounce unstressed *o* as [o]. (See the discussion on page 93.)

LL 2.3.56   Read aloud.

sospiro	[so 'spi ro]
momento	[mo 'men to]
prometto	[pro 'met: to]
toccare	[tok: 'ka re]
spelato	[spe 'la to]
novella	[no 'vɛl: la]
locale	[lo 'ka le]
ottava	[ot: 'ta va]
buffo	['buf: fo]
partorire	[par to 'ri re]

When unstressed *o* is followed by *r* and another *consonant*, pronounce it as [ɔ].

LL 2.3.57   Read aloud.

tor-men-to	[tɔr 'men to]
tor-na-re	[tɔr 'na re]
cor-pet-to	[kɔr 'pet: to]
dor-mi-re	[dɔr 'mi re]

The letter o stressed

When stressed *o* ends a syllable, usually pronounce it as [o].

LL 2.3.58   Read aloud.

so-no	['so no]
mo-stro	['mo stro]
a-mo-re	[a 'mo re]
o-gni	['o ɲi]
ri-go-re	[ri 'go re]
vo-ce	['vo tʃe]

Italian

To-sca	['to ska]
so-la	['so la]

Exceptions: These common words are exceptions to this rule. Pronounce stressed *o* in these words with [ɔ].

LL 2.3.59   Read aloud.

cosa	['kɔ za]	meaning *thing, affair*
core	['kɔ re]	from *cuore*, meaning *heart*
rosa	['rɔ za]	meaning *pink*
sposa	['spɔ za]	meaning *bride*
poco	['pɔ ko]	meaning *little, few*

In the following six circumstances, however, pronounce the stressed *o* that ends a syllable as open [ɔ], and *not* as [o].

1. When *o* ends a stressed antepenult (third-to-last) syllable, pronounce it as [ɔ].

   LL 2.3.60   Read aloud.

po-ve-ro	['pɔ ve ro]
o-pe-ra	['ɔ pe ra]
or-fa-na	['ɔr fa na]
po-po-lo	['pɔ po lo]

   Note: Rely upon the metric stress of the melodic line or consult a dictionary to determine when to give primary stress to the third-to-last syllable.

2. When *o* follows *i* or *u* in a stressed syllable, pronounce it as [ɔ].

   LL 2.3.61   Read aloud.

pio-ve	['pjɔ ve]
io-sa	['jɔ za]
scuo-la	['skwɔ la]
quo-ta	['kwɔ ta]

   Exception: fiore ['fjo re].

   See also rules for *io* (page 91) and *uo* (page 101).

3. When *o* is final and marked with an accent, pronounce it as [ɔ].

   Note: An accent mark over the final vowel indicates that the syllable is stressed.

Italian

LL 2.3.62   Read aloud.

farò	[fa 'rɔ]
salpò	[sal 'pɔ]
ciò	[tʃɔ]
finirò	[fi ni 'rɔ]
tornò	[tɔr 'nɔ]
lascierò	[la ʃɛ 'rɔ]
potrò	[po 'trɔ]
dileguò	[di le 'gwɔ]

4. When stressed *o* is followed by *gli*, pronounce it as [ɔ].

LL 2.3.63   Read aloud.

fo-glio	['fɔ ʎo]
sco-glio	['skɔ ʎo]

5. When stressed *o* is followed by a consonant and a glide, pronounce it as [ɔ].

LL 2.3.64   Read aloud.

glo-ria	['glɔ rja]
To-nio	['tɔ njɔ]
sto-ria	['stɔ rja]
me-mo-ria	[me 'mɔ rja]

6. When stressed *o* is in the noun ending *-oro* or its plural, *-ori*, pronounce it as [ɔ].

LL 2.3.65   Read aloud.

tesori	[te 'zɔ ri]
Lindoro	[lin 'dɔ ro]
Alindoro	[a lin 'dɔ ro]
oro	['ɔ ro]

When stressed *o* is followed by a vowel, usually pronounce it as [ɔ].

LL 2.3.66   Read aloud.

Diphthong:	poi	[pɔːi]
Triphthong:	vuoi	[vwɔːi]
Two syllables:	balboa	[bal 'bɔ a]

See the rules for the letter *o* in consecutive vowel groups on page 98.

When stressed *o* is followed by a consonant in the same syllable, usually pronounce it as [ɔ].

LL 2.3.67   Read aloud.

for-za	['fɔr tsa]
sor-te	['sɔr te]
mor-te	['mɔr te]
por-to	['pɔr to]

Exception: Pronounce these common words with [o]:

LL 2.3.68   Read aloud.

forma	['for ma]	meaning *shape, form*
forse	['for se]	meaning *doubt*
giorno	['dʒor no]	meaning *day*

In the following three circumstances, however, when stressed *o* is followed by a consonant in the same syllable, pronounce it as [o].

1. When stressed *o* is followed by the letter *l* and either *c, f, g, m, p,* or *t*, pronounce *o* as [o].

    LL 2.3.69   Read aloud.

dol-ce	['dol tʃe]
vol-to	['vol to]
col-po	['kol po]
a-scol-to	[a 'skol to]

    Exception: Pronounce the common word *volta* ['vɔl ta] (meaning *turn*) with open [ɔ].

2. When stressed *o* is followed by the letters *mb, mm,* or *mp*, pronounce *o* as [o].

    LL 2.3.70   Read aloud.

om-bra	['om bra]
gom-ma	['gom: ma]
pom-pa	['pom pa]
from-ba	['from ba]

Italian

3. When stressed *o* is followed by a single *n* in the same syllable, pronounce it as [o].

LL 2.3.71 Read aloud.

con	['kon]
r<u>o</u>n-di-ne	['ron di ne]
mon-do	['mon do]
don-de	['don de]

When stressed *o* is followed by a double consonant, check the dictionary. Sometimes it is pronounced [o], sometimes [ɔ].

LL 2.3.72 Compare and contrast.

Close		Open	
sot-to	[sot: to]	lot-to	[lɔt: to]
fos-si	[fos: si]	ap-pog-gio	[ap: 'pod: dʒo]
boc-ca	[bok: ka]	gob-bo	[gɔb: bo]

The letter o in consecutive vowel groups

oa

Pronounce the strong consecutive vowels *oa* as the two syllables [ɔ a].

LL 2.3.73 Read aloud.

bal-bo-a	[bal 'bɔ a]
so-a-ve	[sɔ 'a ve]

oe

See general rules for consecutive vowels on page 68.

Pronounce the strong consecutive vowels *oe* as the two syllables ['ɔ ɛ].

LL 2.3.74 Read aloud.

e-ro-e	[e 'rɔ ɛ]
po-e-ta	[pɔ 'ɛ ta]

Italian

oi

Usually pronounce *oi* as the diphthong [ɔːi].

LL 2.3.75 Read aloud.

poi	[pɔːi]
poiché	[pɔːi ˈke]

Exceptions: In these common words, pronounce the diphthong with [o].

voi	[voːi]
noi	[noːi]
coi	[koːi]

oia, oja

Pronounce *oia* and *oja* as the two syllables [ˈɔ ja].

LL 2.3.76 Read aloud.

gio-ia	[ˈdʒɔ ja]
gio-ja	[ˈdʒɔ ja]

The letter u

When the Italian letter *u* functions as a vowel, it is always pronounced as [u], as in the English word *boot*, never as [ʊ] as in *book*. The sound [ʊ] does not exist in Italian. When [u] is combined with another vowel in a syllable, you need to decide whether to pronounce it as [u] or the glide [w]. See the rules below.

The single letter u

When *u* occurs before a consonant, pronounce it as [u].

LL 2.3.77 Read aloud.

fugare	[fu ˈga re]
pupa	[ˈpu pa]
cucina	[ku ˈtʃi na]
lunga	[ˈluŋ ga]

Italian

When *u* follows a vowel, pronounce it as [u].

LL 2.3.78 Read aloud.

più	[pju]
liuto	[ˈlju to]
pausa	[ˈpaːu za]
Euridice	[eːu ri ˈdi tʃe]

The letter u in consecutive vowel groups

ua

Usually pronounce *ua* as the glide [wa].

LL 2.3.79 Read aloud.

quanto	[ˈkwan to]
graduare	[gra ˈdwa re]
squadare	[skwa ˈda re]
statua	[ˈsta twa]

Pronounce *ua* as the two syllables [ˈu a] in a small word that has no accent mark. Notice that the *u* is stressed.

LL 2.3.80 Read aloud.

tua	[ˈtu a]

ue

Usually pronounce *ue* as the glide [wɛ].

LL 2.3.81 Read aloud.

guerra	[ˈgwɛːˑra]
estinguerà	[e stiŋ gwe ˈra]

Exception: The common words *quello* [ˈkwɛːˑlo] and *questo* [ˈkwe sto] are pronounced with [e].

Pronounce *ue* as the two syllables [ˈu e] in a small word that has no accent mark. Notice that the *u* is stressed.

LL 2.3.82 Read aloud.

tue	[ˈtu e]
due	[ˈdu e]

Italian

ui

Usually pronounce *ui* as the glide [wi].

> Note: When ui follows *q* or *g*, or is in the interior of a word, the result is a glide.
>
> LL 2.3.83 Read aloud.
>
> | qui | [kwi] |
> |---|---|
> | languir' | [laŋ 'gwir] |

When *ui* is final in a small word and there is no accent mark, pronounce it as the two syllables ['u i].

> LL 2.3.84 Read aloud.
>
> | lui | ['lu i] |
> |---|---|
> | cui | ['ku i] |
> | fui | ['fu i] |

uo

Usually pronounce *uo* as the glide [wɔ].

> When the weak vowel *u* is followed by the strong vowel *o* in the initial or interior position of the word, or is final with an accent mark, pronounce the vowel combination as a glide.
>
> LL 2.3.85 Read aloud.
>
> | uomo | ['wɔ mo] |
> |---|---|
> | nuovo | ['nwɔ vo] |
> | può | [pwɔ] |
> | duolo | ['dwɔ lo] |
> | vuole | ['vwɔ le] |
> | dileguò | [di le 'gwɔ] |
> | fuori | ['fwɔ ri] |
> | cuore | ['kwɔ re] |

Pronounce *uo* as the two syllables ['u o] in small words when it is final in the word and there is no accent mark.

> LL 2.3.86 Read aloud.
>
> | tuo | ['tu o] |
> |---|---|
> | suo | ['su o] |

uie

Pronounce *uie* as the triphthong [wjɛ].

LL 2.3.87 Read aloud.

| quiete | [kwjɛ te] |

uio

Pronounce *uio* as the two syllables ['u jɔ].

LL 2.3.88 Read aloud.

| buio | ['bu jɔ] |

uoi

Pronounce *uoi* as the triphthong [wɔːi].

LL 2.3.89 Read aloud.

tuoi	[twɔːi]
suoi	[swɔːi]
vuoi	[vwɔːi]

uoio

Pronounce *uoio* as the two syllables ['wɔ jɔ].

LL 2.3.90 Read aloud.

| muoio | ['mwɔ jɔ] |

Italian Consonants in Detail

Pronounce *b* as [b].

> Note: [b] represents the sound of *b* in the English word *boy*. But in Italian [b] is a "dry" consonant pronounced with less aspiration than in English.

LL 2.4.91   Read aloud.

bocca	['bok: ka]
abisso	[a 'bis: so]
bacio	['ba tʃo]
batti	['bat: ti]
barbara	['bar ba ra]
bambino	[bam 'bi no]

bb

Pronounce *bb* as [b: b].

> Note: Pronounce [b: b] with a longer duration than [b]. Close your lips for the stop portion of the consonant, prolong the stop, and then articulate the plosive part of the consonant.

LL 2.4.92   Compare and contrast.

Examples of [b: b] in English:	
lab bone	
grab back	
Examples in Italian:	
babbo	['bab: bo]
labbro	['lab: bro]
gabbare	[gab: 'ba re]
abbia	['ab: bja]
rabbia	['rab: bja]
abbandonare	[ab: ban do 'na re]

c

When *c* is followed by *a*, *o*, or *u*, pronounce it as [k]. When *c* is pronounced as [k], it is called a *hard c*.

Italian

Note: [k] represents the sound of *k* in the English word *kit*. But in Italian [k] is a "dry" consonant, pronounced with less aspiration than in English.

LL 2.4.93   Read aloud.

canta	['kan ta]
culto	['kul to]
copia	['ko pja]
cura	['ku ra]
stancare	[staŋ 'ka re]
pecora	['pɛ ko ra]

When *cc* is followed by *a, o,* or *u*, pronounce it as [k: k].

Note: Pronounce [k: k] with a longer duration than [k]. Lift the back of your tongue to touch your soft palate for the stop portion of [k]; after a short silent pause, articulate the plosive part of the consonant.

LL 2.4.94   Compare and contrast.

Examples of [k: k] in English :	
pin**k** **c**at	
mil**k** **c**ow	
Examples in Italian:	
bocca	['bok: ka]
sorccoso	[sɔrk: 'ko zo]
ecco	['ɛk: ko]
accusa	[ak: 'ku za]
pecca	['pɛk: ka]
lucca	['luk: ka]

When *c* is followed by *e* or *i*, pronounce it as [tʃ]. A *c* pronounced as [tʃ] is called a *soft c*.

Note: [tʃ] represents the sound of *ch* in the English word *chair*. [tʃ] is an affricative consonant that is made up of the stop of the stop-plosive consonant [t], as in *tip*, combined with the fricative consonant [ʃ], as in *ship*.

LL 2.4.95   Read aloud.

faci	['fa tʃi]
celare	[tʃe 'la re]
certo	['tʃɛr to]

dolce	[ˈdol tʃe]
dieci	[ˈdje tʃi]
Ciro	[ˈtʃi ro]
bacio	[ˈba tʃo]

Note: Even though the *i*, as in *bacio* [ˈba tʃo], is silent, it continues to function as a diacritical mark that softens the pronunciation of *c* to [tʃ]. (See the rule for silent *i* on page 88.)

When *cc* is followed by *e* or *i*, pronounce it as [tː tʃ].

Note: Pronounce [tː tʃ] with longer duration than [tʃ]. Produce [tː tʃ] by lifting the tip of your tongue to touch the back of your upper front teeth for the stop portion of [t]; then after a short silent pause, let the air escape in a fricative [ʃ].

Note: The diacritical mark [ː] indicates the longer duration of the stop portion of [t]. The symbol [t] is written a second time to emphasize the importance of prolonging the doubled consonant in Italian.

LL 2.4.96   Compare and contrast.

Examples of [tː tʃ] in English:	
ha<u>t c</u>heck	
sof<u>t c</u>hair	
Examples in Italian:	
accenti	[atː ˈtʃen ti]
traccia	[ˈtratː tʃa]
braccio	[ˈbratː tʃo]
Puccini	[putː ˈtʃi ni]

When *c* is followed by a consonant other than *c*, pronounce it as [k].

LL 2.4.97   Read aloud.

cla<u>vi</u>cola	[kla ˈvi ko la]
cl<u>i</u>nica	[ˈkli ni ka]
cr<u>e</u>dere	[ˈkre de re]
cr<u>u</u>da	[ˈkru da]
cl<u>a</u>ssico	[ˈklasː si ko]
crescendo	[kre ˈʃen do]

Italian

ch & cch

Pronounce *ch* as [k].

Note: In the digraph *ch*, the *h* is silent. When *ch* occurs before *e* or *i*, the *h* functions as a diacritical mark to harden the pronunciation of *c* to [k].

LL 2.4.98   Read aloud.

che	[ke]
poiché	[poːi 'kɛ]
chiama	['kja ma]
chi	[ki]
chiesi	['kjɛ zi]
inciuchire	[in tʃu 'ki re]

Pronounce *cch* as [kː k].

Note: Pronounce [kː k] with longer duration than [k].

LL 2.4.99   Read aloud.

pacchetto	[pakː 'ketː to]
macchina	['makː ki na]
vecchie	['vekː kje]
acchetare	[akː ke 'ta re]
occhi	['ɔkː ki]

cqu

Pronounce *cqu* as [kː k].

Note: In these words, the *c* is pronounced as [k] and *q* is pronounced as [k], resulting in the prolonged sound [kː k].

LL 2.4.100   Read aloud.

acqua	['akː kwa]
acquieta	[akː 'kwjɛ ta]
acquisire	[akː kwi 'zi re]

Italian

d

Pronounce *d* as [d].

Note: [d] is the sound of *d* in the English word *day*. But in Italian *d* is a dental consonant, not the alveolar *d* used in English. It is also articulated more dryly, with less aspiration, than in English.

LL 2.4.101   Read aloud.

dare	['da re]
deserto	[de 'zɛr to]
diva	['di va]
ind<u>o</u>cile	[in 'dɔ ʧi le]
padre	['pa dre]
dottore	[dot: 'to re]

Pronounce *dd* as [d: d].

Note: Pronounce [d: d] with longer duration than [d]. Place the tip of your tongue on the back of your upper front teeth, and then articulate the plosive part of the consonant.

LL 2.4.102   Compare and contrast.

Examples of [d: d] in English:	
Ne<u>d d</u>id	
be<u>d d</u>own	
Examples in Italian:	
Nedda	['nɛd: da]
freddo	['fred: do]
add<u>i</u>o	[ad: 'di o]
Turiddu	[tu 'rid: du]
bodda	['bɔd: da]
addosso	[ad: 'dɔs: so]

f

Pronounce *f* as [f].

Note: [f] is the sound of *f* in the English word *feet*.

LL 2.4.103   Read aloud.

fato	['fa to]
rifare	[ri 'fa re]
figura	[fi 'gu ra]

Italian

figlia	[ˈfi ʎa]
infelice	[in fe ˈli tʃe]
confessione	[kon fesː ˈsjo ne]

Pronounce *ff* as [fː f].

Note: Pronounce [fː f] with a longer duration than [f].

LL 2.4.104 Compare and contrast.

Examples of [fː f] in English:	
cli**ff** **f**all	
o**ff** **f**ool	
Examples in Italian:	
affanni	[afː fanː ni]
affetto	[afː ˈfɛtː to]
maffia	[ˈmafː fja]
gaffa	[ˈgafː fa]

g

When *g* is followed by *a, o, u*, or a *consonant*, pronounce it as [g]. When *g* is pronounced as [g], it is called a *hard g*.

Note: [g] is the sound of *g* as in the English word *go*. The Italian [g] has a drier, less aspirate sound than in English.

LL 2.4.105 Read aloud.

guarda	[ˈgwar da]
magari	[ma ˈga ri]
gala	[ˈga la]
uguale	[u ˈgwa le]
figura	[fi ˈgu ra]
agonia	[a go ˈni a]
grato	[ˈgra to]
grosso	[ˈgrosː so]

When *g* is followed by *e* or *i*, pronounce it as [dʒ]. When *g* is pronounced as [dʒ], it is called a *soft g*.

Note: [dʒ] is the sound of *dg* as in the English word *fudge*. [dʒ] combines the stop portion of the stop-plosive [d] (as in *dog*) with the fricative [ʒ] (as in the English word *vision*).

Italian

LL 2.4.106 Read aloud.

Gesù	[dʒe ˈzu]
magistero	[ma dʒi ˈstɛ ro]
geo	[ˈdʒɛ ɔ]
gemma	[ˈdʒem: ma]
giorni	[ˈdʒor ni]
bugia	[bu ˈdʒi a]

Note: The *i* (as in *giorno*) is silent and functions as a diacritical mark that softens the pronunciation of *g* to [dʒ]. (See the rule for silent *i* on page 88.)

gg

When *gg* is followed by *a, o, u*, or a *consonant*, pronounce it as [g: g].

Note: Pronounce [g: g] with a longer duration than [g]. Lift the back of your tongue to touch your soft palate for the stop portion of the consonant; after a short pause, articulate the plosive part of the consonant.

LL 2.4.107 Compare and contrast.

Examples of [g: g] in English:	
dog gone	
big gap	
Examples in Italian:	
fugga	[ˈfug: ga]
agguato	[ag: ˈgwa to]
aggrado	[ag: ˈgra do]
leggo	[ˈlɛg: go]
soggolo	[sɔg: ˈgo lo]
reggo	[ˈrɛg: go]

When *gg* is followed by *e* or *i*, pronounce it as [d: dʒ].

Note: Pronounce [d: dʒ] with a longer duration of sound than [dʒ]. The stop portion of [d] is prolonged before the *zh* [ʒ] is articulated.

LL 2.4.108 Compare and contrast.

Examples of [d: dʒ] in English:
mad George
bad gem

Italian

Examples in Italian:

maggio	['mad: dʒo]
guiggiare	[gwid: 'dʒa re]
raggio	['rad: dʒo]
reggia	['rɛd: dʒa]
figge	['fid: dʒe]
loggia	['lɔd: dʒa]

gh

Pronounce *gh* as [g].

Note: In the digraph *gh* the *h* is silent. In Italian, *h* functions as a diacritical mark to harden the sound of *g* before *e* or *i*.

LL 2.4.109   Read aloud.

ghirlanda	[gir 'lan da]
Respighi	[re 'spi gi]
vaghi	['va gi]
ghermita	[ger 'mi ta]
ghetta	['get: ta]
gangherare	[gaŋ ge 'ra re]

gli

Pronounce the letters *gli* as *elya* [ʎ].

Note: A lateral palatal consonant, this sound does not exist in English, but is similar to the [lj] in *mil<u>l</u>ion*. (See page 66 for a full explanation of *elya* [ʎ].)

LL 2.4.110   Read aloud.

foglia	['fɔ ʎa]
consiglio	[kon 'si ʎo]
Pagliacci	[pa 'ʎat: tʃi]
Guglielmo	[gu 'ʎɛl mo]
figlio	['fi ʎo]
moglie	['mɔ ʎe]

Note: When *gli* stands alone in a syllable, without another vowel, the *i* is transcribed as [i].

Italian

LL 2.4.111 Read aloud.

gli	[ʎi]
e-gli	['e ʎi]

gl, gn, & gu

When *gl* is followed by *a, e, o,* or *u,* pronounce it as [gl]. Read aloud.

LL 2.4.112 Read aloud.

glauca	['glaːu ka]
gloria	['glɔ rja]
glutine	[glu 'ti ne]
gleba	['glɛ ba]

Pronounce the digraph *gn* as enya [ɲ].

Note: A nasal, palatal consonant, this sound does not exist in English, but is similar to the [nj] in o*ni*on. (See page 66 for a full explanation of this sound.)

LL 2.4.113 Read aloud.

degno	['de ɲo]
compagno	[kom 'pa ɲo]
bisogna	[bi 'zɔ ɲa]
Signori	[si 'ɲo ri]
gnudo	['ɲu do]
gnocco	['ɲɔkː ko]

When *gu* is followed by a vowel, pronounce it as [gw].

LL 2.4.114 Read aloud.

seguire	[se 'gwi re]
guarda	['gwar da]
guerra	['gwɛːr ra]
guida	['gwi da]

h

The letter *h* is always silent.

LL 2.4.115 Read aloud.

| ho | [ɔ] |
| ha | [a] |

Italian

hai	[aːi]
hanno	['anː no]

Note: In Italian, the silent *h* often follows *c* and *g* and hardens their pronunciation to [k] and [g]. (See the listings for *ch* on page 106; *gh* on page 110.)

LL 2.4.116   Read aloud.

chi	[ki]
ghirlando	[gir 'lan do]
che	[ke]
lunghezza	[lun 'getː tsa]
schiavo	['skja vo]
ghetto	['getː to]

j

Pronounce the letter *j* as [j].
   Note: The letter *j* is only used in older Italian spellings. The name of the symbol [j] is *jot* [jɔt]. It sounds like *y* in *yes*.

LL 2.4.117   Read aloud.

Old spelling:	gaja	['ga ja]
Current spelling:	gaia	['ga ja]

k

The letter *k* is only used in foreign words and would be pronounced as it is in that language.

l

Pronounce the letter *l* as [l].

Note: [l] is the "clear" sound of *l* as in *leap*. Pronounce the lateral consonant [l] as a dental sound. Lift the tip of your tongue to touch the back of your upper front teeth, instead of your alveolar ridge as in English.

LL 2.4.118   Read aloud.

libertà	[li ber 'ta]
fedele	[fe 'de le]

legale	[le ˈga le]
alto	[ˈal to]
luogo	[ˈlwɔ go]
dolore	[do ˈlo re]

Pronounce *ll* as [l: l].

Note: Pronounce [l: l] with a more prolonged sound than [l].

LL 2.4.119 Compare and contrast.

Examples of [l: l] in English:	
te**ll L**assie	
wa**ll l**ight	
Examples in Italian:	
folla	[ˈfɔl: la]
bello	[ˈbɛl: lo]
cartella	[kar ˈtɛl: la]
molle	[ˈmɔl: le]

Pronounce the letter *m* as [m], as in the English word *meat*.

LL 2.4.120 Read aloud.

Marta	[ˈmar ta]
mano	[ˈma no]
amore	[a ˈmo re]
dorma	[ˈdɔr ma]
tema	[ˈte ma]
mondo	[ˈmon do]

Pronounce *mm* as [m: m].

Note: Pronounce [m: m] with a more prolonged sound than [m].

LL 2.4.121 Compare and contrast.

Examples of [m: m] in English:	
du**mb m**an	
Mo**m m**urmured	
Examples in Italian:	
mamma	[ˈmam: ma]
domma	[ˈdɔm: ma]

Italian

gemma	[ˈdʒɛmː ma]
commosso	[komː ˈmɔsː so]
sommetta	[somː ˈmɛtː ta]
vendemmia	[vɛn ˈdɛmː mja]

n

Pronounce the letter *n* as [n], as in the English word *name*.

Note: Italian [n] is pronounced dentally. Place the tip of your tongue on the back of your upper front teeth, instead of your alveolar ridge as in English.

LL 2.4.122   Read aloud.

nome	[ˈno me]
nozze	[ˈnɔtː tse]
numero	[ˈnu me ro]
funesto	[fu ˈnɛ sto]
domani	[do ˈma ni]
cantare	[kan ˈta re]

Pronounce double *nn* as [nː n].

Note: Pronounce [nː n] with a more prolonged sound than [n].

LL 2.4.123   Compare and contrast.

Examples of [nː n] in English:	
Na**n** **k**nits	
ca**n** **n**ever	
Examples in Italian:	
donna	[ˈdɔnː na]
Susanna	[su ˈzanː na]
manna	[ˈmanː na]
nonna	[ˈnɔnː na]

When *n* is followed by the sounds [k] or [g], pronounce it as [ŋ]. (The name of the symbol [ŋ] is *eng*.

Note: Pronounce [ŋ] as *ng* in the English word *hung*. The back of your tongue lifts to touch your soft palate.

LL 2.4.124   Read aloud.

bianco	[ˈbjaŋ ko]
ancora	[aŋ ˈko ra]
lungo	[ˈluŋ go]

Italian

sangue	[ˈsaŋ gwe]
inglese	[iŋ ˈgle ze]
banca	[ˈbaŋ ka]

In words with the initial syllable *in* followed by the sounds [k] or [g], pronounce *n* as [ŋ].

LL 2.4.125   Read aloud.

ingrato	[iŋ ˈgra to]
incluso	[iŋ ˈklu zo]
inganno	[iŋ ˈgan: no]
incolpare	[iŋ kol ˈpa re]

p

Pronounce the letter *p* as [p], as in the English word *put*.

Note: The Italian [p] is pronounced with less aspiration than in English.

LL 2.4.126   Read aloud.

pianto	[ˈpjan to]
porto	[ˈpɔr to]
crepa	[ˈkre pa]
compenso	[kom ˈpen so]
speme	[ˈspɛ me]
placido	[ˈpla tʃi do]

Pronounce *pp* [p: p].

Note: Pronounce [p: p] with a longer duration of sound than [p]. Close your lips for the stop portion of the consonant; prolong the stop, and then articulate the plosive part of the consonant.

LL 2.4.127   Compare and contrast.

Examples of [p: p] in English:	
hel<u>p P</u>aul	
cla<u>p p</u>roudly	
Examples in Italian:	
drappo	[ˈdrap: po]
applauso	[ap: ˈpla:u zo]
supplice	[ˈsup: pli tʃe]
coppa	[ˈkɔp: pa]

Italian

q

Pronounce *qu* as [kw] as in the English word *queen*.

Note: In Italian the letter *q* is always followed by the vowel *u*.

LL 2.4.128 Read aloud.

qua	[kwa]
acqua	[ˈakː kwa]
quota	[ˈkwɔ ta]
questa	[ˈkwe sta]
qui	[kwi]
quando	[ˈkwan do]

r

Pronounce the letter *r* in Italian as either a flipped or trilled *r*. Do not pronounce it as the retroflex *r* of English. (See "Flipped and Trilled r" on page 65.)

Note: If desired, the IPA symbol [ɾ] may be used to represent the flipped *r*. (See page 65.) This text, for simplicity, uses [r] for the flipped and trilled *r*.

When *r* occurs between two vowels, pronounce it as flipped *r*.

LL 2.4.129 Read aloud.

fiore	[ˈfjo re]
severo	[se ˈvɛ ro]
mistero	[mi ˈstɛ ro]
mirare	[mi ˈra re]

Use a trilled *r* when *r* is initial or final, when *r* follows a consonant in the same syllable, or when *r* follows a stressed vowel and precedes a consonant.

Initial *r*:

LL 2.4.130 Read aloud.

rosa	[ˈrɔ za]
rabbia	[ˈrabː bja]
raggio	[ˈradː dʒo]
ruspa	[ˈru spa]
ricatto	[ri ˈkatː to]
ruzza	[ˈrudː dza]

r after a consonant in the same syllable:

LL 2.4.131   Read aloud.

cruda	['kru da]
prosa	['prɔ za]
fronte	['fron te]
struggo	['strug: go]
ingrato	[in 'gra to]
Adrianna	[a 'drjan: na]

r after a stressed vowel and before another consonant:

LL 2.4.132   Read aloud.

parto	['par to]
guarda	['gwar da]
giorno	['dʒor no]
perdono	['pɛr do no]
morte	['mɔr te]
ricordo	[ri 'kɔr do]

Final *r*:

LL 2.4.133   Read aloud.

cantar	[kan 'tar]
morir	[mo 'rir]
danzar	[dan 'tsar]
gioir	[dʒɔ 'ir]
cor	[kɔr]
orror	[ɔr: 'ror]

Some words end in *r* because they are apocopated—that is, shortened, as when *core* appears as *cor*. When such a word ends a phrase or precedes a consonant, trill the *r*; when such a word precedes a vowel, flip the *r*.

Read aloud.

trilled:	un lieto cor!
	un cor di fero
flipped:	un cor amato

Italian

rr

Pronounce *rr* as [rː r] with a more prolonged trill than [r].

Note: A long, trilled *rr* is necessary for correct Italian diction, although to many American ears it seems excessive.

LL 2.4.134   Read aloud.

terra	['tɛrː ra]
errore	[ɛrː 'ro re]
orrido	['ɔrː ri do]
Ferrando	[fɛrː 'ran do]
terrore	[tɛrː 'ro re]
guerra	[gwɛrː ra]

s

When the letter *s* is initial in a word and is followed by a vowel, pronounce it as [s].

LL 2.4.135   Read aloud.

sento	['sɛn to]
sebben	['sɛbː bɛn]
segreto	[se 'gre to]
sempre	['sɛm pre]
sopore	[so 'po re]
sarò	[sa 'rɔ]

When *s* is initial in a syllable, follows a consonant, and precedes a vowel, pronounce it as [s].

LL 2.4.136   Read aloud.

mar-si-na	[mar 'si na]
ten-sio-ne	[tɛn 'sjɔ ne]
men-so-la	['mɛn so la]
ver-so	['vɛr so]
mo-strar-si	[mo 'strar si]
per-so-na	[pɛr 'so na]

Italian

When *s* is initial in a syllable, and precedes an unvoiced consonant, pronounce it as [s].

LL 2.4.137   Read aloud.

sfi-gu-ra-re	[sfi gu 'ra re]
sfor-zan-do	[sfɔr 'tsan do]
sfioc-co	['sfjɔk: ko]
sfac-cia	['sfat: tʃa]
spar-gi	['spar dʒi]
spir-to	['spir to]
scrit-to	['skrit: to]
scre-zio	['skre tsjɔ]
scrol-lo	['scrɔl: lo]
scru-ma-re	[skru 'ma re]
ar-re-sta	[ar: 're sta]
ca-sta	['ka sta]

When the letter *s* is final, pronounce it as [s].

LL 2.4.138   Read aloud.

Radamès	[ra da 'mɛs]
Amneris	[am 'ne ris]

When the letter *s* occurs between vowels, pronounce it as [z].

Note: Pronounce [z] as in the English word *zero*.

LL 2.4.139   Read aloud.

basilica	[ba 'zi li ka]
presa	['pre za]
sposo	['spɔ zo]
spinose	[spi 'no ze]
tesoro	[te 'zɔ ro]
rosario	[ro 'za rjɔ]

Note: Although there are some exceptions to this rule in spoken Italian (most notably *cusa* ['ka sa], *cosa, cosi,* and *desiderio*), most singers sing [z] in these words.

Note: In a few words with prefixes *pre-* and *ri-*, the intervocalic *s* must be pronounced [s]. Check a dictionary.

Italian

When the letter *s* is initial and is followed by a voiced consonant in the same syllable, pronounce it as [z].

LL 2.4.140   Read aloud.

smanie	[ˈzma nje]
sventura	[zvɛn ˈtu ra]
sbarra	[ˈzbarː ra]
sgelo	[ˈzdʒe lo]
sdegnare	[zde ˈɲa re]
slentare	[zlɛn ˈta re]

ss

Pronounce *ss* as [sː s].

Note: Pronounce [sː s] with a more prolonged sound than [s]. Be sure the sound remains unvoiced.

LL 2.4.141   Compare and contrast.

Examples of [sː s] in English:	
succe<u>ss s</u>equence	
ca<u>se s</u>tands	
Examples in Italian:	
cassa	[ˈkasː sa]
lusso	[ˈlusː so]
vissi	[ˈvisː si]
esso	[ˈesː so]
possente	[posː ˈsɛn te]
oppresso	[opː ˈprɛsː so]

sc, sch

When *sc* is followed by *a*, *o*, or *u*, pronounce it as [sk].

LL 2.4.142   Read aloud.

scusare	[sku ˈza re]
cascare	[ka ˈska re]
scolta	[ˈskol ta]
riscontro	[ri ˈskon tro]
scuola	[ˈskwɔ la]
discordare	[di skɔr ˈda re]

When *sc* is followed *e* or *i*, pronounce it as [ʃ].

> Note: Pronounce [ʃ] as *sh* in the English word <u>she</u>. The name of the symbol [ʃ] is *esh* [ɛʃ].
>
> LL 2.4.143   Read aloud.
>
> | scena | [ˈʃɛ na] |
> |---|---|
> | scelta | [ˈʃɛl ta] |
> | ruscello | [ru ˈʃɛlː lo] |
> | scintilla | [ʃin ˈtilː la] |
> | sciolto | [ˈʃɔl to] |
> | bascia | [ˈba ʃa] |
>
> Note: Even though the *i*, as in *sciolto*, is silent, it continues to act as an agent to soften the *sc* to [ʃ]. (See the rule for silent *i* on page 88).

Pronounce *sch* as [sk].

> Note: When *h* occurs after *c* and before *e* or *i*, it hardens *c* to [k].
>
> LL 2.4.144   Read aloud.
>
> | scherzo | [ˈskɛr tso] |
> |---|---|
> | luschero | [ˈlu ske ro] |
> | rischioso | [ri ˈskjɔ zo] |
> | schiaffare | [skjafː ˈfa re] |
> | schema | [ˈske ma] |
> | immischiarsi | [imː mi ˈskjar si] |

Pronounce the letter *t* as [t] as in the English word *team*.

> Note: In Italian, [t] is a dental, dry consonant. Place the tip of your tongue on the back of your upper front teeth, instead of your alveolar ridge as in English, and give less aspiration on the plosive part of the consonant.
>
> LL 2.4.145   Read aloud.
>
> | timore | [ti ˈmo re] |
> |---|---|
> | punto | [ˈpun to] |
> | guinta | [ˈgwin ta] |
> | bistro | [ˈbi stro] |
> | terzo | [ˈter tso] |

Italian

tanto	['tan to]
mite	['mi te]

Pronounce *tt* as [tː t] with a longer duration than t [t].

> Note: Pronounce [tː t] with a longer duration than [t]. Place the tip of your tongue on the back of your upper front teeth. Your tongue tip remains in that position for a brief pause, then releases plosively, but with a drier, less aspirate sound than in English.
>
> LL 2.4.146   Compare and contrast.

Examples of [tː t] in English:	
Pat tells	
met Tim	
Examples in Italian:	
ditta	['ditː ta]
moffetta	[mofː 'fetː ta]
ricetta	[ri tʃetː ta]
batti	['batː ti]
Masetto	[ma 'zetː to]
Violetta	[vjɔ 'letː ta]

Pronounce the letter *v* as [v], as in the English word *victor*.

LL 2.4.147   Read aloud.

avanti	[a 'van ti]
virtù	[vir 'tu]
voce	['vo tʃe]
viola	['vjɔ la]
favore	[fa 'vo re]
malvivo	[mal 'vi vo]

Pronounce *vv* as [vː v].

> Note: Pronounce [vː v] with a more prolonged sound than [v].
>
> LL 2.4.148   Compare and contrast.

Examples of [vː v] in English:
have verses
save Victor

Italian

Examples in Italian:

avverso	[avːˈvɛr so]
avvolto	[avːˈvɔl to]

W

The letter *w* is used only in foreign words. Pronounce it as you would in that language.

X

The letter *x* is used only in foreign words. Pronounce it as you would in that language.

Y

The letter *y* is used only in foreign words. Pronounce it as you would in that language.

Z

The consonant *z* in Italian has two pronunciations: [ts] (as in *eats*) or [dz] (as in *beads*). There are no consistent rules for determining which pronunciation to use, although [ts] is more frequent. Consult a reliable dictionary for correct pronunciation.

Note: The following words use the unvoiced combination sound [ts], which is composed of the stop portion of [t] followed by the fricative [s].

LL 2.4.149   Read aloud.

zio	[ˈtsi o]
terzo	[ˈtɛr tso]
zitto	[ˈtsitː to]
grazia	[ˈɡra tsja]
danza	[ˈdan tsa]
delizia	[de ˈli tsja]

The following words use the voiced combination sound [dz], which is composed of the stop portion of [d] followed by the fricative [z].

LL 2.4.150   Read aloud.

zelo	[ˈdze lo]
Zerlina	[dzɛr ˈli na]

Italian

bronzo	[ˈbrɔn dzo]
donzella	[don ˈdzɛlː la]
Azucena	[a dzu ˈtʃe na]
Zuniga	[dzu ˈni ga]

The letter group zz is pronounced either as [tː ts] or [dː dz]. Consult a dictionary to determine whether a word should be pronounced with [tː ts] or [dː dz]. Pronounce the zz with a more prolonged sound than a single z.

Pay attention to the difference between the sounds of [dz] and [dʒ]. Do not confuse these two sounds.

LL 2.4.151   Read aloud.

Examples in English comparing [dz] with [dʒ]:	
feeds	[fidz]
fudge	[fʌdʒ]
beads	[bidz]
budge	[bʌdʒ]

LL 2.4.152   Read aloud.

Examples in Italian comparing [dː dz] with [dː dʒ]:	
vizza	[vidː dza]
figge	[fidː dʒe]
mezzo	[mɛdː dzo]
reggia	[rɛdː dʒa]

Pronounce these words with [tː ts].

LL 2.4.153   Read aloud.

mezzo	[ˈmetː tso]	(of fruit, over-ripe)
nozze	[ˈnɔtː tse]	
guizzare	[gwitː ˈtsa re]	
mazza	[ˈmatː tsa]	
pizza	[ˈpitː tsa]	

Pronounce these words with [dː dz].

LL 2.4.154   Read aloud.

mezzo	[ˈmɛdː dzo]	(half, medium, mezzo-soprano)
Mezzana	[mɛdː ˈdza na]	
bizzarro	[bidː ˈdza ro]	
gazza	[ˈgadː dza]	

Latin

Latin Diction

Latin

Chart of Latin Sounds

The following chart lists the sounds of Latin in alphabetical order. Refer to this chart to quickly check the sound of a spelling. For special circumstances and exceptions to the sounds that cannot be presented easily in a simple chart, see the discussions of the individual sounds later in this chapter.

	Italian Letter and Position in Word		IPA	Example	and IPA	Page
a	a		[ɑ]	mala	[ˈmɑ lɑ]	137
	æ		[ɛ]	æternæ	[ɛ ˈtɛr nɛ]	133, 137
	au	(diphthong)	[ɑːu]	causa	[ˈkɑːu zɑ]	137
	ay	(diphthong)	[ɑːi]	Raymundi	[rɑːi ˈmun di]	138
b	b		[b]	bonæ	[ˈbɔ nɛ]	142
c	c, cc	before *a, o, u,* or a *consonant*	[k]	corda	[ˈkɔr dɑ]	142
	c, cc	before *e, æ, œ, i* or *y*	[tʃ]	lucis	[ˈlu tʃis]	142
	c	between *ex* and *e, æ, œ, i,* or *y*	[ʃ]	excelsis	[ɛk ˈʃɛl sis]	142
	c	final	[k]	fac	[fɑk]	142
	ch		[k]	Christum	[ˈkri stum]	142
d	d		[d]	domine	[ˈdɔ mi nɛ]	143
e	e		[ɛ]	testi	[ˈtɛ sti]	138
	eu	(diphthong)	[ɛːu]	euge	[ˈɛːu dʒɛ]	138
	eu	(two syllables)	[ɛ u]	Deum	[ˈdɛ um]	138
f	f		[f]	finis	[ˈfi nis]	144
g	g	before *a, o, u,* or a *consonant*	[g]	plagas	[ˈplɑ gɑs]	144
	g	before *e, æ, œ, i,* or *y*	[dʒ]	regina	[rɛ ˈdʒi nɑ]	144
	gn		[ɲ]*	Agnus	[ˈɑ ɲus]	144, 147
h	h		silent	Hosanna	[ɔ ˈzɑnː nɑ]	145
		exceptions: nihil, mihi	[k]	nihil, mihi	[ˈni kil] [ˈmi ki]	145
i	i		[i]	liber	[ˈli bɛr]	139
	i	between two *vowels*	[j]	alleluia	[ɑlː lɛ ˈlu jɑ]	139
j	j		[j]	Jesu	[ˈjɛ zu]	145

* *The IPA symbol enya* [ɲ] *represents a sound similar to the* ni *of the English word* onion [ˈʌn jən].
See page 144.

Latin

Italian Letter and Position in Word		IPA	Example and	IPA	Page
k		[k]	kalendæ	[ka 'lɛn dɛ]	145
l		[l]	laudamus	[lɑːu 'da mus]	146
m		[m]	morte	['mɔr tɛ]	146
n		[n]	non	[nɔn]	146
n	before [kt]	[ŋ]	sancto	['saŋ ktɔ]	146
n	before g in separate syllable	[n]	conglorificatur	[kɔn glɔ ri fi 'ka tur]	146
	but sometimes	[ŋ]	sanguis	['saŋ gwis]	146
o		[ɔ]	nobis	['nɔ bis]	140
œ		[ɛ]	cœlestis	[tʃɛ 'lɛs tis]	140
p		[p]	pater	['pa tɛr]	147
ph		[f]	Prophetas	[prɔ 'fɛ tas]	147
qu		[kw]	quoniam	['kwɔ ni am]	148
r	flipped	[ɾ]	Maria	[ma 'ri a]	148
	(optional) trilled	[r]	regina	[rɛ 'dʒi na]	148
s	usually	[s]	tristis	['tri stis]	149
s	between two *vowels**	[z]	miserere	[mi zɛ 'rɛ ɾɛ]	149
s	final usually	[s]	vivos	['vi vɔs]	149
s	final after a *final voiced consonant*	[z]	omnipotens	[ɔ 'mni pɔ tɛnz]	149
sc	before *a, o, u,* or a *consonant*	[sk]	scuto	['sku tɔ]	150
sc	before *e, æ, œ, i,* or *y*	[ʃ]	scio	['ʃi ɔ]	150
sch	before *a, o,* or *u*	[sk]	Pascha	['pa ska]	150
t		[t]	tantum	['tan tum]	150
ti	following a *vowel* and preceding a letter other than *s, t,* or *x*	[tsi]	gratia	['gra tsi a]	150
th		[t]	Sabaoth	['sa ba ɔt]	150
u		[u]	crucem	['kru tʃɛm]	140
u	following *ng* or *q* and preceding a *vowel*	[w]	qui	[kwi]	140
			sanguis	['saŋ gwis]	140
v		[v]	vivos	['vi vɔs]	151

*An s between two vowels is pronounced as a softened s, a sound between [s] and [z].

Latin

Italian Letter and Position in Word			IPA	Example	and IPA	Page
w	w	(not used in Latin)				151
x	x	in initial *ex* and *exs* before a *vowel*	[gs]*	exalto	[ɛg ˈsɑl tɔ]*	151
				exsules	[ɛg ˈsu lɛs]*	151
		before a *consonant*	[ks]	extendo	[ɛk ˈstɛn dɔ]	151
				exspiro	[ɛk ˈspi ɾɔ]	151
		before silent *h*	[gs]*	exhibeo	[ɛg ˈsi bɛ ɔ]*	151
	x	in initial *exc* before a *forward vowel*	[kʃ]	excelsis	[ɛk ˈʃɛl sis]	151
		before a *back vowel*	[ksk]	excuso	[ɛk ˈsku zɔ]	151
	x	in the interior of a word	[ks]	dextro	[ˈdɛk strɔ]	151
	x	final	[ks]	pax	[pɑks]	151
y	y		[i]	hymnus	[ˈi mnus]	141
z	z		[dz]	Lazaro	[ˈlɑ dzɑ ɾɔ]	153

* *In words pronounced with* [gs], *some people choose to use an acceptable variation of* [gz]: exalto [ɛg ˈzɑl tɔ].

Latin

Special Features of Latin

Liturgical Latin

There are two systems of pronunciation in Latin. One is liturgical and the other is classical.

Classical Latin is the original language attributed to Caesar and Cicero. Although classical Latin has had a long history, it is not currently spoken by any culture as a native tongue and exists only as a scholarly language.

Liturgical, Roman, or ecclesiastical Latin is the language used in the vocal literature of the church. The system of pronunciation presented in this book is liturgical Latin and is appropriate for choral masses, cantatas, and oratorios. The material follows the guidelines set forth by Rev. Michael de Angelis in a publication entitled *The Correct Pronunciation of Latin According to Roman Usage*, St. Gregory Guild, 1937.

Latin rules of pronunciation are consistent and straightforward. Vowels usually have only one possible pronunciation; there are only three diphthongs. Other consecutive vowels are pronounced as two syllables. Many consonants have similarities to other languages, although there is one consonant, the letter *x* as in *excelsis*, which often poses pronunciation questions. See "The Letter X" on page 151 for information about pronouncing this letter.

Perhaps the greatest challenge in Latin diction is to determine the stress patterns of the words. There are no easy, regular rules. Therefore, we have indicated primary stress in the IPA transcriptions and have included a complete IPA transcription and translation for the five parts of the Ordinary of the Mass. For words not included in this book, refer to a dictionary, a *Liber usualis*, or other sources listed in the bibliography. Within these sources you can find translations and pronunciation transcriptions for many other sacred Latin texts.

Syllabification

Single Consonant Between Vowels

When a single consonant stands between vowels, place the consonant with the second vowel.

LL 3.2.01   Read aloud.

mi-se-re-re	[mi zɛ ˈrɛ rɛ]
a-men	[ˈɑ mɛn]

The small diacritical mark, ['], placed above and before a syllable in IPA transcription indicates that syllable receives primary stress: miserere [mi zɛ ˈrɛ rɛ]

Latin

no-bis	['nɔ bis]
na-tu-ra	[na 'tu ra]
glo-ri-a	['glɔ ri a]
sa-lu-ta-re	[sa lu 'ta rɛ]

Exception: In compound words, put the consonant with the preceding syllable.

LL 3.2.02   Read aloud.

ad-i-re	[ad 'i rɛ]
in-i-qui-ta-tis	[in i kwi 'ta tis]

The consonant *x* is usually placed with the preceding vowel. (The letter *x* has several pronunciations. See page 151.)

LL 3.2.03   Read aloud.

dix-it	['dik sit]
ex-au-di	[eg 'sau di]
dex-te-ram	['dɛk stɛ ram]

Two Consecutive Consonants

In Latin, as in Italian, you lengthen the sound of double consonants. In IPA, lengthened double consonants are transcribed with the symbol [ː] and a repeated consonant symbol to indicate that the sound should be prolonged.

Usually divide syllables between two consecutive consonants.

LL 3.2.04   Read aloud.

tor-men-tum	[tɔr 'mɛn tum]
mun-di	['mun di]
tan-go	['taŋ gɔ]
mit-to	['mitː tɔ]

However, there are many instances when you will place consonant combinations with the second of two syllables:

1. Divide syllables before the consonant digraphs *ch, gn, ph,* or *th* (combined letters pronounced as a single sound).

LL 3.2.05   Read aloud.

ma-chi-na	['ma ki na]
a-gnus	['a ɲus]
Pro-phe-tas	[prɔ 'fɛ tas]
Ca-tho-li-cam	[ka 'tɔ li kam]

2. When *l, r,* or *t* follows *b, c, d, g,* or *p*, place both consonants with the syllable that follows.

Latin

LL 3.2.06   Read aloud.

bl, br:	te-ne-bræ	[ˈtɛ nɛ brɛ]
cl, cr, ct:	fa-ctum	[ˈfɑ ktum]
	sæ-clum	[ˈsɛ klum]
pl, pr, pt:	pro-pter	[ˈprɔ ptɛɾ]

3) Place *qu*, *mn*, *sc*, *sp*, *st* and *tr* with the syllable that follows.

LL 3.2.07   Read aloud.

qu:	re-qui-em	[ˈrɛ kwi ɛm]
mn:	o-mnes	[ˈɔ mnɛs]
sc:	a-scen-dit	[ɑ ˈʃɛn dit]
sp:	in-spe-ra-tus	[in spɛ ˈrɑ tus]
st:	Chri-stum	[ˈkri stum]
tr:	Patris	[ˈpɑ tris]

Three Consecutive Consonants

Usually divide three consonants as one followed by two.

LL 3.2.08   Read aloud.

san-cto	[ˈsɑŋ ktɔ]
cun-cta	[ˈkuŋ ktɑ]
Ec-cle-si-a	[ɛkː ˈklɛ zi ɑ]

Put the combination *str* with the second syllable.

LL 3.2.09   Read aloud.

| no-stri | [ˈnɔ stri] |

Exception: Prefixes are put in separate syllables and may not follow the previous rules for syllabification.

LL 3.2.10   Read aloud.

| ab-sti-ne-o | [ɑb sti ˈnɛ ɔ] |

Consecutive Vowels

Most consecutive vowels form two syllables, although some form diphthongs. (See the detailed discussion of consecutive vowels on page 133.)

Latin

Divide these vowels into two syllables.

LL 3.2.11 Read aloud.

De-o	['dɛ ɔ]
glo-ri-a	['glɔ ri ɑ]
fi-li-um	['fi li um]
per-pe-tu-a	[pɛr 'pɛ tu ɑ]
re-qui-em	['rɛ kwi ɛm]
di-es i-ræ	['di ɛs 'i rɛ]

Stress

The topic of primary stress in Latin is complex and requires familiarity with the language. The rules presented here are meant to be simple guidelines. A singer can rely on the metric setting of the words in the musical score, can refer to the IPA transcriptions located throughout this chapter, or can refer to a dictionary for additional help with stressing.

The second-to-last syllable is also called the penultimate syllable. The third-to-last syllable is also called the antepenultimate syllable.

Two Syllables

In words of two syllables, give the primary stress to the second-to-last syllable.

LL 3.2.12 Read aloud.

tan-go	['tɑŋ gɔ]
De-us	['dɛ us]
un-de	['un dɛ]

More Than Two Syllables

Sometimes in words of more than two syllables, the primary stress is given to the second-to-last syllable.

LL 3.2.13 Read aloud.

Ray-mun-dus	[rɑːi 'mun dus]
be-a-ta	[bɛ 'ɑ tɑ]

Otherwise, the primary stress is given to the third-to-last syllable.

LL 3.2.14 Read aloud.

Do-mi-nus	['dɔ mi nus]
glo-ri-a	['glɔ ri ɑ]

Latin

Elision

In certain words with a dropped final *e*, retain the primary stress of the original spelling.

LL 3.2.15   Read aloud.

tan-ton	[tɑn 'tɔn]	for	tan-to-ne	[tɑn 'tɔ nɛ]
il-lic	[ilː 'litʃ]	for	il-li-ce	[ilː 'li tʃɛ]

Latin Vowels

Latin is a language of pure vowels. There are only five pure vowel sounds, [ɑ, ɛ, i, ɔ, u], although there are six letters, *a, e, i, o, u,* and *y*. In Latin, the two letters *i* and *y* have the same pronunciation: [i], as the *ee* in *beet*.

The pronunciation of Latin vowels is not influenced by stressing and unstressing as it is in English and Italian. The vowels *e* and *o* are always pronounced [ɛ] and [ɔ]. The unstressed schwa [ə] sound does not exist in Latin. The only time a vowel has a pronunciation that is different than the five vowel sounds listed above is when *i* and *u* are pronounced as glides.

The letters *i* and *u* are pronounced as the glides [j] and [w] when they adjoin certain letters. When *i* stands between two vowels, as in *alleluia* [ɑlː lɛ 'lu jɑ], it is pronounced as the glide [j]. When the letter *u* follows *q* or *ng* and precedes another vowel, as in *qui* [kwi] or *sanguis* ['sɑŋ gwis], it is pronounced as the glide [w].

There are only three diphthongs in Latin: *ay, au,* and *eu*. Latin diphthongs are transcribed in IPA as two pure vowels (as [ɑu] in *laudamus*) and both vowels must be pronounced clearly and distinctly. The duration of the two vowels differs, however: the first sound is longer and the second is shorter. English speakers must be careful not to reduce the second vowel sound to a brief glide, but to give it the full vowel value.

Pronouncing Consecutive Vowels

Most consecutive vowels in Latin constitute two syllables, as in *be-a-ta* or *De-o*. However, in Latin, two consecutive vowels may be pronounced as either a single vowel, a diphthong, a glide, or as two separate syllables.

Single Vowel Sound

The digraphs æ and œ are a single vowel sound.

Latin

A digraph is a combination of two or more letters that represent a single sound.

Pronounce the digraphs printed as æ and œ as the single sound *eh* [ɛ] as in *bed*.

LL 3.2.16   Read aloud.

cæ-li	[ˈtʃɛ li]
hœ-dis	[ˈɛ dis]
cœ-lum	[ˈtʃɛ lum]
sæ-cu-lum	[ˈsɛ ku lum]
bo-næ	[ˈbɔ nɛ]
mœ-re-bat	[me ˈrɛ bɑt]

Two dots over a vowel is called a dieresis [daɪ ˈɛ rə sɪs].

However, when there is a dieresis over one of the vowels, treat the vowels as two distinct sounds.

LL 3.2.17   Read aloud.

Mi-cha-ël	[ˈmi kɑ ɛl]
Ra-pha-ël	[ˈrɑ fɑ ɛl]
Is-rä-el	[ˈis rɑ ɛl]
po-ë-ma	[pɔ ˈɛ mɑ]

Diphthongs

The vowels *au, ay,* and *eu* combine to form diphthongs.

The vowel combinations *au* and *ay* are always pronounced as diphthongs, and *eu* is sometimes a diphthong. Both vowel sounds of a diphthong are distinctly articulated, with the first vowel longer and the second one shorter in duration.

When a single diphthong is written under a series of notes, vocalize on the first vowel and move to the second vowel at the last moment before the next syllable, with an assigned metrical time appropriate to the musical context. But be careful that the second vowel is given full vowel value and is not reduced to a glide.

Pronounce *au* and *ay* as diphthongs.

LL 3.2.18   Read aloud.

lau-da-mus	[lɑːu ˈdɑ mus]
ex-au-di	[eg ˈsɑːu di]
Ray-mun-di	[rɑːi ˈmun di]

Pronounce *eu* sometimes as a diphthong, sometimes as two syllables.

Latin

When *eu* begins a word, it tends to be a diphthong.

LL 3.2.19   Read aloud.

eu-ge	[ˈɛːu dʒɛ]
Eu-se-bi-i	[ɛːu ˈzɛ bi i]

When *eu* does not begin a word, it is pronounced as two syllables.

LL 3.2.20   Read aloud.

me-us	[ˈmɛ us]

Glides

The vowels *u* and *i* are sometimes pronounced as the glides [w] and [j].

When there is a combination of two vowels and the first vowel is either the glide [w] or [j], pronounce the second vowel with greater stress and longer duration.

The glide [w] occurs when *u* follows *q* or *ng* and precedes another vowel.

LL 3.2.21   Read aloud.

qu:	qui	[kwi]
	quo-ni-am	[ˈkwɔ ni ɑm]
ngu:	san-guis	[ˈsɑŋ gwis]

The glide [j] occurs when *j* precedes another vowel.

LL 3.2.22   Read aloud.

Ju-dex	[ˈju dɛks]
Je-sus	[ˈjɛ zus]

The glide [j] occurs when *i* is between two vowels.

LL 3.2.23   Read aloud.

al-le-lu-ia	[ɑlː lɛ ˈlu jɑ]

Two Syllables

Consecutive vowels are usually pronounced as two separate syllables, except for the spellings previously listed. The following spellings are examples:

LL 3.2.24   Read aloud.

ai:	la-i-cus	[ˈlɑ i kus]
	a-it	[ˈɑ it]

In Latin [ɑi] and [ou] are always pronounced as two separate syllables, not as diphthongs as in English.

Each vowel, including a repeated vowel in such words as filii *or* Aaron, *must be clearly articulated—in a smooth, not staccato, manner.*

Latin

ou:	pro-ut	[ˈprɔ ut]
	co-u-tun-tur	[kɔ u ˈtun tur]
ei:	me-i	[ˈmɛ i]
	de-i-tas	[ˈdɛ i tɑs]
	e-le-i-son	[ɛ ˈlɛ i zɔn]

One exception: The interjection *hei* [ɛi] is a single syllable.

LL 3.2.25   Read aloud.

ea:	be-a-ta	[bɛ ˈɑ tɑ]
eo:	De-o	[ˈdɛ ɔ]
ie:	Ky-ri-e	[ˈki ri ɛ]
ia:	me-mo-ri-a	[mɛ ˈmɔ ri ɑ]
	glo-ri-a	[ˈglɔ ri ɑ]
ua:	per-pe-tu-a	[pɛr ˈpɛ tu ɑ]
uo:	tu-o	[ˈtu ɔ]
eu:	me-us	[ˈmɛ us]
ii:	fi-li-i	[ˈfi li i]
	a-tri-is	[ˈɑ tri is]
aa:	A-a-ron	[ˈɑ ɑ rɔn]

Latin Vowels in Detail

Vowels in Latin are extremely easy to pronounce because of the few variations. Single vowels are, for the most part, pronounced with a single sound.

The letter

a

The letter *a* is always pronounced [ɑ], the sound of *ah* as in *father*, with the one exception of the digraph *æ*, which is pronounced [ɛ], as the sound of *e* in *bet*. As an American singer, you must be cautious never to use the neutral sounds of *uh* [ʌ] as in *up* or schwa [ə] as in *above* in Latin. In addition, the [ɑ] sound must be clear and open, never rounded as the sound of *aw* [ɔ] in *caw* or *caught*.

LL 3.3.01   Read aloud.

tu-ba	['tu bɑ]
sal-va	['sɑl vɑ]
spar-gens	['spɑr dʒɛnz]
gra-tis	['grɑ tis]
ma-la	['mɑ lɑ]
a-ni-mas	['ɑ ni mɑs]

ae

The letters *æ* form a digraph and are pronounced as the single vowel sound [ɛ] as in *bet*.

LL 3.3.02   Read aloud.

æ-ter-næ	[ɛ 'tɛr nɛ]
mæ-re-bat	[mɛ 'rɛ bɑt]
vi-æ	['vi ɛ]
me-æ	['mɛ ɛ]
cæ-lis	['tʃɛ lis]
bo-næ	['bɔ nɛ]

au

Pronounce *au* as the diphthong [ɑːu]. Give the first vowel longer duration than the second, but give the full vowel quality to both vowel sounds.

Latin

LL 3.3.03	Read aloud.
cau-sa	[ˈkɑːu zɑ]
au-di-ti-o-ne	[ɑːu di tsi ˈɔ nɛ]

ay

Pronounce *ay* as the diphthong [ɑːi]. Give the first vowel longer duration than the second, but give the full vowel quality to both vowels. Be careful not to use the more open vowel [ɪ] as in the English word *bid*. Keep the vowel *i* pure [i].

LL 3.3.04	Read aloud.
Ray-mun-di	[rɑːi ˈmun di]

The letter e

There are differing opinions among authorities about whether to pronounce the vowels *e*, *æ*, and *œ* as close [e] or open [ɛ]. Some suggest that all of these vowels should be pronounced as close [e] as in *chaotic*, while others suggest that these vowels be pronounced as open [ɛ]. A third group of Latin scholars prefers a combination of [e] and [ɛ]. In this book, we suggest that you always pronounce the letters *e*, *æ*, and *œ* with the sound of open [ɛ] as in *bet*.

Be sure that the sound of [ɛ] is well articulated. Do not open it so far that it resembles the sound of [æ] as in *bat*. The vowels in the words *bet*, *bed*, *head*, *said*, and *pet* can be a guide.

LL 3.3.05	Read aloud.
per-fru-i	[ˈpɛr fru i]
est	[ɛst]
te-sti	[ˈtɛ sti]
e-va-de-re	[ɛ ˈvɑ dɛ ɾɛ]
tre-mor	[ˈtrɛ mɔr]
mi-se-re-re	[mi zɛ ˈɾɛ ɾɛ]
eleison	[ɛ ˈlɛ i zɔn]
deo	[ˈdɛ ɔ]

eu

Pronounce *eu* as a diphthong only when it is initial in a word.

LL 3.3.06   Read aloud.

eu-ge	[ˈɛːu ʤɛ]
Eu-se-bi-i	[ɛːu ˈzɛ bi i]

Note: The word *eun-tes* [ˈɛuːn tɛs] has an irregular stress. Longer duration is given to the second vowel.

Otherwise, pronounce *eu* as two syllables.

LL 3.3.07   Read aloud.

me-us	[ˈmɛ us]
De-um	[ˈdɛ um]
De-us	[ˈdɛ us]

The letter *i* is always pronounced as [i], the sound of *ee* in *beet*, with one exception: when *i* stands between two vowel sounds, it is pronounced as the glide [j], the sound of *y* in *you*. This vowel is never pronounced [ɪ] as in *bit*.

The letter

LL 3.3.08   Read aloud.

i-ræ	[ˈi rɛ]
Ju-di-can-ti	[ju di ˈkɑn ti]
di-es	[ˈdi ɛs]
ul-ti-o-nis	[ul tsi ˈɔ nis]
stri-cte	[ˈstri ktɛ]
il-lis	[ˈilː lis]
scri-ptus	[ˈskri ptus]
mi-rum	[ˈmi rum]
li-ber	[ˈli bɛr]
sit	[sit]

LL 3.3.09   Read aloud.

al-le-lu-ia	[ɑlː lɛ ˈlu jɑ]
e-ia	[ˈɛ jɑ]

Be aware of the difference between the sound of [j] and [i] in words with consecutive vowels. Read this common word aloud pronouncing *ia* as two syllables. Do not use a glide:

LL 3.3.10

glo-ri-a	[ˈglɔ ri ɑ]

Latin

The letter o

The letter *o* is always pronounced as open [ɔ] as in *bought, awe,* or *autumn*. Be sure to articulate [ɔ] with rounded lips. Many American singers fail to adequately round their lips, and [ɔ] begins to sound like [ɑ].

Read aloud using a well-formed [ɔ].

LL 3.3.11   Read aloud.

non	[nɔn]
la-bor	['lɑ bɔɾ]
cor	[kɔɾ]
le-o-nis	[le 'ɔ nis]
vo-ca	['vɔ kɑ]
do-lo-ro-sa	[dɔ lɔ 'rɔ zɑ]
o-ra	['ɔ ɾɑ]
no-bis	['nɔ bis]

œ

The letters *œ* are a digraph pronounced as the single sound of [ɛ] as in *bet*.

LL 3.3.12   Read aloud.

cœ-le-stis	[tʃɛ 'le stis]

The letter u

The letter *u* is pronounced as [u], the sound of *oo* in the word *boot*, with only one exception (noted below), when it is pronounced as the glide [w] as in *were*. In Latin, this vowel is never pronounced as [ʊ] as in *book* or as the diphthong [ju] as in the English word *abuse* or *fuse*.

LL 3.3.13   Read aloud.

u-nam	['u nɑm]
fa-ci-mus	['fɑ tʃi mus]
tu	['tu]
san-ctus	['sɑŋ ktus]
Je-su	['je zu]
mun-di	['mun di]
la-cu	['lɑ ku]
cru-cem	['kru tʃɛm]

Read these words with *u* before or after another vowel aloud.

LL 3.3.14   Read aloud.

per-pe-tu-a	[pɛr 'pɛ tu ɑ]
me-us	['mɛ us]
al-le-lu-ia	[ɑlː lɛ 'lu jɑ]
lau-da-mus	[lɑːu 'dɑ mus]
fi-li-um	['fi li um]
mor-tu-os	['mɔr tu ɔs]

Exception: When the letter *u* follows *ng* or *q* and precedes another vowel, pronounce *u* as the glide [w].

LL 3.3.15   Read aloud.

qu:	qua-rum	['kwɑ rum]
	tam-quam	['tɑm kwɑm]
	qui	[kwi]
	quod	[kwɔd]
	quæ-rens	['kwɛ rɛnz]
ngu:	san-guis	['sɑŋ gwis]

The letter *y* has only one sound. It is always pronounced as [i], the sound of *ee* as in *beet*.

LL 3.3.16   Read aloud.

hy-mnus	['i mnus]
mar-ty-res	['mɑr ti rɛs]

The letter *y* is also pronounced [i] in the diphthong *ay*:

LL 3.3.17   Read aloud.

Ray-mun-dus	[rɑːi 'mun dus]

The letter

Latin

§ Latin Consonants in Detail

Many of the Latin consonants have the same sounds as English or Italian and their pronunciation is very consistent. The relative simplicity of the pronunciation choices for Latin consonants make Latin an easy language to learn to pronounce.

b

Pronounce *b* as [b], as in the English word *bone*.

LL 3.4.01   Read aloud.

li-be-ra	['li bɛ ɾa]
bo-næ	['bɔ nɛ]

c

The following rules relate to the pronunciation of *c* or *cc* before a vowel or consonant, and of *c* when it occurs as the final letter of a word. For the pronunciation of *sc*, see page 150. Also see "The Letter X" on page 151.

Pronounce *c* or *cc*, before *a*, *o*, *u*, or a *consonant*, as [k], as in the English word *kit*. When *c* is pronounced as [k], it is called *hard c*.

Read these words aloud using *c* before *a*, *o*, or *u*.

LL 3.4.02   Read aloud.

cum	[kum]
cor-da	['kɔr da]
sæ-cu-la	['sɛ ku la]
lu-cam	['lu kam]
cau-sa	['kaːu za]
pec-ca-ta	[pekː 'ka ta]
cre-do	['krɛ dɔ]
lo-cu-tus	[lɔ 'ku tus]

Read these words aloud using *c* before a consonant.

LL 3.4.03   Read aloud.

cre-a-tu-ra	[krɛ a 'tu ɾa]
fa-ctum	['fa ktum]
la-cri-mo-sa	[la kri 'mɔ za]
sæ-clum	['sɛ klum]

Latin

Pronounce *c* or *cc* before *e, æ, œ, i,* or *y* as [tʃ], as *ch* in the English word *chair*. When *c* is pronounced [tʃ], it is called *soft c*.

LL 3.4.04   Read aloud.

lu-ce-at	[ˈlu tʃɛ ɑt]
lu-cis	[ˈlu tʃis]
ci-nis	[ˈtʃi nis]
ac-ci-pe	[ˈɑtː tʃi pɛ]
ec-ce	[ˈɛtː tʃɛ]
be-ne-di-ci-mus	[bɛ nɛ ˈdi tʃi mus]

Pronounce *c* as [ʃ], the sound of *sh* in the English word *she*, when *c* stands between *ex* and the vowel *e, æ, œ, i,* or *y*. The symbol [ʃ] is called *esh* [ɛʃ]. (See "The Letter X" on page 151, for a full description.)

LL 3.4.05   Read aloud.

ex-cel-sis	[ɛk ˈʃɛl sis]

Pronounce final *c* as [k].

LL 3.4.06   Read aloud.

fac	[fɑk]
nunc	[nuŋk]

Pronounce *ch* as [k].

LL 3.4.07   Read aloud.

Chri-stum	[ˈkri stum]
ma-chi-na	[ˈmɑ ki nɑ]

Pronounce the letter *d* as the sound of *d* in *dog*. However, the Latin *d* is more dental and less aspirate than the English *d*.

LL 3.4.08   Read aloud.

do-mi-ne	[ˈdɔ mi nɛ]
De-um	[ˈdɛ um]
a-do-ra-tur	[ɑ dɔ ˈrɑ tur]
De-i	[ˈdɛ i]

Latin

f

Pronounce the letter *f* as in the English word *feet*.

LL 3.4.09   Read aloud.

of-fe-ri-mus	[ɔfː 'fɛ ɾi mus]
fi-nis	['fi nis]
fa-vil-la	[fɑ 'vilː lɑ]
fons	[fɔnz]

g

Pronounce *g* as [g] when it occurs before *a, o, u,* or a *consonant* other than *n*. The sound [g], as in the English word *gone*, is called *hard g*. However, the Latin *g* is less aspirate than English *d*.

LL 3.4.10   Read aloud.

a-gas	['ɑ gɑs]
gla-di-us	['glɑ di us]
pla-ga	['plɑ gɑ]
er-go	['ɛr gɔ]
glo-ri-a	['glɔ ɾi ɑ]

Pronounce *g* before *e, æ, œ, i,* or *y* as [ʤ] as in the English word *fudge*. When *g* is pronounced as [ʤ], it is called *soft g*.

LL 3.4.11   Read aloud.

vir-gi-ne	['vir ʤi nɛ]
ge-re	['ʤɛ ɾɛ]
re-sur-get	[rɛ 'sur ʤɛt]
re-gi-na	[rɛ 'ʤi nɑ]
co-get	['kɔ ʤɛt]
ge-ni-tum	['ʤɛ ni tum]
in-ge-mi-sco	[in ʤɛ 'mi skɔ]

gn

Pronounce *gn* as [ɲ]. The symbol enya [ɲ] represents a sound similar to the *ni* in *onion* ['ʌn jən]. However, [ɲ] is a palatal consonant, made with a single articulatory action. The blade of the tongue lifts to touch the boundary between the teeth ridge and the hard palate.

LL 3.4.12 Read aloud.

A-gnus	[ˈɑ ɲus]
di-gnæ	[ˈdi ɲɛ]
re-gni	[ˈrɛ ɲi]
i-gnem	[ˈi ɲɛm]

The letter *h* is silent in Latin.

LL 3.4.13 Read aloud.

Ho-san-na	[ɔ ˈzɑnː nɑ]
ho-di-e	[ˈɔ di ɛ]
ho-mi-ni-bus	[ɔ ˈmi ni bus]

Exceptions: In these two words, *h* is pronounced [k]. In ancient manuscripts these words were spelled *nichel* and *michi*.

LL 3.4.14 Read aloud.

ni-hil	[ˈni kil]
mi-hi	[ˈmi ki]

The letter *j* is pronounced as the glide jot [j]. The symbol [j] represents the sound of *y* in *you* and is often called a *semi-consonant* or *semi-vowel*.

LL 3.4.15 Read aloud.

Je-su	[ˈjɛ zu]
ma-je-sta-tis	[mɑ jɛ ˈstɑ tis]
cu-jus	[ˈku jus]
ju-di-ca-re	[ju di ˈkɑ rɛ]

Pronounce *k* as [k], as in the English word *kit*. The Latin [k] is less aspirate than the English [k].

LL 3.4.16 Read aloud.

ka-len-dæ	[kɑ ˈlɛn dɛ]
kæ-sa	[ˈkɛ zɑ]

Latin

l

The letter *l* is pronounced as "clear" *l* [l], the sound of *l* as in *leap*. The Latin *l* is articulated more dentally than in English.

LL 3.4.17 Read aloud.

la-tro-nem	[lɑ 'trɔ nɛm]
lu-ce-at	['lu ʧɛ ɑt]
tol-lis	['tɔl: lis]
il-lud	['il: lud]
lu-mi-ne	['lu mi nɛ]

For details on how to pronounce a dental [l], see "The Consonant l" on page 62.

m

Pronounce *m* as [m], as in the English word *me*.

LL 3.4.18 Read aloud.

me	[mɛ]
mor-te	['mɔr tɛ]
sum	[sum]
mun-di	['mun di]
do-mi-ne	['dɔ mi nɛ]
sæ-clum	['sɛ klum]

n

Pronounce *n* as [n], as in the English word *note*.

LL 3.4.19 Read aloud.

ne	[nɛ]
in-cli-na-to	[in kli 'nɑ tɔ]
sunt	[sunt]
tre-men-da	[trɛ 'mɛn dɑ]
venit	['vɛ nit]
an-ge-li-cus	[ɑn 'ʤɛ li kus]

Exception: When *n* occurs before *g* in a separate syllable, the *n* is pronounced [n], as in *angelicus*. However, in a few words, *n* before *g* is pronounced as [ŋ] : *sanguis* ['sɑŋ gwis], and *tango* ['tɑŋ gɔ].

Latin

gn

Pronounce *gn* as enya [ɲ] when the letters occur in the same syllable. (See page 66.)

LL 3.4.20   Read aloud.

A-gnus	[ˈɑ ɲus]
ma-gna	[ˈmɑ ɲɑ]

nct

Pronounce *n* before *ct* [kt] as [ŋ]. The symbol eng [ŋ] represents the *ng* in *song*. English words also use [ŋ] before [kt], as in *banked*.

LL 3.4.21   Read aloud.

san-cto	[ˈsɑŋ ktɔ]
san-ctus	[ˈsɑŋ ktus]

Note: The *n* before *c* in the word *nunc* [nuŋk] is also pronounced [ŋ].

p

The letter *p* is pronounced [p], as in the English word *put*. The Latin *p* is less aspirate than in English.

LL 3.4.22   Read aloud.

pi-e	[ˈpi ɛ]
pro-pter	[ˈprɔ ptɛɾ]
pi-us	[ˈpi us]
pa-ter	[ˈpɑ tɛɾ]
Spi-ri-tu	[ˈspi ɾi tu]
Pi-la-to	[pi ˈlɑ tɔ]

Pronounce *ph* as [f].

LL 3.4.23   Read aloud.

Pro-phe-tas	[prɔ ˈfɛ tɑs]
phre-ne-ti-ci	[frɛ ˈnɛ ti tʃi]

Latin

q

In Latin, *q* always combines with *u* and is pronounced as [kw].

LL 3.4.24   Read aloud.

quæ-rens	[ˈkwɛ rɛnz]
re-qui-em	[ˈrɛ kwi ɛm]
qua-si	[ˈkwɑ zi]
quo-ni-am	[ˈkwɔ ni ɑm]
fi-li-o-que	[fi li ˈɔ kwɛ]

r

The Latin *r* is pronounced as flipped [ɾ] or trilled [r], as in Italian. It is never the retroflex *r* of English, as in the word *run*. When *r* stands between two vowels or is final, pronounce it as flipped *r*.

Read these words aloud with *r* between two vowels.

LL 3.4.25   Read aloud.

Ky-ri-e	[ˈki ɾi ɛ]
e-rat	[ˈɛ ɾat]
glo-ri-a	[ˈglɔ ɾi ɑ]
me-mo-ra-ri	[mɛ mɔ ˈɾa ɾi]
o-re-mus	[ɔ ˈɾɛ mus]
sa-lu-ta-re	[sɑ lu ˈtɑ ɾɛ]

Pronounce these words with final *r*.

LL 3.4.26   Read aloud.

sem-per	[ˈsɛm pɛɾ]
con-fun-dar	[kɔn ˈfun dɑɾ]
mi-ser	[ˈmi zɛɾ]
cla-mor	[ˈklɑ mɔɾ]

When *r* is not between two vowels or final, pronounce it with either flipped or trilled *r*. Soloists usually use the trilled *r* in these words, whereas choral singers use flipped *r*.

Read aloud these words with an *r* before a vowel.

LL 3.4.27   Read aloud.

re-gi-na	[rɛ ˈdʒi nɑ]
no-stri	[ˈnɔ stri]
re-spi-ce	[rɛ ˈspi tʃɛ]
Chri-stum	[ˈkri stum]

Latin

Read aloud these words with a double *rr*.

LL 3.4.28 Read aloud.

ter-ra	[ˈtɛrː rɑ]
ter-ræ	[ˈtɛrː rɛ]

Read these words aloud with *r* preceding a consonant.

LL 3.4.29 Read aloud.

per-so-næ	[pɛr ˈsɔ nɛ]
mor-ti-us	[ˈmɔr ti us]
æ-ter-na	[ɛ ˈtɛr nɑ]
a-sper-ges	[ɑ ˈspɛr ʤɛs]

S

The letters *s* and *ss* are usually pronounced [s] as in the English word *sit*.

LL 3.4.30 Read aloud.

re-mis-si-o-nem	[rɛ misː si ˈɔ nɛm]
ba-ptis-ma	[bɑ ˈptis mɑ]
tri-stis	[ˈtri stis]
di-scus-si-o	[di ˈskusː si ɔ]
sunt	[ˈsunt]
spi-ri-tum	[ˈspi ɾi tum]
al-tis-si-mus	[ɑl tisː si mus]
sa-lu-tem	[sɑ ˈlu tɛm]
est	[ɛst]

When *s* stands between two vowels, pronounce it as the voiced [z] sound as in the English word *zero*.

LL 3.4.31 Read aloud.

mi-se-re-re	[mi zɛ ˈrɛ ɾɛ]
Je-su	[ˈjɛ zu]
Ec-cle-si-am	[ɛkː ˈklɛ zi ɑm]

When *s* is final, usually pronounce it as [s].

LL 3.4.32 Read aloud.

vi-vos	[ˈvi vɔs]
e-is	[ˈɛ is]
mor-tu-os	[ˈmɔr tu ɔs]
tu-is	[ˈtu is]

In some words (as miserere*), when s occurs between two vowels, it is pronounced with a sound that is halfway between [s] and [z]. Some systems of pronunciation use [s] instead of [z] for this intervocalic s to transcribe the sound.*

Latin

re-ges	['rɛ ʤɛs]
se-des	['sɛ dɛs]

When final *s* follows a final voiced consonant, it is pronounced [z] as in the English word *tens* [tɛnz].

LL 3.4.33   Read aloud.

o-mni-po-tens	[ɔ 'mni pɔ tɛnz]

sc

When *sc* occurs before *a, o, u,* or a *consonant*, pronounce it as [sk].

LL 3.4.34   Read aloud.

sca-bel-lum	[skɑ 'bɛl: lum]
scu-to	['sku tɔ]
re-qui-e-scat	[rɛ kwi 'ɛ skɑt]
Scri-ptu-ras	[skri 'ptu rɑs]

When *sc* occurs before *e, æ, œ, i,* or *y*, pronounce it as [ʃ].

LL 3.4.35   Read aloud.

su-sci-pi-at	['su ʃi pi ɑt]
sci-o	['ʃi ɔ]
a-scen-dit	[ɑ 'ʃɛn dit]
su-sci-pe	['su ʃi pɛ]

sch

When *sch* occurs before *a, o,* or *u*, pronounce it as [sk].

LL 3.4.36   Read aloud.

scho-la-sti-ca	[skɔ 'lɑ sti kɑ]
Pa-scha	['pɑ skɑ]
scho-la	['skɔ lɑ]

t

Pronounce the letter *t* [t] as in the English word *tote*. However, the Latin *t* is more dental and less aspirate than in English.

LL 3.4.37   Read aloud.

et	[ɛt]
tan-tum	['tɑn tum]

Latin

tem-po-ra	[ˈtɛm pɔ ɾa]
i-te-rum	[ˈi tɛ ɾum]
te-sta-men-tum	[tɛ stɑ ˈmɛn tum]

Pronounce the letters *ti* as [tsi] when they follow any vowel or consonant and precede any letter except *s, t,* or *x*. Otherwise, *ti* is pronounced [ti], as in *majestatis* [mɑ jɛ ˈstɑ tis].

LL 3.4.38   Read aloud.

gra-ti-a	[ˈgrɑ tsi ɑ]
ter-ti-a	[ˈtɛr tsi ɑ]
Pon-ti-o	[ˈpɔn tsi ɔ]
o-ra-ti-o-nem	[ɔ ɾɑ tsi ˈɔ nɛm]

The letters *th* form a digraph that is pronounced with the single sound [t].

LL 3.4.39   Read aloud.

Sa-ba-oth	[ˈsɑ bɑ ɔt]
Ca-tho-li-cam	[kɑ ˈtɔ li kɑm]
thro-num	[ˈtrɔ num]

V

Pronounce the letter *v* as in the English word *vet*.

LL 3.4.40   Read aloud.

vox	[vɔks]
vi-sce-ra	[ˈvi ʃɛ ɾɑ]
vi-vos	[ˈvi vɔs]
no-vum	[ˈnɔ vum]
vo-lun-ta-tis	[vɔ lun ˈtɑ tis]
vi-si-bi-li-um	[vi zi ˈbi li um]

W

The letter *w* is not used in Latin.

X

The letter *x* appears in Latin words in initial, medial, and final syllables.

Latin

It has several different pronunciations, [gs], [ks], [kʃ], and [ksk], depending upon its position in the word and the adjoining letters. The spellings for these pronunciations are listed below.

In initial *ex* and *exs* before a vowel, pronounce *x* as [gs].

LL 3.4.41   Read aloud.

ex-al-to	[ɛg 'sɑl tɔ]
ex-sur-ge	[ɛg 'sur dʒɛ]
ex-er-ce-o	[ɛg 'sɛr tʃɛ ɔ]
ex-su-les	[ɛg 'su lɛs]
ex-o-plo	[ɛg 'sɔ plɔ]

Note: The sound of [ɛgs] can be heard in the English words *egg sandwich*.

Note: In words pronounced with [gs], some people choose to use an acceptable variation of [gz]: [ɛg 'zal tɔ].

In initial *ex* and *exs* before a consonant, pronounce x as [ks].

LL 3.4.42   Read aloud.

ex-po-sci-te	[ɛk 'spɔ ʃi tɛ]
ex-ster-no	[ɛk 'stɛr nɔ]
ex-pu-ngo	[ɛk 'spun gɔ]
ex-spe-cto	[ɛk 'spɛ ktɔ]
ex-ten-do	[ɛk 'stɛn dɔ]
ex-spi-ro	[ɛk 'spi rɔ]

Note: Hard [ks] can be heard in the English words *licks* and *hex*.

Exception: In initial *ex* before the silent consonant *h*, pronounce *x* as [gs].

LL 3.4.43

ex-hi-be-o	[ɛg 'si bɛ ɔ]

In initial *exc* before a forward vowel (*i, e, ae, oe,* or *y*), pronounce *x* as [kʃ].

LL 3.4.44   Read aloud.

ex-cel-sis	[ɛk 'ʃɛl sis]
ex-ces-sus	[ɛk 'ʃɛː sus]

Note: The sound [ʃ], called *esh*, is the sound of *sh* in *she*. The sound of [kʃ] can be heard in the English words *pink shells* or *peck shells*.

Latin

In initial *exc* before a back vowel (*a, o,* or *u*), pronounce *x* as [ksk].

LL 3.4.45   Read aloud.

ex-can-to	[ɛk ˈskɑn tɔ]
ex-car-ni-fi-ca-re	[ɛk skɑr ni fi ˈkɑ ɾɛ]
ex-cu-so	[ɛk ˈsku zɔ]

Note: The sound of [ksk] can be heard in the English words *Nick's car*.

Pronounce medial *x* as [ks].

LL 3.4.46   Read aloud.

re-sur-rex-it	[rɛ zurː ˈrɛk sit]
dex-te-ram	[ˈdɛk stɛ ɾɑm]
e-rex-it	[ɛ ˈrɛk sit]
cru-ci-fi-xus	[kru ʧi ˈfik sus]

Pronounce final *x* as [ks].

LL 3.4.47   Read aloud.

pax	[pɑks]
vox	[vɔks]
lux	[luks]
sup-plex	[ˈsupː plɛks]

Z

The letter *z* is pronounced as [dz], as in the English word *beads* [bidz]. It is never [ts] as it sometimes is in Italian.

LL 3.4.48   Read aloud.

La-za-ro	[ˈlɑ dzɑ ɾɔ]

Latin

154

 The Ordinary of the Mass

Kyrie

Kyrie eleison.
['ki ri ɛ ɛ 'le i zɔn]
Lord, have mercy.

Christe eleison.
['kri ste ɛ 'le i zɔn]
Christ, have mercy.

Kyrie eleison.
['ki ri ɛ ɛ 'le i zɔn]
Lord, have mercy.

Gloria

Gloria in excelsis Deo.
['glɔ ri a in ɛk 'ʃɛl sis 'de ɔ]
Glory to God in the highest.

Et in terra pax hominibus bonæ voluntatis.
[ɛt in 'tɛrː ra paks ɔ 'mi ni bus 'bɔ ne vɔ lun 'ta tis]
And on earth peace to men of good will.

Laudamus te. Benedicimus te.
[laːu 'da mus te be ne 'di tʃi mus tɛ]
We praise You. We bless You.

Adoramus te. Glorificamus te.
[a dɔ 'ra mus te glɔ ri fi 'ka mus tɛ]
We worship You. We glorify You.

Gratias agimus tibi propter magnam gloriam tuam.
['gra tsi as 'a dʒi mus 'ti bi 'prɔ ptɛr 'ma ɲam 'glɔ ri am 'tu am]
We give You thanks for Your great glory.

Domine Deus, Rex cœlestis, Deus Pater omnipotens,
['dɔ mi ne 'de us rɛks tʃe 'lɛ stis 'de us 'pa tɛr ɔ 'mni pɔ tɛnz]
Lord God, heavenly King, God the Father almighty.

Domine Fili unigenite, Jesu Christe.
['dɔ mi ne 'fi li u ni 'dʒɛ ni te 'je zu 'kri stɛ]
Lord Jesus Christ, the only-begotten Son.

Domine Deus, Agnus Dei, Filius Patris.
['dɔ mi ne 'de us 'a ɲus 'de i 'fi li us 'pa tris]
Lord God, Lamb of God, Son of the Father.

Qui tollis peccata mundi,
[kwi 'tɔlː lis pɛkː 'ka ta 'mun di]
You, Who take away the sins of the world,

Latin

Ordinary of the Mass

miserere nobis.
    [mi zɛ 'rɛ rɛ   'nɔ bis]
        have mercy on us.

Qui tollis peccata mundi,
    [kwi 'tɔlː lis pɛkː 'ka ta 'mun di]
        You, Who take away the sins of the world,

suscipe deprecationem nostram.
    ['su ʃi pɛ dɛ prɛ ka tsi 'ɔ nɛm 'nɔ stram]
        receive our prayer.

Qui sedes ad dexteram Patris,
    [kwi 'sɛ dɛs ad 'dɛk stɛ ram 'pa tris]
        You, Who sit at the right hand of the Father,

miserere nobis.
    [mi zɛ 'rɛ rɛ   'nɔ bis]
        have mercy on us.

Quoniam tu solus sanctus. Tu solus Dominus.
    ['kwɔ ni am tu 'sɔ lus 'saŋ ktus tu 'sɔ lus 'dɔ mi nus]
        For You alone are holy. You alone are Lord.

Tu solus Altissimus, Jesu Christe.
    [tu 'sɔ lus al 'tisː si mus 'jɛ zu 'kri stɛ]
        You alone are most high, O Jesus Christ,

Cum Sancto Spiritu,
    [kum 'saŋ ktɔ 'spi ri tu]
        With the Holy Spirit,

in gloria Dei Patris. Amen.
    [in 'glɔ ri a 'dɛ i 'pa tris 'a mɛn]
        in the glory of God the Father. Amen.

Credo

Credo in unum Deum,
    ['krɛ dɔ in 'u num 'dɛ um]
        I believe in one God.

Patrem omnipotentem, factorem cœli et terræ,
    ['pa trɛm ɔ mni pɔ 'tɛn tɛm fa 'ktɔ rɛm 'tʃɛ li ɛt 'tɛrː rɛ]
        The Father almighty, maker of heaven and earth,

visibilium omnium, et invisibilium.
    [vi zi 'bi li um 'ɔ mni um ɛt in vi zi 'bi li um]
        of all things visible and invisible.

Et in unum Dominum Jesum Christum,
    [ɛt in 'u num 'dɔ mi num 'jɛ zum 'kri stum]
        And I believe in one Lord, Jesus Christ,

Latin

Ordinary of the Mass

Filium Dei unigenitum.
['fi li um 'de i u ni 'dʒe ni tum]
the only-begotten Son of God.

Et ex Patre natum ante omnia sæcula.
[ɛt ɛks 'pɑ trɛ 'nɑ tum 'ɑn tɛ 'ɔ mni ɑ 'sɛ ku lɑ]
Born of the Father before all ages.

Deum de Deo, lumen de lumine,
['dɛ um dɛ 'dɛ ɔ 'lu mɛn dɛ 'lu mi nɛ]
God of God, Light of Light,

Deum verum de Deo vero.
['dɛ um 'vɛ rum dɛ 'dɛ ɔ 've rɔ]
true God of true God.

Genitum, non factum,
['dʒɛ ni tum nɔn 'fɑ ktum]
Begotten, not made,

consubstantialem Patri:
[kɔn sub stɑn tsi 'ɑ lɛm 'pɑ tri]
of one substance with the Father:

per quem omnia facta sunt.
[pɛr kwɛm 'ɔ mni ɑ 'fɑ ktɑ sunt]
By Whom all things were made.

Qui propter nos homines,
[kwi 'prɔ ptɛr nɔs 'ɔ mi nɛs]
Who for us men

et propter nostram salutem
[ɛt 'prɔ ptɛr 'nɔ strɑm sɑ 'lu tɛm]
and for our salvation

descendit de cælis.
[dɛ 'ʃɛn dit dɛ 'tʃɛ lis]
came down from heaven.

Et incarnatus est de Spiritu Sancto
[ɛt in kɑr 'nɑ tus ɛst dɛ 'spi ri tu 'sɑŋ ktɔ]
And He became flesh by the Holy Spirit

ex Maria Virgine: Et homo factus est.
[ɛks mɑ 'ri ɑ 'vir dʒi nɛ ɛt 'ɔ mɔ 'fɑ ktus ɛst]
of the Virgin Mary: And was made man.

Crucifixus etiam pro nobis:
[kru tʃi 'fik sus 'ɛ tsi ɑm prɔ 'nɔ bis]
He was also crucified for us,

sub Pontio Pilato passus, et sepultus est.
[sub 'pɔn tsi ɔ pi 'lɑ tɔ 'pɑsː sus ɛt sɛ 'pul tus ɛst]
suffered under Pontius Pilate, and was buried.

Latin

Ordinary of the Mass

Et resurrexit tertia die,
    [ɛt rɛ zurː ˈrɛk sit ˈtɛr tsi ɑ ˈdi ɛ]
        And on the third day He rose again,

secundum Scripturas.
    [sɛ ˈkun dum skri ˈptu ɾas]
        according to the Scriptures.

Et ascendit in cælum:
    [ɛt ɑ ˈʃɛn dit in ˈtʃɛ lum]
        He ascended into heaven

sedet ad dexteram Patris.
    [ˈsɛ dɛt ɑd ˈdɛk stɛ ɾam ˈpɑ tris]
        and sits at the right hand of the Father.

Et iterum venturus est cum gloria,
    [ɛt ˈi tɛ ɾum vɛn ˈtu ɾus ɛst kum ˈglɔ ɾi ɑ]
        He will come again in glory

judicare vivos et mortuos:
    [ju di ˈkɑ ɾɛ ˈvi vɔs ɛt ˈmɔr tu ɔs]
        to judge the living and the dead:

cujus regni non erit finis.
    [ˈku jus ˈrɛ ɲi nɔn ˈɛ ɾit ˈfi nis]
        And of His kingdom there will be no end.

Et in Spiritum Sanctum Dominum et vivificantem:
    [ɛt in ˈspi ɾi tum ˈsaŋ ktum ˈdɔ mi num ɛt vi vi fi ˈkan tɛm]
        And I believe in the Holy Spirit, the Lord and Giver of life,

qui ex Patre Filioque procedit.
    [kwi ɛks ˈpɑ trɛ fi li ˈɔ kwɛ prɔ ˈtʃɛ dit]
        Who proceeds from the Father and the Son.

Qui cum Patre et Filio simul adoratur
    [kwi kum ˈpɑ trɛ ɛt ˈfi li ɔ ˈsi mul ɑ dɔ ˈɾɑ tuɾ]
        Who together with the Father and the Son is adored

et conglorificatur:
    [ɛt kɔn glɔ ɾi fi ˈkɑ tuɾ]
        and glorified,

qui locutus est per Prophetas.
    [kwi lɔ ˈku tus ɛst pɛɾ prɔ ˈfɛ tas]
        and Who spoke through the prophets.

Et unam sanctam catholicam
    [ɛt ˈu nam ˈsaŋ ktam kɑ ˈtɔ li kam]
        and one holy, Catholic,

et apostolicam Ecclesiam.
    [ɛt ɑ pɔ ˈstɔ li kam ɛkː ˈklɛ zi ɑm]
        and Apostolic Church.

Latin

Ordinary of the Mass

Confiteor unum baptisma
    [kɔn 'fi te ɔr 'u num ba 'ptis ma]
        I confess one baptism

in remissionem peccatorum.
    [in rɛ misː si 'ɔ nɛm pekː ka 'tɔ ɾum]
        for the remission of sins.

Et expecto resurrectionem mortuorum.
    [ɛt ɛk 'spɛ ktɔ rɛ zurː rek tsi 'ɔ nɛm mɔr tu 'ɔ ɾum]
        And I await the resurrection of the dead.

Et vitam venturi sæculi. Amen.
    [ɛt 'vi tam vɛn 'tu ɾi 'sɛ ku li 'a mɛn]
        And the life of the world to come. Amen.

Sanctus

Sanctus, Sanctus,
    ['saŋ ktus 'saŋ ktus]
        Holy, holy

Sanctus Dominus Deus Sabaoth.
    ['saŋ ktus 'dɔ mi nus 'dɛ us 'sa ba ɔt]
        holy Lord God of hosts.

Pleni sunt cæli et terra gloria tua.
    ['plɛ ni sunt 'tʃɛ li ɛt 'tɛrː ra 'glɔ ɾi a 'tu a]
        Heavens and earth are filled with Your glory.

Hosanna in excelsis.
    [ɔ 'zanː na in ɛk 'ʃɛl sis]
        Hosanna in the highest.

Benedictus

Benedictus qui venit in nomine Domini
    [bɛ nɛ 'di ktus kwi 'vɛ nit in 'nɔ mi nɛ 'dɔ mi ni]
        Blessed is He Who comes in the name of the Lord.

Hosanna in excelsis.
    [ɔ 'zanː na in ɛk 'ʃɛl sis]
        Hosanna in the highest.

Agnus Dei

Agnus Dei qui tollis peccata mundi:
    ['a ɲus 'dɛ i kwi 'tɔlː lis pekː 'ka ta 'mun di]
        Lamb of God, who takes away the sins of the world:

miserere nobis.
    [mi zɛ 'rɛ ɾɛ 'nɔ bis]
        have mercy on us.

Latin

Ordinary of the Mass

Agnus Dei qui tollis peccata mundi:
    ['ɑ ɲus 'dɛ i kwi 'tɔl: lis pɛk: 'kɑ tɑ 'mun di]
        Lamb of God, who takes away the sins of the world:

dona nobis pacem.
    ['dɔ nɑ 'nɔ bis 'pɑ ʧɛm]
        grant us peace.

Latin
160

German

German Diction

The accepted standard of German for public performance is called Bühnenaussprache, or Stage German. In this book we follow Bühnenaussprache.

To many Americans, German sounds dark and guttural—probably because it contains several sounds and speech patterns foreign to American English. In reality, though, the majority of German vowels and consonants are clear and forward, promoting good vocalism.

As you begin to study German diction, you will find that you often turn to the structure of the language. To apply rules of pronunciation, for instance, you learn to pull apart prefixes, suffixes, verb inflection endings, and compound words. It can seem daunting at first, but several traits of the language will ease your work. For instance, you see fewer exceptions in *general* rules than in Italian or English. And the majority of exceptions you do find occur in prefixes and suffixes, which you can learn to identify. You can also learn to spot verb inflections with a few examples. You will notice usually no more than one or two pronunciations of a letter, and few orthographic spellings for a particular sound. And you will see clear principles of syllabification, helping you recognize sound groups to guide your pronunciation.

You will also find many sounds common to German and English. Other sounds are closely related to their English allophones; you make only minor adjustments in the articulators to produce the German sounds.

You will discover several unfamiliar vowel sounds (called *mixed vowels*) represented by the orthographic symbols ö and ü, and two other new sounds to Americans: the *ichlaut* and *achlaut*—the fricative pronunciations of *ch*. As you read the descriptions and go through the exercises, you will learn to feel the shapes of these German sounds as well as how they can enhance your singing.

To begin your adventure with German, we suggest you first orient yourself to the unfamiliar sounds, reading "Distinctive German Vowels" on page 173, paying special attention to the umlauted vowels, and "Distinctive German Consonants" on page 184, paying special attention to the consonant *ch*. Next, jump back to the Chart of German Sounds, noticing the letter contexts that guide you in applying rules of pronunciation, allowing an overview to emerge. With the unfamiliar now familiar and an overview to orient you, finally begin the "Syllabification" section and work your way straight through the text.

German

Chart of German Sounds

The following chart lists the letters of German in alphabetical order. Refer to this chart to quickly check the sound of a spelling. Although German is quite regular in its forms, there are some special circumstances and exceptions that cannot be presented easily in a simple chart. For details, see the discussions of the individual sounds later in this chapter.

German Letter and Position in Word		IPA	Example and	IPA	Page
a	a	before *one* consonant	[aː]	Vater	[ˈfaː tər]	192
	aa		[aː]	Saal	[zaːl]	192
	ah	in same syllable	[aː]	Mahl	[maːl]	193
	a	before *two* consonants usually	[a]	Wasser	[ˈva sər]	193
	ai		[ae]	Mai	[mae]	182, 193
	ay		[ae]	Bayern	[ˈbae ərn]	182, 193
	au		[ao]	Baum	[baom]	182, 194
	ä*	before *one* consonant	[ɛː]	spät	[ʃpɛːt]	194
	äh*	in same syllable	[ɛː]	Krähe	[ˈkrɛː ə]	195
	ä*	before *two* consonants usually	[ɛ]	Männer	[ˈmɛ nər]	195
	äu		[ɔø]	Träume	[ˈtrɔø mə]	182, 196
b	b	initial in word or syllable	[b]	Bube, geben	[ˈbuː bə] [ˈgeː bən]	211
	b	final in word or syllable	[p]	Dieb	[diːp]	211
	b	before *t* and *st*	[p]	lebst	[leːpst]	211
c	c	before a *front* vowel sound	[ts]	Citrone	[tsi ˈtroː nə]	211
	c	before a *back* vowel sound or a consonant (except *h*)	[k]	Café	[ka ˈfe]	211
	ch	after a *front* vowel, consonant, umlauted vowel, or diphthong (except *au*)	[ç]	ich, welche	[ɪç] [ˈvɛl çə]	184, 213
	ch	after a *back* vowel or diphthong *au*	[x]	Bach, doch	[bax] [dɔx]	184, 212
	chs	when *s* is part of the root word	[ks]	sechs	[zɛks]	215
	ck		[k]	backen	[ˈba kən]	212
d	d	initial in word or syllable	[d]	anders	[ˈan dərs]	185, 216
	d	final in word or syllable	[t]	Tod, Widmung	[toːt] [ˈvɪt mʊŋ]	185, 216
	dt		[t]	Stadt	[ʃtat]	215
e	e	in a stressed syllable and before *one* consonant	[eː]	ewig, beten	[ˈeː vɪç] [ˈbeː tən]	197
	ee		[eː]	Seele	[ˈzeː lə]	197
	eh	in same syllable	[eː]	sehr	[zeːr]	199

The umlauts ä, ö, and ü are sometimes written ae, oe, and ue. These spellings do not alter the pronunciation.

German

German Letter and Position in Word		IPA	Example and	IPA	Page
e	before *two* consonants usually	[ɛ]	Bett, helfen	[bɛt] ['hɛl fən]	197
e	final or in an unstressed syllable	[ə]	Liebe, gesund	['liː bə] [gə 'zʊnt]	198
ei		[ae]	ein	[aen]	182, 200
ey		[ae]	Meyer	['mae ər]	182, 200
eu		[ɔø]	heulen	['hɔø lən]	182, 200
f		[f]	fein, Tafel	[faen] ['taː fəl]	216
g	initial in word or syllable	[g]	Gott, fragen	[gɔt] ['fraː gən]	216
g	final in word or syllable	[k]	Tag, Flugzeug	[taːk] ['fluːk ˌtsɔøk]	216
g	before *t* or *st*	[k]	fragst	[fraːkst]	217
g	in suffix *-ig*	[ç]	König, Ewigkeit	['køː nıç] ['eː vıç kaet]	217
g	in some words of French origin	[ʒ]	Genie	[ʒe 'niː]	218
h	initial in a word or element**	[h]	Held, Gottheit	[hɛlt] ['gɔt haet]	218
h	after a vowel in same syllable	*silent*	Wahn, gehen	[vaːn] ['geː ən]	218
i	before one consonant	[iː]	Bibel	['biː bəl]	200
ie	"	[iː]	Liebe	['liː bə]	202
ih	in same syllable	[iː]	ihr	[iːr]	202
ieh	in same syllable	[iː]	Vieh	[fiː]	202
i	in the *stressed* ending *-ik*	[iː]	Musik	[mu 'ziːk]	200
i	before *two* consonants	[ɪ]	Kinder, ist	['kɪn dər] [ɪst]	200
i	in the suffixes *-in*, *-nis*	[ɪ]	Müllerin, Bildnis	['my lə rɪn] ['bɪlt nɪs]	200
i	in the suffix *-ig*	[ɪ]	willig	['vɪ lıç]	217
i	in the *unstressed* ending *-ik*	[ɪ]	Lyrik	['lyː rɪk]	200
j	usually	[j]	Jahr, ja	[jaːr] [ja]	219
j	in some words of French origin	[ʒ]	Journalist	[ʒur na 'lɪst]	219
k		[k]	Klause zurück	['klao zə] [tsu 'rʏk]	219
l		[l]	hell, loben	[hɛl] ['loː bən]	219
m		[m]	Mode träumen	[moː də] ['trɔø mən]	220
n		[n]	Nonne, Wein	['nɔ nə] [vaen]	220
ng	in same element**	[ŋ]	lang, si-ngen	[laŋ] ['zɪ ŋən]	220, 221
ng	in separate elements**	[n g]	hin-gehen	['hɪn geː ən]	220, 221

*** For a definition of* element, *see page 166.*

German

German Letter and Position in Word		IPA	Example and	IPA	Page
n	nk in one element**	[ŋk]	dank-en	[ˈdaŋ kən]	221
	nk in separate elements**	[n k]	An-klang	[ˈan klaŋ]	221
o	o before *one* consonant	[oː]	Rose, Ton	[ˈroː zə] [toːn]	203
	oh in same syllable	[oː]	Sohn, wohl	[zoːn] [voːl]	203
	oo	[oː]	Moos, Boot	[moːs] [boːt]	203
	o before *two* consonants usually	[ɔ]	Ort, kommen	[ɔrt] [ˈkɔmː mən]	203
	ö* before *one* consonant	[øː]	Öde, hören	[ˈøː də] [ˈhøː rən]	205
	öh* in same syllable	[øː]	Höhe, fröhlich	[ˈhøː ə] [ˈfrøː lɪç]	206
	ö* before *two* consonants usually	[œ]	göttlich	[ˈgœt lɪç]	205
p	p	[p]	prosit, Puppe	[ˈproː zɪt] [ˈpʊ pə]	218
	pf	[pf]	Pferd, stumpf	[pfɛrt] [ʃtʊmpf]	218
	ph	[f]	phantastisch	[fan ˈtas tɪʃ]	218
q	qu	[kv]	Quelle erquicken	[ˈkvɛ lə] [ɛr ˈkvɪ kən]	222
r	r flipped or trilled; *never* the American [ɹ]	[r]	Regen, Herr	[ˈreː gən] [hɛr]	223
s	s initial in word or element	[z]	Silber, Absicht	[ˈzɪl bər] [ˈap zɪçt]	223
	s between vowels	[z]	Rose	[ˈroː zə]	223
	s final in word or syllable	[s]	Glas, lösbar	[glaːs] [ˈløːs bar]	224
	ss, ß	[s]	müssen, Kuß	[ˈmʏ sən] [kʊs]	224
	sch in *same* element**	[ʃ]	schnell, Tisch	[ʃnɛl] [tɪʃ]	224
	sch in *two* elements**	[s ç]	Häus-chen	[ˈhɔøs çən]	224
	sp initial in word or element**	[ʃp]	Aussprache	[ˈaos ʃpra xə]	225
	sp in all other positions	[sp]	Knospe	[ˈknɔs pə]	225
	st initial in word or element**	[ʃt]	Stein, Frühstück	[ʃtaen] [ˈfryː ʃtʏk]	225
	st in all other positions	[st]	ist, trösten	[ɪst] [ˈtrøː stən]	225
t	t	[t]	Ton, Sonntag	[toːn] [ˈzɔn taːk]	185, 226
	th in *same* element**	[t]	Thema, Theater	[ˈteː ma] [te ˈaː tər]	226
	th in *two* elements**	[t | h]	Rathaus, mithören	[ˈraːt ˌhaos] [ˈmɪt høː rən]	226
	ti in the endings *-tion, -tient*	[tsj]	Nation, Patient	[na ˈtsjoːn] [pa ˈtsjɛnt]	226
	tsch in *same* element**	[tʃ]	deutsch	[dɔøtʃ]	227
	tz	[ts]	Platz, sitzen	[plats] [ˈzɪ tsən]	227

* The umlauts ä, ö, and ü are sometimes written ae, oe, and ue. These spellings do not alter the pronunciation.
**For a definition of element, see page 166.

German

German Letter and Position in Word			IPA	Example and	IPA	Page
u	u	before *one* consonant	[uː]	Blume	[ˈbluː mə]	207
	uh	in same syllable	[uː]	Stuhl, Uhr	[ʃtuːl] [uːr]	208
	u	before *two* consonants usually	[ʊ]	Mutter, Bruch	[ˈmʊ tər] [brʊx]	207
	ü*	before *one* consonant	[yː]	für, grün	[fyːr] [gryːn]	208
	üh*	in same syllable	[yː]	fühlen	[ˈfyː lən]	210
	ü*	before *two* consonants usually	[ʏ]	Müller, Glück	[ˈmʏ lər] [glʏk]	208
v	v	in all German words, or final in foreign words	[f]	Vater, brav	[ˈfaː tər] [braːf]	227
	v	other positions in foreign words	[v]	Vase, November	[ˈvaː zə] [no ˈvɛm bər]	227
w	w		[v]	Welt, Schwester	[vɛlt] [ˈʃvɛ stər]	228
x	x		[ks]	Hexe	[ˈhɛ ksə]	228
y	y	in derivations from Greek: before *one* consonant	[y]	Lyrik, Physik	[ˈlyː rɪk] [ˈfyː zɪk]	210
		before *two* consonants	[ʏ]	Rhythmus idyllisch	[ˈrʏt mʊs] [i ˈdʏ lɪʃ]	210
	y	in derivations from other languages	[i] or [j]	Tyrol, Pyjama York	[ti ˈrɔl] [pi ˈdʒa ma] [jɔrk]	210
z	z		[ts]	Zimmer, Herz	[ˈtsɪ mər] [hɛrts]	228
	zw		[tsv]	zwei, zwischen	[tsvae] [ˈtsvɪ ʃən]	228

* The umlauts ä, ö, and ü are sometimes written ae, oe, and ue. These spellings do not alter the pronunciation.
**For a definition of element, see page 166.

German

Special Features of German

Syllabification

To apply rules of pronunciation, you must learn to break words into smaller units. To learn this process in German, you must think conceptually at two overlapping levels: *syllables* and *elements*.

A syllable, the smallest unit in a word, contains a single vowel (or single diphthong). A syllable may be a self-contained word (as in *Mond*) or it may be a member of a multi syllabic word (as in *A-bend*).

An element is a word, prefix, or suffix, which forms a self-contained unit within a larger word. An element may contain a single syllable or multiple syllables.

To illustrate the overlapping levels, consider the following examples:

In the compound word *Hundehaus* (dog house), there are two elements (*Hunde-* and *haus*) and three syllables (*Hun-de-haus*). The first element, *Hunde*, has two syllables; the second, *haus*, one syllable.

In the compound word *Abendessen* (evening meal), made up of two elements, *Abend* is one element composed of two syllables and *essen* is one element composed of two syllables.

In *gegeben*, there are three syllables and two elements. The prefix *ge-* is an element and the root verb *geben* is an element.

Generally, first divide a word into its elements and then the elements into syllables. Sometimes, however, as you will see, you need to look across element boundaries to determine a pronunciation. Let's begin with the letter contexts that tell us where to divide words into syllables.

Single Consonant between Vowels

When a single consonant stands between two vowels, put the consonant with the second syllable.

LL 4.2.01 Read aloud.

Va-ter	['faː tər]
Flü-gel	['flyː gəl]
he-ran	[hɛ 'ran]
ge-ge-ben	[gə 'geː bən]
Stra-ße	['ʃtraː sə]

The consonant ß, called Eszett [ɛs 'tsɛt], is a single consonant pronounced [s] and can also be written as ss.

Example: Stra-ße ['ʃtraː sə] or Stras-se ['ʃtraː sə].

German

Exception: When *h* follows a vowel, put it with the first syllable. The *h* is silent and tells you to pronounce the preceding vowel close and long in duration.

LL 4.2.02   Read aloud.

ruh-ig	[ˈruː ɪç]
müh-e	[ˈmyː ə]
eh-e	[ˈeː ə]
Hohl-mass	[ˈhoːl mas]
steh-len	[ˈʃteː lən]
müh-se-lig	[ˈmyː zeː lɪç]

For the meaning of close *and* long *vowels, as well as* open *and* short *vowels, see "General Rules for Pronouncing German Vowels" on page 175—a primary key for understanding German diction.*

However, when *h* is part of the suffix *-heit* or *-haft*, or when it begins the second element of a compound word, put it with the second syllable and pronounce the *h*.

LL 4.2.03   Read aloud.

Ho-heit	[ˈhoː haet]
Hun-de|haus	[ˈhʊn də ˌhaos]

Treat *ß* and the digraphs *ch*, *ck*, *ng*, *ph*, *sch*, and *th* as *single* consonants that begin the next syllable.

LL 4.2.04   Read aloud.

ch	[ç]	Bü-cher	[ˈbyː çər]
	[x]	Spra-che	[ˈʃpraː xə]
ck	[k]	be-glü-cken	[bə ˈglyː kən]
ng	[ŋ]	Wa-nge	[ˈva ŋə]
ph	[f]	Pro-phet	[pro ˈfeːt]
sch	[ʃ]	lau-schen	[ˈlao ʃən]
th	[t]	Zi-ther	[ˈtsɪ tər]

In orthographic spellings, we use a vertical bar to show the two words of a compound spelling. In IPA transcriptions, however, note that a vertical bar indicates a glottal stop (also called a glottal stroke). For details see page 189.

Multiple Consonants

When two or more consonants stand between two vowels, divide the word between the consonants and put the last consonant with the second syllable.

LL 4.2.05   Read aloud.

Hol-de	[ˈhɔl də]
wer-den	[ˈveːr dən]
be-merk-ten	[bə ˈmɛrk tən]
steh-len	[ˈʃteː lən]
Ar-beits	[ˈar baets]

The combination of two or more written consonants that produce a single consonant sound (such as ch, ph, th) *is called a* digraph.

Exception: When *st* is initial in a word or word element, put both *s* and *t* with the second syllable. (See page 225 for more information about *st*.)

LL 4.2.06   Read aloud.

st	[st]	schön-stem	[ˈʃøːn stəm]
		tief-stem	[ˈtiːf stəm]
		Lieb-ste	[ˈliːp stə]
st	[ʃt]	Feld-stein	[ˈfɛlt ʃtaen]
		Früh-stück	[ˈfryː ʃtʏk]

Exception: Because they are digraphs—two letters that represent a single consonant sound—put *ß, ck, ch, ng, ph, sch,* and *th* with the second syllable. (See previous rule for single consonant between two vowels.)

Prefixes and Suffixes

Prefixes and suffixes are separate elements. Notice how the words divide into separate elements—the root as one element, and the prefix or suffix as another.

LL 4.2.07   Read aloud.

Prefixes	
zu ǀ gleich	[tsu ˈglaeç]
be ǀ glü-cken	[bə ˈglʏ kən]
Zu ǀ eig-nung	[ˈtsuː ˌaeg nʊŋ]
ab ǀ bren-nen	[ˈap ˌbrɛ nən]
durch ǀ spie-len	[ˈdʊrç ʃpiː lən]

LL 4.2.08   Read aloud.

Suffixes	
Mäd ǀ chen	[ˈmɛːt çən]
Rös ǀ lein	[ˈrøːz ˌlaen]
Land ǀ schaft	[ˈlant ʃaft]
Fröh ǀ lich ǀ keit	[ˈfrøː lɪç ˌkaet]
scherz ǀ haft	[ˈʃɛrts ˌhaft]

While you must know which parts are prefixes and which are root words, you can learn to recognize common prefixes and suffixes, as shown below.

German

LL 4.2.09 Read aloud.

Common prefixes			
ab-	[ap]	her-	[heːr]
an-	[an]	hin-	[hɪn]
auf-	[aof]	miß-	[mɪs]
be-	[bə]	nach-	[nax]
bei-	[bae]	über-	[ˈyː bər]
da-	[daː]	um-	[ʊm]
dar-	[dar]	un-	[ʊn]
durch-	[dʊrç]	unter-	[ˈʊn tər]
ein-	[aen]	ur-	[uːr]
ent-	[ɛnt]	ver-	[fɛr]
er-	[er]	vor-	[foːr]
fort-	[fɔrt]	weg-	[vɛk]
ge-	[gə]	zer-	[tsɛr]
		zu-	[tsuː]

Exception: While you would normally divide a word into separate elements, in the prefixes *her-*, *hin-*, *dar-*, or *vor*, look across the element boundary and notice whether the next element begins with a vowel. When any of these four prefixes join another prefix that begins with a vowel, begin the next syllable with the final consonant of the first prefix. For instance, *her + ab = he-rab*. (See "Medial Position" on page 189.)

LL 4.2.10 Read aloud.

Common suffixes	
-bar	[baːr]
-chen	[çən]
-haft	[haft]
-keit	[kaet]
-lein	[laen]
-lich	[lɪç]
-los	[loːs]
-nis	[nɪs]
-sal	[zaːl]
-sam	[zaːm]
-schaft	[ʃaft]
-tum	[tʊm]
-wärts	[vɛrts]

German

Compound Words

Divide a compound word between the word elements and then by syllables.

LL 4.2.11   Read aloud.

Zug	luft	['tsuːk ˌlʊft]
Don-ners	tag	['dɔ nərs ˌtaːk]
Ar-beits	tisch	['ar baets ˌtɪʃ]
A-bend	es-sen	['aː bənt ˌe sən]

Often, you can recognize a compound word by the syllables *e*, *en*, *er*, and *es* connecting the two words.

LL 4.2.12   Read aloud.

e as in Scheide	gruss	['ʃae də ˌgruːs]
en as in Linden	baum	['lɪn dən ˌbaom]
er as in Räder	gebraus	['reː dər gə ˌbraos]
es as in Liebes	gaben	['liː bəs ˌgaː bən]

Nouns and words used as nouns are always capitalized in German.

Stress

German, like English, is metric, rising and falling with similar patterns of primary stress, secondary stress, and unstressed syllables. *Primary stress* occurs in most German words on the root syllable, which is usually the first syllable in simple words. In IPA, we indicate the stressed syllable with diacritical mark ['] placed above and before the syllable. *Secondary stress* occurs in multi-syllabic and compound words, which we indicate with the diacritical mark [ˌ] placed below and before the syllable. We don't mark all secondary stress syllables in this text; we only mark them when they help clarify pronunciation. An *unstressed* syllable occurs when the single letter *e* occurs in any of four particular contexts. (See "Unstressed Syllables" on page 173.) With unstressed syllables, we simply pronounce *e* as schwa [ə].

Follow these rules to determine the stressing of syllables. Keep in mind that these rules are *general* and a particular sentence may vary from them. When in doubt, determine the primary stress by observing the stress of the melodic line of your music or check a reliable dictionary.

Simple words: In simple words, stress the first syllable.

LL 4.2.13   Read aloud.

Mut-ter	['mʊ tər]
Schu-le	['ʃuː lə]
le-ben	['leː bən]
ha-ben	['haː bən]

German

Compound words: In compound words, place the stress according to the following context:

Nouns: Stress the *first element* in compound nouns. Secondary stress may be placed on the second element.

LL 4.2.14   Read aloud.

Haus│tür	['haos ˌtyːr]
Schnee│ball	['ʃneː ˌbal]
Früh│jahr	['fryː jaːr]
Dank│sa-gung	['daŋk ˌzaː gʊŋ]
Wald│ein-sam-keit	['valt ˌaen zaːm kaet]

Adverbs: Stress the *second element* in compound adverbs. You can find most of the elements that make up compound adverbs in the list of common prefixes. See "Prefixes and Suffixes" on page 168.

LL 4.2.15   Read aloud.

hi-nauf	[hɪ 'naof]
hi-naus	[hɪ 'naos]
he-rein	[hɛ 'raen]
da-her	[da 'heːr]
um-sonst	[ʊm 'zɔnst]
da-für	[da 'fyːr]

Prefixes: Notice that the stressed syllable varies in words with prefixes according to the following context:

In words with one of these seven prefixes *emp-, ent-, er-, ver-, zer-, be-,* and *ge-,* stress the *root word*.

LL 4.2.16   Read aloud.

[ɛ]			
emp-	[ɛmp]	emp-fin-den	[ɛmp 'fɪn dən]
ent-	[ɛnt]	ent-flieh-en	[ɛnt 'fliː ən]
er-	[ɛr]	er-reicht	[ɛr 'raeçt]
ver-	[fɛr]	Ver-ständ-en	[fɛr 'ʃtɛn dən]
zer-	[tsɛr]	zer-reiß-en	[tsɛr 'rae sən]
[ə]			
be-	[bə]	be-glü-cken	[bə 'glʏ kən]
ge-	[gə]	ge-ge-ben	[gə 'geː bən]

Other than these seven prefixes, usually stress the *prefix*.

German

For instance, in words with the common prefixes *ab-, an-, aus-, auf-, bei-, ein-, mit-,* and *ur-,* stress the *prefix*

LL 4.2.17 Read aloud.

ab ǀ wärts	['ap vɛrts]
aus ǀ geh-en	['aos geː ən]
Bei ǀ fall	['baɛ fal]
ein ǀ si-ngen	['aen zɪ ŋən]
Mit ǀ leid	['mɪt laɛt]
ur ǀ al-te	['uːr ǀ al tə]

Or in the words with the common prefixes *da-, dar-, durch-, her-, hin-, in-, miß-, ob-, über-, um-, un-, unter-, voll-, vor-,* and *zu-,* usually stress the *prefix*.

LL 4.2.18 Read aloud.

durch ǀ zieh-en	['dʊrç tsiː ən]
Miß ǀ brauch	['mɪs braox]
Vor ǀ sicht	['foːr zɪçt]
zu ǀ kom-men	['tsuː kɔ mən]
Um ǀ weg	['ʊm veːk]
un ǀ klar	['ʊn klaːr]
her ǀ kom-men	['heːr kɔ mən]

Here are two exceptions to this rule:

LL 4.2.19 Read aloud.

| zu ǀ frie-den | [tsu 'friː dən] |
| miß ǀ gönnt | [mɪs 'gœnt] |

Foreign Origin

In words of foreign origin, usually stress the last syllable.

In borrowed words and in German words of foreign origin, such as those that end with *-ei,* stress the last syllable.

LL 4.2.20 Read aloud.

Stu-dent	[ʃtu 'dɛnt]
Pa-pier	[pa 'piːr]
Phy-sik	[fy 'ziːk]
Bi-bli-o-tek	[bɪ bli o 'teːk]
Ma-le-rei	[ma lə 'raɛ]

When a prefix separates from its verb and stands alone at the end of a phrase or sentence, it takes the primary stress of the sentence: "Ich komme vom Gebirge her" [ɪç 'kɔmə fɔm gə'bɪrgə 'heːr] *(Schubert,* Der Wanderer*).*

Speakers sometimes shift the stress of the prefix to the root word for emphasis or to change the connotation of the word: un̲menschlich *means inhuman (cruel);* unmen̲schlich *means inhuman—(excessive)-as in* "an inhuman pace."

German

However, in the ending *-ieren*, which is also borrowed, stress the *-ie*.

LL 4.2.21   Read aloud.

| hal-bie-ren | [hal ˈbiː rən] |

You will often need to look up a word in the dictionary to determine whether it is borrowed or not. Words ending in -ie *or* -ieren *give you a starting point.*

Unstressed Syllables

In German, as in English and French, stress patterns include weak stressing, which we call *unstressing*, and the unstressed vowel is usually a neutral sound, most often *schwa* [ə].

You want to be aware of several considerations about unstressing. First, notice that unstressing occurs on different vowels in various languages. In English, any vowel might be reduced to a neutral [ə] in an unstressed syllable. For example, the following vowels may be reduced to [ə]: *a* in *breakfast* [ˈbrɛk fəst]; *o* in *contain* [kən ˈteɪn]; *u* in *suppose* [sə ˈpoʊz]. But in French and German, only an unstressed *e* reduces to [ə].

Second, you want to know when to unstress a syllable. See the rule on page 198 for the four contexts where *e* becomes unstressed in German.

Next isolate the German pronunciation of [ə], which is slightly different from other languages. In English, you sing [ə] much like its stressed partner [ʌ], but less open. In French, you articulate [ə] with very round lips, like a close [ø] (umlauted ö). In German, you produce [ə] like an open umlauted [œ]. You shape your lips like "aw" [ɔ] and simultaneously raise and arch your tongue forward to "eh" [ɛ]. Avoid opening the vowel as much as "uh" [ʌ] or "eh" [ɛ] or rounding as much as [o].

Last, although [ə] is a neutral sound, sing it with good resonance, consistent with the other vowels in your songs, counteracting a tendency to sing it wth a dull sound. As an American singer, you may need diligence when singing this neutral sound because, in English, we often hear it when people hesitate and can't remember what to say—a dull, flat sound, devoid of vibrant resonance. It can be easy to transfer this unfocused stressed "uh" [ʌ]—and its partner unstressed [ə]—into your singing.

Distinctive German Vowels

The German vowels *a*, *e*, *o* differ from their American counterparts in a few ways. They need special attention so that your articulation habits from American speech do not carry over.

German

The letter a

Pronounce the letter *a* only as [aː] or [a], never rounding it to [ɔ] or [ə], as you might in English.

LL 4.2.22   Compare and contrast.

English		German	
America	[ə ˈmɛ rɪ kə]	Amerika	[a ˈmeː ri ka]
altar	[ˈɔl tər]	Altar	[al ˈtaːr]

The letter e

Pronounce the letter *e* only as [eː], [ɛ], or [ə], never as the diphthong [eɪ] as you normally do in English. Also pronounce the German [eː] with a closer position than the American [e], placing the arch of your tongue more forward and closer to the teeth ridge than in English, creating a sound approaching [i].

LL 4.2.23   Compare and contrast.

English		German	
sail	[seɪl]	Seele	[ˈzeː lə]
way	[weɪ]	Weh	[veː]

Pronounce the unstressed German [ə] similar to the sound of the mixed vowel open *ö* [œ], rounding your lips slightly more than you would for the American [ə] and placing your tongue in a higher position, leaning toward pronouncing [œ]. Be careful never to pronounce the German [ə] as [ɛ] or [ʌ].

LL 4.2.24   Compare and contrast.

English		German	
comma	[ˈkɑ mə]	komme	[ˈkɔ mə]
about	[ə ˈbaʊt]	gebaut	[gə ˈbaot]

The letter o

Pronounce the letter *o* only as [o] or [ɔ], always as a pure [o], never the common English diphthong [oʊ]. Also pronounce the German [o] with more closed, firmly rounded lips than in English.

LL 4.2.25   Compare and contrast.

English		German	
note	[noʊt]	Not	[noːt]
sew	[soʊ]	Sohn	[zoːn]

German

General Rules for Pronouncing German Vowels

In German each vowel has a *close* and an *open* pronunciation—and this key concept will guide you with regularity. To undestand this concept, the terms *close* and *open* refer to the *space between the tongue and the roof of the mouth*. The rule is simple: When the arch of your tongue is closer to the roof of your mouth, the vowel is *close*; When your tongue is further from the roof of your mouth, the vowel is *open*. For example, *i* can be pronounced as close *ee* [iː] or open *ih* [ɪ], two similar sounds that differ in how *close* the tongue is from the roof of the mouth.

The general rules, which apply to all German vowels, indicate when to pronounce vowels as close or open in individual words. For example, one rule says that *before a single consonant in a syllable of primary stress, vowels are usually close*; therefore the letter *u* in *Bruder* is close [u]—because *u* is in the stressed syllable *Bru*. Another rule states that *before double or multiple consonants, vowels are usually open*; therefore the letter *u* in *unter* is open [ʊ]—because *u* comes before the two consonants *n* and *t*.

Besides open and close, the general rules also specify a *long* or *short* pronunciation, referring to the *duration of the sound*. Here, the rules are also simple: letting a vowel sound with a longer duration is called a *long vowel*; with shorter duration, a *short vowel*. The difference between long and short vowels, simple as it is, characterizes German diction distinctly—and deserves special attention. In IPA transcriptions, you use the symbol [ː] to indicate a long vowel. To indicate a short vowel, simply write the vowel without [ː].

Usually combine the close/open and long/short distinctions: pronounce close vowels with a long duration; open vowels with a short duration. In the example above, pronounce the letter *u* in *Bruder* [uː] as both close and long; likewise, pronounce the letter *u* in *unter* [ʊ] as both open and short.

In music, where duration values are fixed, you can suggest the duration: Sustain the vowel as long as possible before pronouncing the following consonant for long vowels; slightly anticipate the following consonant for short vowels.

The following rules for pronouncing German vowels are more consistent than in other languages. Once you know them, you can apply them equally to all vowels, across letter contexts. Common exceptions to these rules are included in the detailed discussion of vowels in the "German Vowels in Detail" section beginning on page 191.

Study the chart below and keep the close/long, and open/short character of each vowel in mind while learning the general rules.

German

LL 4.2.26   Read aloud.

Letter	Close/long	Open/short
i	[iː]	[ɪ]
e	[eː]	[ɛ]
o	[oː]	[ɔ]
ö	[øː]	[œ]
u	[uː]	[ʊ]
ü	[yː]	[ʏ]
y	[yː]	[ʏ]

Written *a* and *ä* are slightly different: distinguish them primarily by duration, rather than close/open pronunciation—same sound, only longer or shorter. You nevertheless determine the duration by following the same rules for close/long and open/short vowels. (See page 191 and 194 for a more detailed discussion of the letter *a* and *ä*.)

LL 4.2.27   Read aloud.

	Long	Short
a	[aː]	[a]
ä	[ɛː]	[ɛ]

Close and Long Vowels

In syllables of primary stress, pronounce vowels close and long in the following contexts.

1. When vowels are doubled, pronounce them close and long.

   LL 4.2.28   Read aloud.

Seele	[ˈzeː lə]
Moos	[moːs]
Meer	[meːr]
Saal	[zaːl]

2. When a vowel is followed by *h* in the same syllable, leave the *h* silent and pronounce the preceding vowel close and long.

   LL 4.2.29   Read aloud.

mehr	[meːr]
Sohne	[ˈzoː nə]
zählen	[ˈtsɛː lən]
ihrer	[ˈiː rər]
Frühe	[ˈfryː ə]
sahe	[ˈzaː ə]

German

ruhe	[ˈruː ə]
wohl	[voːl]
fröhlich	[ˈfrøː lɪç]

3. When vowels occur before a single consonant, usually pronounce them close and long, as illustrated in these contexts:

In *polysyllables*, pronounce stressed vowels before a single consonant as close and long. (See "Stress" on page 170.)

LL 4.2.30   Read aloud.

Bru-der	[ˈbruː dər]
re-den	[ˈreː dən]
Flü-gel	[ˈflyː gəl]
ö-de	[ˈøː də]

In *monosyllables*, usually pronounce vowels before a single consonant close and long.

LL 4.2.31   Read aloud.

Grab	[graːp]
schon	[ʃoːn]
dir	[diːr]
Ton	[toːn]
für	[fyːr]
rot	[roːt]

Exception: vowels in some monosyllables vary in their close/long and open/short character and you will need to consult a dictionary. Here is a list of common monosyllables and their close/long, open/short character.

LL 4.2.32   Read aloud.

Close and long		Open and short	
nun	[nuːn]	zum	[tsʊm]
		um	[ʊm]
schon	[ʃoːn]	von	[vɔn]
		vom	[vɔm]
		ob	[ɔp]
Weg (noun)	[veːk]	weg (adverb)	[vɛk]
her	[heːr]	es	[ɛs]
der	[deːr]	des	[dɛs]

German

für	[fyːr]		
		in	[ɪn]
		im	[ɪm]
		mit	[mɪt]
dir	[diːr]	bin	[bɪn]
		hin	[hɪn]

4. When vowels are final in a monosyllable, pronounce them close and long.

LL 4.2.33   Read aloud.

du	[duː]
Knie	[kniː]
wo	[voː]
zu	[tsuː]
die	[diː]
wie	[viː]

For some verbs, nouns, and adjectives, you must retain the the close and long character of the *root word's vowel*, even when the vowel changes in the different forms of the root word (from [e] to [i], for instance).

Verbs: Determine the pronunciation of the root verb and, throughout its different inflections, maintain the close/long character of its vowel, regardless of the letter endings that follow the vowel. In the following example, for instance, consider the root verb *geben*. Because the *e* comes before a single vowel, pronounce it close and long. When the verb changes form, to *gibt*, the vowel changes from *e* to *i*. The vowel *i* now comes before two consonants, *bt*, which would usually tell you to open and shorten the vowel. But with this verb, you must retain the close/long character of the root verb *geben* and pronounce *gipt* with the close/long [iː], as in [giːpt], not [gɪpt].

LL 4.2.34   Read aloud.

leben	[ˈleː bən]	*to live*	becomes	lebt	[leːpt]	*he lives*
geben	[ˈgeː bən]	*to give*	becomes	gibt	[giːpt]	*he gives*

Note: To apply this rule, you must first know the root verb, which you can often see in a dictionary. You can also anticipate the root word by recognizing common letter endings of verb inflections through the sample conjugation of *leben* (to live).

German

ich lebe	I live
wir leben	we live
du lebst	you live
ihr lebt	you live
er lebt	he lives
sie leben	they live

Nouns: When a noun becomes plural with an umlaut, maintain the close/long character of the root word's vowel.

LL 4.2.35   Read aloud.

Buch	[buːx]	book	becomes	Bücher	[ˈbyː çər]	books

Adjectives: When the adjective changes degree with an umlaut, also maintain the close/long character of the root word's vowel.

LL 4.2.36   Read aloud.

hoch	[hoːx]	high
höher	[ˈhøː ər]	higher
höchst	[ˈhøːçst]	highest
rot	[roːt]	red
rötlich	[ˈrøːt lıç]	reddish

Vowels That are Close but not Long:

In syllables that do not carry primary stress, close vowels are not long. Notice the unstressed letters *i, e, a, o* in the following:

LL 4.2.37   Read aloud.

A-li-bi	[ˈaː li bi]
de-fi-ni-ti<u>o</u>n	[ˌde fi ni ˈsjoːn]
fa-bu-l<u>ie</u>-ren	[ˌfa bu ˈliː rən]
j<u>e</u>t-zo	[ˈjeːt tso]

Close vowels are not long in unstressed monosyllable words within a sentence (such as words for the English articles *the* and *an*).

LL 4.2.38   Read aloud.

der	[der]
den	[den]
dem	[dem]

German

Open and Short Vowels

Pronounce vowels as open and short in the following contexts:

1. Usually pronounce vowels before double or multiple consonants as open and short.

   LL 4.2.39   Read aloud.

Double:	Sonne	[ˈzɔ nə]
	schlaf-fen	[ˈʃla fən]
Multiple:	un-ter	[ˈʊn tər]
	hel-fen	[ˈhɛl fən]

   Note: Double and multiple consonants do not need to be in the same syllable with the vowel to affect the open character of the vowel.

2. Pronounce *all* vowels before *ck* [k], *ng* [ŋ], and *sch* [ʃ] as open and short.

   LL 4.2.40   Read aloud.

ck:	schickt	[ʃɪkt]
	pflücken	[ˈpflʏ kən]
	Blicke	[ˈblɪ kə]
	Stock	[ʃtɔk]
ng:	Hoffnung	[ˈhɔf nʊŋ]
	Finger	[ˈfɪ ŋər]
	singen	[ˈzɪ ŋən]
sch:	Tisch	[ˈtɪʃ]
	Busche	[ˈbʊ ʃə]
	Fische	[ˈfɪ ʃə]

3. Pronounce vowels before the letter *x* [ks] as open and short.

   LL 4.2.41   Read aloud.

Hexe	[ˈhɛk sə]
exakt	[ɛk ˈsakt]

4. Before *ch*, *ß* (Eszett) and *ss*:

   Always pronounce the forward vowels *e* and *i* as open and short.

   LL 4.2.42   Read aloud.

ch:	ich	[ɪç]
	nicht	[nɪçt]
	mich	[mɪç]
	Becher	[ˈbɛ çər]

German

ß:	vergiß	[fɛr ˈgɪs]
ss:	essen	[ˈɛ sən]
	wissen	[ˈvɪ sən]

5. Vowels other than *e* and *i* have variable pronunciations before *ch*, *ß*, and *ss*. You will need to consult a dictionary.

LL 4.2.43 Read aloud.

	Open and Short		Close and Long	
ch:	doch	[dɔx]	hoch	[hoːx]
	noch	[nɔx]	suchen	[ˈzuː xən]
	Dach	[dax]	Sprach	[ʃpraːx]
	Nacht	[naxt]	stach	[ʃtaːx]
			Fluch	[fluːx]
ß:	abschluß	[ˈap ʃlʊs]	flößen	[fløː sən]
ss:	Fluss	[flʊs]	Fuss	[fuːs]
	Kuss	[kʊs]	Gruss	[gruːs]
	Küssen	[ˈkʏ sən]	Schoss	[ʃoːs]
	muss	[mʊs]	gross	[groːs]
	Ross	[rɔs]		

6. Before *st*, all vowels have variable close/long and open/short pronunciations. You will need to consult a dictionary.

LL 4.2.44 Read aloud.

	Open and Short		Close and Long	
st:	kosten	[ˈkɔ stən]	Trost	[troːst]
			löst	[løːst]

7. Before the combination of *r* plus *d, t, l,* or *n*, all vowels also have variable pronunciations. Again, consult a dictionary.

LL 4.2.45 Read aloud.

	Open and Short		Close and Long	
rd:			werden	[ˈveːr dən]
			Pferd	[pfeːrt]
rt:			Geburt	[gə ˈbuːrt]
	Hirt	[hɪrt]	zart	[tsaːrt]
	Pforten	[ˈpfɔr tən]	Bart	[baːrt]
rl:			perlig	[ˈpeːr lɪç]

German

See the chart of prefixes and suffixes on page 168 for many of the common exceptions to the rules for open and close vowels.

In the prefixes *her-*, *da-*, or *dar-* when followed by a consonant, you must first determine stressing to know how to pronounce the vowel. When the prefix is stressed, pronounce the vowel as close and long; when unstressed, pronounce it as open and short. Consult a dictionary for stressing.

LL 4.2.46   Read aloud.

Close and Long (stressed)		Open and Short (unstressed)	
*her*stellen	['heːr ʃtel ən]	*her*nieder	[her 'niː dər]
		*da*durch	[da 'dʊrç]

Mixed Vowel Sounds

German has four mixed vowel sounds, which are indicated by an umlaut (¨) over the letters *ö* and *ü*, as in *schön* and *früh*.

> Note: The umlaut vowels *ö* and *ü* can also be written by eliminating the dots and adding the letter *e*: *oe* and *ue* as in *schoen* and *frueh*. These two spellings are interchangeable.

To pronounce a mixed vowel sound, combine—or *mix*—different lip and tongue positions: round your lips for a back vowel while raising and arching your tongue for a forward vowel. For example, round your lips to the position of *oo* [u] as in *boot* and then, *without moving your lips,* arch your tongue into the forward position for *ee* [i] as in *beet*. Add voice, and, though unfamiliar, you will hear the close mixed vowel sound of *ü* [y], a blending of the back vowel sound of [u] and the forward vowel sound of [i].

LL 4.2.47   Read aloud.

Chart of Lip and Tongue Positions for the Mixed Vowels					
	Lip position		Tongue position		Mixed vowel
closed ü	[u]	+	[i]	=	[yː]
open ü	[ʊ]	+	[ɪ]	=	[ʏ]
closed ö	[o]	+	[e]	=	[øː]
open ö	[ɔ]	+	[ɛ]	=	[œ]

Authorities vary their opinons about transcribing the sounds of the German diphthongs. Siebs, who wrote for a German-speaking audience, used [ae], [ao], and [ɔø]. Other authorities employ [aɪ], [aʊ], and [ɔɪ] or [ɔy] or [ɔʏ]. In this text, we use the symbols [ae], [ao], and [ɔø].

Diphthongs

German has three diphthongs. Each is pronounced with the first vowel sound receiving longer duration. Compared to English diphthongs, German diphthongs have a darker quality, which adds to the characteristic sound of the German language.

German

The Diphthong [ae]

Pronounce the letter combinations *ai*, *ay*, *ei*, or *ey* as [ae]. The sound of the German diphthong is similar to the diphthong [aɪ] in the English word *bite*, but darker in quality because of [e] as the second sound

LL 4.2.48   Compare and contrast.

English		German	
my	[maɪ]	Mai	[mae]
dine	[daɪn]	dein	[daen]

Examples:

LL 4.2.49   Read aloud.

Feil'	[fael]
Bayern	['bae ərn]
Reich	[raeç]
Meyer	['mae ər]

The Diphthong [ao]

Pronounce the letter combination *au* as [ao]. The sound of the German diphthong [ao] is similar to the diphthong [aʊ] in the English word *house* [haʊs], but darker in quality because of the more rounded [o] for the second sound.

LL 4.2.50   Compare and contrast.

English		German	
house	[haʊs]	Haus	[haos]
about	[ə 'baʊt]	baut	[baot]

LL 4.2.51   Read aloud.

auf	[aof]
faul	[faol]
auch	[aox]
Tau	[tao]

Shift from the first vowel to the second vowel of a German diphthong by changing the tongue and/or lip position, but not by lowering the jaw.

The Diphthong [ɔø]

Pronounce the letter combinations *eu* and *äu* as [ɔø]. The sound of the German diphthong [ɔø] is similar to the diphthong [ɔɪ] in the English word *boy*, but darker in quality because of the more rounded [ø] for the second sound. When you pronounce the German [ɔø], protrude and round your lips energetically and feel the arch of your tongue moving forward as you glide from [ɔ] to [ø].

German

LL 4.2.52 Compare and contrast.

English		German	
Troy	[trɔɪ]	treu	[trɔø]

LL 4.2.53 Read aloud.

neu	[nɔø]
heute	['hɔø tə]
Bäume	['bɔø mə]
läute	['lɔø tə]

Distinctive German Consonants

The Consonant ch

Pronounce the letters *ch* with two different sounds in German, both unfamiliar to English speakers. These are the *ichlaut* [ç] and the *achlaut* [x]. Pronounce both the *ichlaut* and the *achlaut* as voiceless consonants.

Ichlaut [ç]

Pronounce the letter *ch* as *ichlaut* [ç] after forward vowels, umlauts, diphthongs (other than *au*), and consonants.

You can discover [ç] when you say the initial *h* in the name *Hugh* using a high, forward arch of the tongue and emphasizing the initial aspirate sound. Isolate the initial sound [ç ç ç ç], then precede it with a bright [i], [iç iç iç iç], allowing an energetic stream of air to flow over your arched tongue. You will feel the air flow between the center of your tongue arch and your teeth ridge.

> To pronounce the German word *ich*, repeat the process above using the vowel [ɪ], [ɪç ɪç ɪç ɪç]. Once you find the sound, you will notice that the sound naturally adjusts its position slightly, depending on the sounds surrounding it. The ichlaut remains an aspirated sound, however, and never becomes the fricative [ʃ] or plosive [k].

LL 4.2.54 Compare and contrast.

English		German	
dish	[dɪʃ]	dich	[dɪç]
wrecked	[ɹɛkt]	Recht	[rɛçt]

Achlaut [x]

Pronounce the letters *ch* after back vowels and the diphthong *au* as *achlaut* [x]. The voiceless sound of [x] resembles the sound of a whispered *ah* [a].

Allow the air to rush between the velum and the arched back of the tongue. Isolate the sound [x x x x], then precede it with [a], to pronounce [ax ax ax ax]. Note that the *achlaut* is always aspirated and never pronounced with the stop of the plosive [k].

LL 4.2.55   Compare and contrast.

English		German	
box	[bɑks]	Bachs	[baxs]
fluke	[fluk]	Fluch	[fluːx]

Ichlaut and Achlaut with Forward and Back Vowels

The following progression of ichlauts and achlauts moves from the most forward to the most back position. Read the syllables, which may feel very unfamiliar, then read again reversing the pattern.

LL 4.2.56   Read aloud.

ichi eche ächä	[içi eçe ɛçɛ]
acha ocho uchu	[axa oxo uxu]

Dental Consonants D, T, N, and L

Make dental consonants with the tip of your tongue touching the gum line behind your upper teeth. In German there are four dental consonants: *d*, *t*, *n*, and *l* (all, oddly enough, found in the English word d<u>ental</u>.) For German dental consonants place the tip of your tongue more forward than for their English counterparts.

[d] and [t]

In German, allow less air to escape with the explosion of *d* and *t* than in English, producing what is sometimes called a *dry* sound.

[n]

Pronounce [n] with the tip of the tongue more forward than in English.

[l]

Pronounce [l] as a clear *dental* sound, somewhat like the *l* in the English word *let*. Avoid the *alveolar* dark *l* as in *all*, which is the most common sound of *l* in English.

LL 4.2.57   Read aloud.

English		German	
dandy	[dæn dɪ]	dadurch	[da 'dʊrç]

German

total	[toʊ təl]	total	[toː ˈtal]
none	[nʌn]	Nonne	[ˈnɔ nə]

Voicing and Unvoicing b, d, g

Pronounce the consonants *b, d,* and *g* as either voiced or unvoiced, depending on the following contexts:

1. When they are initial in a word or syllable, pronounce the consonants *b, d,* and *g* with their normal, voiced sound.

   LL 4.2.58   Read aloud.

Bett	[bɛt]
Ge-dicht	[gə ˈdɪçt]
Lie-be	[ˈliː bə]
We-ge	[ˈveː gə]

2. However, pronounce the consonants *b, d,* and *g* as unvoiced *p, t,* and *k* when they are final in a word or syllable or when they occur before *t* or *st.*

   LL 4.2.59   Read aloud.

Dieb	[diːp]
end-lich	[ˈɛnt lɪç]
ab-fahren	[ˈap faː rən]
lebt	[leːpt]
trägst	[trɛːkst]
Tod	[toːt]
Weg	[veːk]
er-folg-reich	[ɛr ˈfɔlk raeç]
Magd	[maːkt]

   Whether you voice or unvoice the single consonants *b, d,* and *g* depends entirely upon the position of the consonant in the word. The pronunciation may even change in different forms of the same word. For example, notice the pronunciation of the final *g* and *d* in the following words as the form of the word changes.

   LL 4.2.60   Read aloud.

Weg	[veːk]	*becomes*	Wege	[ˈveː gə]
Leid	[laet]	*becomes*	Leider	[ˈlae dər]

3. When the combinations of *-bt* and *-gd* are final in a word, pronounce them unvoiced.

German

LL 4.2.61   Read aloud.

| Jagd | [jakt] | gibt | [giːpt] |

Exception: When the letters *-ig* are final in words or syllables, pronounce the letters as [ɪç].

LL 4.2.62   Read aloud.

| billig | ['bɪ lɪç] | emsig | ['ɛm zɪç] |
| wichtig | ['vɪç tɪç] | Ewigkeit | ['eː vɪç kaet] |

4. When the digraph *ng* occurs in a word, the letters are pronounced as [ŋ]. The *g* is not pronounced.

LL 4.2.63   Read aloud.

| singen | ['zɪ ŋən] | Hoffnung | ['hɔf nʊŋ] |

Occasionally, Germans contract a word by omitting the letter *e*. When a voiced *b*, *d*, or *g* occurs in such a contracted word, and when it occurs before *l*, *n*, or *r*, still pronounce the stop-plosive consonant as voiced and pronounce it with the second syllable.

LL 4.2.64   Read aloud.

Wa-ge-ner	['vaː gə nər]	becomes	Wa-gner	['vaː gnər]
re-ge-net	['reː gə nət]	becomes	re-gnet	['reː gnət]
gol-de-ne	['gɔl də nə]	becomes	go-ldne	['gɔ ldnə]
Wan-de-rer	['van də rər]	becomes	Wan-drer	['van drər]

Interpretive Use of Consonants

German consonants carry expressiveness to an even greater degree than in Italian or English and must be articulated precisely and clearly. The great German artists sing energetic consonants to shape their words and enhance the meaning of the text. They emphasize consonants by lengthening their duration or increasing their loudness, using artistic freedom to articulate consonant sounds richly.

Refer to a word-by-word translation of the text to become sensitive to the meaning of the words and to determine which consonants to emphasize. In German, as in English, you may shift the emphasis when words are repeated. However, emphasize consonants only to enliven the expression. Be careful not to destroy the vocal line!

When emphasizing consonants, follow these guidelines:

> Pronounce initial consonants before the musical beat and the vowel on the beat to avoid slowing the tempo.
>
>> Note: It may be helpful to think of linking initial consonants to the end of the preceding word.

German

In consonant clusters, emphasize only one consonant. The consonant you choose to emphasize will generally be the one that can be the loudest or longest of the group. For example, lengthen the *s* in *stille*, not the *t*, *stille*; and the *r* in *frisch*, not the *f*, *frisch*.

Within a word, emphasize only the consonants that follow an open, short vowel, as in wu*n*derhe*ll*.

Do not emphasize a consonant after a close, long vowel.

Double Consonants

In speech, Germans usually pronounce a double consonant only slightly longer than a single consonant. They use the double consonant to essentially open and shorten the preceding vowel rather than focus on the consonant.

However, you can often lengthen double consonants for emphasis and expressiveness. Where we might say, *Everything's going my way*, a German would exclaim, *Es geht mir alles gut!* and lengthen the *ll*. Outstanding singers of German Lieder enliven both diction and meaning this way.

> Note: The long duration of a consonant is indicated in IPA transcriptions by a colon [ː]. In this text, we transcribe double consonants with a single symbol and use the [ː] and doubled consonants only where context warrants their use.

LL 4.2.65   Read aloud.

Himmel	[ˈhɪmː məl]
Wonne	[ˈvɔnː nə]
bitter	[ˈbɪtː tər]

When the final consonant of the first word is the same as the first consonant of the second word, lengthen the consonant. You essentially stop the first consonant and explode the second. A similar sound occurs in English when the same consonant ends one word and begins the next.

LL 4.2.66   Read aloud.

English	German	
ba*n* *n*oise	hi*n* *n*ehmen	[ˈhɪnː neː mən]
qui*t* *t*alking	Fes*t* *t*ag	[ˈfɛstː ˌtaːk]

German

Glottal Stop

A *glottal stop* is articulated by a brief, but complete closing of the glottis in the larynx. You can hear a glottal stop between these two example English words: *the answer*.

Unlike the French or Italians, who link sounds across syllables, Germans insert glottal stops in the following contexts:

Initial position

Usually precede words beginning with a vowel with a glottal stop, being careful not to link it to the previous word.

LL 4.2.67   Read aloud.

an alle	[an ǀ ˈa lə]
Am offenen Abend	[am ǀ ˈɔfənən ǀ ˈaːbənt]
Dein Abschied	[daen ǀ ˈapʃiːt]
Etwas in ihm ist anders	[ˈɛtwas ǀ ɪn ǀ iːm ǀ ɪst ǀ ˈandərs]

Medial Position

Within a word, use a glottal stop in two instances:

In a *compound word*, when the second element begins with a vowel, separate it from the first element with a glottal stop.

LL 4.2.68   Read aloud.

Land ǀ urlaub	[ˈlant ǀ ˌurlaop]
Mannes ǀ art	[ˈma nəs ǀ ˌart]
Ein ǀ akter	[ˈaen ǀ ˌaktər]
Erd ǀ apfel	[ˈeːrt ǀ ˌapfəl]

When a prefix is a separate element, separate the prefix from the root word with a glottal stop.

LL 4.2.69   Read aloud.

Er ǀ innerung	[ɛr ǀ ˈɪnəruŋ]
aus ǀ atmen	[ˈaos ǀ atmən]
über ǀ all	[ˈyː bər ǀ al]
un ǀ endlich	[ʊn ǀ ˈɛnt ǀ lɪç]
hin ǀ arbeiten	[ˈhɪn ǀ arbaetən]
Vor ǀ ahnung	[ˈfoːr ǀ aː nuŋ]

German

Exception: When the prefixes *her-*, *hin-*, *dar-*, and *vor-* are combined with another prefix that begins with a vowel, do not use a glottal stop. Begin the second syllable with the medial consonant. Refer to the chart on page 168 to help you recognize prefixes that may be combined.

LL 4.2.70   Read aloud.

her + ab = he-rab	[he 'rap]
dar + an = da-ran	[da 'ran]
hin + ein = hi-nein	[hɪ 'naen]
vor + aus = vo-raus	[fo 'raos]

German

German Vowels in Detail

The German language contains six vowels plus three umlauted vowels. Each vowel letter has a close and open sound; *e* and *y* each have an additional sound. The letters and their respective sounds are indicated in the chart below.

Letter	Close/Long	Open/Short	Other	
i	[iː]	[ɪ]		
e	[eː]	[ɛ]	[ə]	
o	[oː]	[ɔ]		
u	[uː]	[ʊ]		
y	[yː]	[ʏ]	[i]	[j]
ö	[øː]	[œ]		
ü	[yː]	[ʏ]		

	Long	Short
a	[aː]	[a]
ä	[ɛː]	[ɛ]

You contrast the two possible pronunciations of *a* ([aː] and [a]) and *ä* ([ɛː] and [ɛ]) by their long or short duration. To know which duration, apply the rules for close/long and open/short vowels, but maintain the same vowel sound.

Pronounce the German letter *a* as either long [aː] or short [a].

Under the section of "General Rules for Pronouncing German Vowels" on page 175 in *Special Features of German*, you can read the generally consistent rules for pronouncing close/long vowels and open/short vowels. However, as demonstrated in the Vowel Chart above, the letter *a* does not fit into the pattern for close and open, but does fit the pattern of long and short vowels. In German, the long or short *duration* of the vowel *a* is of greater importance than its close and open character. Although the duration of the vowel is predetermined by the melodic notes in singing, you can nevertheless define the duration of short [a] by moving more quickly to the consonant that follows.

> Pronounce *a* as long [aː] when the spelling of a German word follows the rule for a close/long vowel.
>
> Pronounce *a* as short [a] when the spelling of a German word follows the rule for an open/short vowel.

The letter

a

German

Read aloud to compare and contrast the long and short duration of these vowels.

LL 4.3.01 Read aloud.

[aː]		[a]	
Kahn	[kaːn]	kann	[kan]
Abend	[ˈaː bənt]	Apfel	[ˈap fəl]
Wahl	[vaːl]	Wald	[valt]
Sahne	[ˈzaː nə]	sandte	[ˈzan tə]
Vater	[ˈfaː tər]	Wasser	[ˈva sər]

Caution: As an English-speaking American, you must be careful never to pronounce the German letter *a* as [ɔ] or [ə].

Note: Some German authorities use the symbol [ɑ] to represent the close/long pronunciation and the symbol [a] to represent the open/short pronunciation of the vowel *a*. In this text, we eliminate the symbol [ɑ] because the contrast between the sound of [ɑ] and [a] is subtle in singing.

a, aa

When *a* or *aa* are followed by a single consonant in a primary stressed syllable, usually pronounce *a* or *aa* as long [aː].

LL 4.3.02 Read aloud.

Vater	[ˈfaː tər]
Grab	[graːp]
Staat	[ʃtaːt]
Saal	[zaːl]

Exception: In several prefixes when *a* is followed by a single consonant, pronounce it as short [a].

LL 4.3.03 Read aloud.

ab-ordnen	[ˈap	ɔrdnən]
an-erkannt	[ˈan	ɛrkant]

Exception: In several one-syllable words, when *a* is followed by a single consonant, pronounce it as short [a].

LL 4.3.04 Read aloud.

am	[am]
man	[man]
das	[das]

German

When *a* is followed by double or multiple consonants, usually pronounce it as short [a].

> Note: The double or multiple consonants do not need to be in the same syllable to affect the open/short pronunciation of the vowel. However, they must be in the same word element.

LL 4.3.05   Read aloud.

Tasse	['ta sə]
halt	[halt]
anders	['an dərs]
allen	['a lən]

Exception: Because it varies, you cannot apply a rule to know how to pronounce the vowel *a* before *ch*, *ß* (Eszett), *ss*, and *st*. (See "General Rules for Pronouncing German Vowels" on page 175, or consult a dictionary.)

ah

Pronounce the letter combination *ah* in the same syllable as long [aː].

When a vowel is followed by *h* in the same syllable, the *h* is silent, signalling you to pronounce the vowel as close and long.

LL 4.3.06   Read aloud.

| Bahn | [baːn] |
| fahren | ['faː rən] |

ai, ay

Pronounce *ai* and *ay* as the diphthong [ae]. The sound [ae] is similar to the diphthong found in the English word *bite*, but darker in quality because of the use of [e] as the second sound.

LL 4.3.07   Read aloud.

Mai	[mae]
Laich	[laeç]
Kaiser	['kae zər]
Saite	['zae tə]
Bayern	['bae ərn]
Tokayer	[to 'kae ər]

German

au

Pronounce *au* as the diphthong [ao]. The sound of [ao] is similar to the diphthong found in the English word *house*, but darker in quality because of the use of more rounded [o] for the second sound.

LL 4.3.08   Read aloud.

Haus	[haos]
Laub	[laop]
Auge	['ao gə]
auf	[aof]
Faust	[faost]
lauschen	['lao ʃən]

ä

Pronounce the German letter *ä* as long [ɛː] or short [ɛ].

Under "General Rules for Pronouncing German Vowels" on page 175 in *Special Features of German,* you can read the generally consistent rules for pronouncing close/long vowels and open/short vowels. However, as demonstrated in the Vowel Chart above, the letter *ä* does not fit into the pattern for close and open, but it does fit the pattern for long and short vowels. In German, the long or short *duration* of the vowel *ä* is of greater importance than its close and open character. Although the duration of the vowel is predetermined by the melodic notes in singing, you can nevertheless define the duration of short [ɛ] by moving more quickly to the consonant that follows.

Pronounce *ä* as [ɛː] when the spelling of a German word follows the rule for a close/long vowel.

Pronounce *ä* as [ɛ] when the spelling of a German word follows the rule for an open/short vowel.

When *ä* is followed by a single consonant in a primary stressed syllable, usually pronounce it as long [ɛː].

LL 4.3.09   Read aloud.

bäten	['bɛː tən]
Bäder	['bɛː dər]
Väter	['fɛː tər]
Schwäne	['ʃvɛː nə]

German

spät	[ʃpɛːt]
erklären	[ɛr ˈkleː rən]
Schären	[ˈʃɛː rən]
Mädchen	[ˈmɛːt çən]

When *ä* is followed by double or multiple consonants, usually pronounce it as short [ɛ].

Note: The double or multiple consonants do not need to be in the same syllable to apply this rule. However, the multiple consonants must be in the same word element.

LL 4.3.10   Read aloud.

Äpfel	[ˈɛp fəl]
Kälte	[ˈkɛl tə]
stärke	[ˈʃtɛr kə]
ärgern	[ˈɛr gən]
lässig	[ˈlɛ sıç]
schwärmenden	[ˈʃvɛr mən dən]

In *Mädchen* [ˈmɛːt çən], a common word with the suffix *-chen*, notice that the multiple consonants are not in the same element. Therefore pronounce *ä*, followed by only the single consonant *d* in the first element, as long [ɛː].

Exception: The vowel *ä* has variable pronunciations before *ch*, *ß* (Eszett), *ss*, and *st*, and when before the combination of *r* plus *d, t, l,* and *n*. (For more information, see *"General Rules for Pronouncing German Vowels" on page 175*, or consult a dictionary.)

äh

Pronounce *äh* in the same syllable as [ɛː].

When a vowel is followed by *h* in the same syllable, the *h* is silent, signalling you to pronounce the vowel as close and long.

LL 4.3.11   Read aloud.

ähnlich	[ˈɛːn lıç]
nähen	[ˈnɛː ən]
Krähe	[ˈkrɛː ə]
erwähnen	[ɛr ˈvɛːn ən]

German

äu

Pronounce *äu* as the diphthong [ɔø].

> Note: When you pronounce the German [ɔø], round your lips more than for the English [ɔɪ] as in the word *boy*. Protrude your lips energetically and feel the arch of the tongue move forward as you glide from [ɔ] to [ø].

LL 4.3.12   Read aloud.

Fräulein	['frɔø laen]
Bäume	['bɔø mə]
Häuser	['hɔø zər]
läuten	['lɔø tən]
Bläue	['blɔø ə]
Täubchen	['tɔøp çən]

The letter e

Pronounce the letter *e* in one of three ways: close/long [eː], open/short [ɛ], and unstressed schwa [ə].

Pronounce the German [eː] with the high arch of your tongue closer to the roof of your mouth than for an American [e], and without a trace of the diphthongal [ɪ] used in our language. When pronounced correctly, "*O, Weh!*" [o 'veː] sounds almost like [o 'viː] to our American ears.

Pronounce the German [ɛ] with your tongue slightly more foward and your jaw more open than an English [ɛ].

Pronounce the German *schwa* with the lips slightly rounded toward [œ]. The sound quality varies slightly in openness according to its position in the word, but you will feel your tongue consistently more forward and higher than for either the English [ʌ] or [ə]. Be careful not to open *schwa* all the way to [ɛ] or over-round it to the French *schwa*.

LL 4.3.13   Compare [eː] and [ɛ].

[eː]		[ɛ]	
den	[deːm]	denn	[dɛn]
beten	['beː tən]	betten	['bɛ tən]
stehlen	['ʃteː lən]	stellen	['ʃtɛ lən]

When *e* and *ee* are followed by a single consonant in a primary stressed syllable, usually pronounce *e* and *ee* as [eː].

LL 4.3.14   Read aloud.

ewig	['eː vɪç]
Regen	['reː gən]
der	[deːr]
Seele	['zeː lə]
Elend	['eː lənt]
er	[eːr]

Exception: In some monosyllables when *e* occurs before a single consonant, pronounce it as open/short [ɛ].

LL 4.3.15   Read aloud.

es	[ɛs]
des	[dɛs]
wes	[vɛs]

Note: In some prefixes when *e* is followed by a single consonant, pronounced it as [ɛ].

LL 4.3.16   Prefixes.

| er- | [ɛr] | as in *erachten* | [ɛr \| 'ax tən] |
| her- | [hɛr] | as in *herauf* | [hɛ 'raof] |

Note: Always pronounce the noun *Weg,* written with capital W, as [veːk]. But pronounce the adverb, prefix, and suffix *weg* as [vɛk].

When *e* is followed by double or multiple consonants, usually pronounce it as open/short [ɛ].

Note: To apply this rule, the double or multiple consonants do not need to be in the same syllable, but they must be in the same element.

LL 4.3.17   Read aloud.

Welt	[vɛlt]
emsig	['ɛm zɪç]
Herz	[hɛrts]
wenn	[vɛnn]

Exception: Because the pronunciations vary, you cannot apply this rule before *st*. (See "General Rules for Pronouncing German Vowels" on page 175.)

German

Exception: In some verbs, nouns, and adjectives, you need to retain the close/long character of the root word's vowel as it changes form. For example, pronounce the *e* before two consonants in *lebst* as close/long because the original vowel is before a single consonant in the root verb *leben* (to live). (See page 178.)

| ich lebe | (*I live*) |
| du lebst | (*you live*) |

When single *e* occurs in an unstressed syllable, generally pronounce it as *schwa* [ə]. Germans unstress syllables in four circumstances.

1. When the single letter *e* occurs as the final letter or in a suffix of a word, usually pronounce *e* as [ə].

   LL 4.3.18   Read aloud.

Final letter:	
Wege	['veː gə]
habe	['haː bə]
Freude	['frɔø də]
Seele	['zeː lə]
Schule	['ʃuː lə]
komme	['kɔ mə]

   LL 4.3.19   Read aloud.

Suffix:	
kleinen	['klae nən]
langem	['la ŋəm]
alles	['a ləs]
bitter	['bɪ tər]
schaffend	['ʃa fənt]
schwendelt	['ʃvɛn dəlt]

2. When single *e* is in the unstressed prefixes *be-* or *ge-* before a root word, pronounce *e* as [ə].

   LL 4.3.20   Read aloud.

begangen	[bə 'gaŋ ən]
geliebtes	[gə 'liːp təs]
betrogen	[bə troː gən]
gesucht	[gə 'zuːxt]
beglücken	[bə 'glʏ kən]
benehmen	[bə 'neː mən]

German

gegeben	[gə ˈgeː bən]
Gebot	[gə ˈboːt]

Note: In words such as *geben* [ˈgeː bən] and *gehen* [ˈgeː ən], *ge-* is part of the root word and not a prefix. You can identify root words when the final unstressed syllable cannot stand alone. In the two syllable words above, *ge-* is a part of the root word because *-ben* and *-bot* cannot stand alone: therefore, *ge* receives primary stress.

3. When the single letter *e* occurs in the final syllable of a word element or as a common connective syllable which often occurs in a compound word, pronounce *e* as [ə].

   LL 4.3.21   Read aloud.

e as in Hundehaus	[ˈhʊn də ˌhaos]
e as in Scheidegruss	[ˈʃae də ˌgruːs]
en as in Lindenbaum	[ˈlɪn dən ˌbaom]
er as in Rädergebraus	[ˈrɛː dər gə ˌbraos]
es as in Liebesgaben	[ˈliː bəs ˌgaː bən]

4. When the single letter *e* is in a consecutive syllable and when an adjective ending is added to a verb form, pronounce *e* as [ə].

   LL 4.3.22   Read aloud.

helfen	[ˈhɛl fən]	*becomes*	helfenden	[ˈhɛl fən dən]
brennen	[ˈbrɛ nən]	*becomes*	brennenden	[ˈbrɛ nən dən]
schaffen	[ˈʃa fən]	*becomes*	schaffenden	[ˈʃa fən dən]
spiegeln	[ˈʃpiː gəln]	*becomes*	spiegelnden	[ˈʃpiː gəln dən]

Nouns and words used as nouns are always capitalized in German.

eh

Pronounce *eh* in the same syllable as [eː].

When a vowel is followed by *h* in the same syllable, the *h* is silent, signalling you to pronounce the vowel as close and long.

LL 4.3.23   Read aloud.

mehr	[meːr]
stehlen	[ˈʃteː lən]

German

ei, ey

Pronounce *ei* and *ey* as the diphthong [ae].

The pronunciation of the diphthong [ae] is similar to the [aɪ] pronounced in the English word *height* [haɪt], but darker in quality because of the [e] as the second sound.

LL 4.3.24 Read aloud.

dein	[daen]
Leib	[laep]
bleiben	['blae bən]
Veilchen	['fael çən]
Heine	['hae nə]
Meyer	['mae ər]

eu

Pronounce *eu* as the diphthong [ɔø].

The sound of [ɔø] is similar to the diphthong found in the English word *boy*, but darker in quality because of the more rounded [ø] for the second sound. When you pronounce the German [ɔø], protrude and round your lips energetically and feel the arch of the tongue move forward as you glide from [ɔ] to [ø].

LL 4.3.25 Read aloud.

neu	[nɔø]
heute	['hɔø tə]
Reue	['rɔø ə]
Freude	['frɔø də]
treulich	['trɔø lıç]
Atreus	['a trɔøs]

The letter

Pronounce the letter *i* as [iː] or [ɪ], not ever as the diphthong [aɪ], as in the English word *might*.

When followed by a single consonant in a primary stressed syllable, usually pronounce *i* as [iː].

LL 4.3.26 Read aloud.

| Mine | ['miː nə] |
| Sirup | ['ziː rʊp] |

Exception: In the combination -*ik,* when the syllable is stressed, pronounce *i* as [iː], and when the syllable is unstressed, pronounce *i* as [ɪ].

LL 4.3.27   Read aloud.

Mus*ik*	[mu ˈziːk]
Fab*rik*	[fab ˈriːk]
T*ragik*	[ˈtraː gɪk]
L*yrik*	[ˈlyː rɪk]

Exception: In the following words and suffixes, when *i* occurs before a single consonant, pronounce it as [ɪ].

LL 4.3.28   Read aloud.

in, im	[ɪn] [ɪm]	bin	[bɪn]
bis	[bɪs]	mit	[mɪt]
hin	[hɪn]	April	[a ˈprɪl]

LL 4.3.29   Suffixes. Read aloud.

-ig	[ɪç]	as in *fertig*	[ˈfɛr tɪç]
-nis	[nɪs]	as in *Bildnis*	[ˈbɪlt nɪs]
-in	[ɪn]	as in *Studentin*	[ʃtu ˈdɛn tɪn]

Exception: Pronounce *i* as the glide [j] in a small group of words borrowed from foreign languages that end in -*ie,* -*ien,* and -*ient*. (See sample words under the heading "ie" below.)

When *i* occurs before double or multiple consonants, usually pronounce it as [ɪ].

Note: The double or multiple consonants do not need to be in the same syllable with the vowel to affect the open character of the vowel, but do need to be in the same element.

LL 4.3.30   Read aloud.

bitte	[ˈbɪ tə]
Winter	[ˈvɪn tər]
spricht	[ʃprɪçt]
frisch	[frɪʃ]

Exception: When it occurs before *st,* the vowel *i* has variable pronunciations. (See "General Rules for Pronouncing German Vowels" on page 175, or consult a dictionary.)

Exception: The close/long character of the vowel in the original form of certain verbs, nouns, and adjectives is retained in the changed forms. For example, in the following example, even

German

though the vowel changes and occurs before two consonants, the close/long character of [e:] in the verb *geben* is kept in the close/long character of [i:] in *gibt*. (See page 178.)

| geben | ['ge: bən] | *to give* | becomes | gibt | [gi:pt] | *he gives* |

ie

Pronounce *ie* as [i:].

In German the letters *ie* form a unit and are pronounced [i:]

LL 4.3.31   Read aloud.

Liebe	['li: bə]
hier	[hi:r]
wie	[vi:]
Lied	[li:t]
Melodie	[me lo 'di:]
Phantasie	[fan ta 'zi:]

Exception: The letters *ie* do not form a unit in a small group of words borrowed from foreign languages that end in *-ie*, *-ien*, and *-ient*. Pronounce *i* as the glide [j].

LL 4.3.32   Read aloud.

Lilie	['lɪ: ljə]
Familie	[fa 'mi ljə]
Italien	[i 'ta: ljən]
Patient	[pa 'tsjɛnt]
Portier	[pɔr 'tje:]

ih

Pronounce *ih* in the same syllable as [i:].

When a vowel is followed by *h* in the same syllable, the *h* is silent and the vowel is pronounced close and long.

LL 4.3.33   Read aloud.

ihr	[i:r]
ihm	[i:m]

German

The letter O

The German letter *o* has two pronunciations: close and long [oː] and open and short [ɔ]. The vowel *o* [oː] is a long, pure sound, more rounded than in English and with no trace of the English diphthong [oʊ].

LL 4.3.34   Compare and contrast.

German pure [oː]		English diphthong [oʊ]	
Rose	['roː zə]	rose	[roʊz]
Hof	[hoːf]	hope	[hoʊp]

The German open/short [ɔ] is pronounced with lips slightly more protruded and rounded than for its English equivalent in the word *caught* [kɔt].

LL 4.3.35   Compare and contrast.

The German pure [oː]		The German [ɔ]	
wohne	['voː nə]	Wonne	['vɔ nə]
Ofen	['oː fən]	offen	['ɔ fən]

When followed by a single consonant in a primary stressed syllable, usually pronounce *o* as [oː].

LL 4.3.36   Read Aloud.

loben	['loː bən]
Boden	['boː dən]
Ode	['oː də]
Omen	['oː mən]
nobel	['noː bəl]
Mode	['moː də]

Exceptions: When followed by a single consonant, several words are pronounced with open/short [ɔ].

LL 4.3.37   Read aloud.

op	[ɔp]
von	[fɔn]
vom	[fɔm]
Marmor	['mar mɔr]
Bischof	['bɪ ʃɔf]
Doktor	['dɔk tɔr]

German

When followed by a single cononant in a monosyllable, usually pronounce *o* as close and long, but not always. Consult a dictionary.

LL 4.3.38   Read aloud.

schon	[ʃoːn]
rot	[roːt]
Brot	[broːt]
Strom	[ʃtroːm]
Ton	[toːn]
vor	[foːr]
Flor	[floːɹ]
Not	[noːt]

When *o* is the final letter in a monosyllable, pronounce it as [oː].

LL 4.3.39   Read aloud.

wo	[voː]

When followed by a double or multiple consonants, usually pronounce *o* as [ɔ].

Note: The doubled or multiple consonants do not need to be in the same syllable with the vowel to affect the open character of the vowel, but do need to be in the same element.

LL 4.3.40   Read aloud.

Sommer	[ˈzɔ mər]
voll	[fɔl]
Dorf	[dɔrf]
sonst	[zɔnst]
kommt	[kɔmt]
Gott	[gɔt]

Exception: The close/long character of *o* in the original form of certain verbs, nouns, and adjectives is retained in the changed forms. For example, the vowel from the verb *stoßen* retains its close/long character in the following chart, even when *o* changes to *ö* and occurs before two consonants. (See page 178.)

LL 4.3.41   Read aloud.

stoßen	[ˈʃtoː sən]	*to bump*	becomes	er stößt	[eːr ˈʃtøːst]	*he bumps*

German

Exception: In one important word, the letter *o* is pronounced as close/long [oː] when followed by two consonants:

LL 4.3.42 Read aloud.

| Mond | [moːnt] |

Exception: The vowel *o* has variable pronunciations in these spellings: when before *ch*, *ß* (Eszett), *ss*, and *st*; when before the combination of *r* plus *d, t, l,* and *n*. (See "General Rules for Pronouncing German Vowels" on page 175, or consult a dictionary.)

ö, oe

The German letters *ö* and *oe* have two pronunciations: close and long [ø] and open and short [œ]. (The letter *ö* is sometimes written as *oe*; this spelling does not alter the pronunciation of *ö*.) For example:

LL 4.3.43 Read aloud.

schön	=	schoen	[ʃøːn]	In both words, the vowel is close/long
können	=	koennen	[ˈkœ nən]	In both words, the vowel is open/short

Close/long ö [ø] is a mixed vowel produced by simultaneously forming the lip vowel [o] and the tongue vowel [e]. In pronouncing the umlauted sounds, be sure to avoid any trace of a diphthong. Maintain your rounded lip position until the beginning of the next sound.

Open/short ö [œ] is a mixed vowel produced by simultaneously forming the lip vowel [ɔ] and the tongue vowel [ɛ]. In pronouncing the umlauted sounds, be sure to avoid any trace of a diphthong. Maintain your rounded lip position until the beginning of the next sound.

When followed by a single consonant in a primary stressed syllable, usually pronounce *ö* as [ø].

LL 4.3.44 Read aloud.

König	[ˈkøː nɪç]
öde	[ˈøː də]
lösen	[ˈløː sən]
knöten	[ˈknøː tən]
Köder	[ˈkøː dər]
Flöte	[ˈfløː tə]

German

Exception: When *ö* occurs before a single consonant in monosyllables, as in *schön*, pronounce it as close/long [ø], but not always. Consult a dictionary.

When followed by double or multiple consonants, usually pronounce *ö* and *oe* as [œ].

Note: Double or multiple consonants do not need to be in the same syllable with the vowel to affect the open character of the vowel, but do need to be in the same element.

LL 4.3.45   Read aloud.

Götter	['gœ tər]
können	['kœ nən]
Hölle	['hœ lə]
plötzlich	['plœts lıç]

Exception: The close/long character of the vowel in the original form of verbs, nouns, and adjectives is retained in the changed form. For example, the *ö* keeps its close/long character before two consonants in the following chart. (See page 178, or consult a dictionary.)

LL 4.3.46   Read aloud.

hören	['hø: rən]	*to hear*	becomes	hörst	['hø:rst]	*(you) hear*

Exception: The vowel *ö* has variable pronunciations in these spellings: when before *ch*, *ß* (Eszett), *ss*, and *st*; when before the combination of *r* plus *d, t, l,* and *n*. (See "General Rules for Pronouncing German Vowels" on page 175, or consult a dictionary.)

öh

Pronounce *öh* in the same syllable as [ø].

When a vowel is followed by *h* in the same syllable, the *h* is silent and the vowel is pronounced close and long.

LL 4.3.47   Read aloud.

löhnen	['lø: nən]
Söhne	['zø: nə]

German

The letter u

The German vowel *u* is always the pure sound [u] or [ʊ]. It never has the glide [j] of the English diphthong [ju] as in the word *music* ['mju zɪk].

When *u* occurs before a single consonant in a primary stressed syllable, usually pronounce it as [uː].

LL 4.3.48 Read aloud.

Mut	[muːt]
du	[duː]
Muse	['muː zə]
nur	[nuːr]
zu	[tsuː]
nun	[nuːn]

Exceptions: When *u* occurs in monosyllables, prefixes, or before a single consonant or digraph, the letter *u* has variable prounciations. (See "General Rules for Pronouncing German Vowels" on page 175, or consult a dictionary.)

In the following monosyllables and prefixes, pronounce the letter *u* as [ʊ].

LL 4.3.49 Read aloud.

Monosyllable		Prefix			
um	[ʊm]	un-	[ʊn]	as in *unendlich*	[ʊn | 'ɛnt lɪç]
zum	[tsʊm]	um-	[ʊm]	as in *umarmen*	[ʊm | 'ar mən]

When final in a monosyllable, pronounce *u* as [uː].

LL 4.3.50 Read aloud.

zu	[tsuː]
du	[duː]

When followed by double or multiple consonants, usually pronounce *u* as [ʊ].

Pronounce [ʊ] like the *oo* sound in the English word *look*, but with the lips more rounded and slightly protruded.

LL 4.3.51 Read aloud.

German

Mutter	[ˈmʊ tər]
drucken	[ˈdrʊ kən]
Sturm	[ʃtʊrm]
Busch	[bʊʃ]

Exception: The close/long character of the vowel in the original form of certain verbs, nouns, and adjectives is retained even when it occurs before two consonants in the changed form. (See page 178.)

Exception: The vowel *u* has variable pronunciations in these spellings: when before *ch*, *ß* (Eszett), *ss* and *st*; when before the combination of *r* plus *d, t, l,* and *n*. (See "General Rules for Pronouncing German Vowels" on page 175, or consult a dictionary.)

uh

Pronounce *uh* in the same syllable as [uː].

When a vowel is followed by *h* in the same syllable, the *h* is silent and the vowel is pronounced close and long.

LL 4.3.52   Read aloud.

fuhren	[ˈfuː rən]
Ruhe	[ˈruː ə]
Buhle	[ˈbuː lə]

ü

The German letter *ü* has two pronunciations: close and long [yː] and open and short [ʏ].

Close/long *ü* is a mixed vowel produced by simultaneously forming the lip vowel [u] and the tongue vowel [i]. You will feel a downward pull on your upper lip, creating a beak-like sensation. The proper shape may also be found by whistling a pitch at medium range and then, without changing your mouth formation, shifting from a whistle to a vocal sound. In pronouncing the umlauted sounds, be sure to avoid any trace of a diphthong. Maintain your rounded lip position until the beginning of the next sound.

Open/short *ü* [ʏ] is a mixed vowel produced by simultaneously forming the lips for [ʊ] and the tongue for [ɪ]. Although the shape is more relaxed than [yː], your lips must maintain enough rounding to prevent

German

stücken [ˈʃtʏ kən] from becoming confused with *sticken* [ˈʃtɪ kən]. In pronouncing the umlauted sounds, be sure to avoid any trace of a diphthong. Maintain your rounded lip position until the beginning of the next sound.

ü, ue

When followed by a single consonant in a primary stressed syllable, usually pronounce *ü* and *ue* as [yː].

LL 4.3.53   Read aloud.

üben	[ˈyː bən]
Flügel	[ˈflyː gəl]
grün	[gryːn]
süd	[zyːt]
für	[fyːr]
müde	[ˈmyː də]

Note: The letter *ü* is sometimes written as *ue*. This spelling does not alter the pronunciation of *ü*.

üben	=	ueben	=	[ˈyː bən]
Müllerin	=	Muellerin	=	[ˈmʏ lə rɪn]

When followed by double or multiple consonants, pronounce *ü* as [ʏ].

Note: Double or multiple consonants do not need to be in the same syllable with the vowel to affect the open character of the vowel, but do need to be in the same element.

LL 4.3.54   Read aloud.

Hütte	[ˈhʏ tə]
Glück	[glʏk]
Müllerin	[ˈmʏ lə rɪn]
pflücken	[ˈpflʏ kən]

Exception: The close/long character of the vowel in the original form of verbs, nouns, and adjectives is retained even when before two consonants in the changed form. For example, in the following words, the *u* in *Buch* retains a close/long character with *ü* in *Bücher*. (See page 178.)

LL 4.3.55   Read aloud.

Buch	[buːx]	book	Bücher	[ˈbyː çər]	books

Exception: The vowel *ü* has variable pronunciations in these spellings: when before *ch*, *ß* (Eszett), *ss*, and *st*; when before

German

üh

Pronounce *üh* in the same syllable as [yː].

When a vowel is followed by *h* in the same syllable, the *h* is silent and the vowel is pronounced close and long.

LL 4.3.56 Read aloud.

glühen	[ˈglyː ən]
rühmlich	[ˈryːm lɪç]
kühn	[kyːn]

The letter y

The letter *y* appears only in words of foreign origin and has four pronunciations: [yː], [ʏ], [i], and [j]. In the majority of cases, the German derivation is from Greek and *y* will follow the rules for the letter *ü*. Words of other derivations are given the sound found in the original language, usually *i*. When in question, refer to a dictionary.

In these words, pronounce the letter *y* as close/long [yː].

LL 4.3.57 Read aloud.

Lyrik	[ˈlyː rɪk]
typisch	[ˈtyː pɪʃ]
Mythe	[ˈmyː tə]

In these words, pronounce the letter *y* as open/short [ʏ].

LL 4.3.58 Read aloud.

Nymphe	[ˈnʏm fə]
Myrte	[ˈmʏr tə]
Zephyr	[ˈtseː fʏr]

In these words, pronounce the letter *y* as [i].

LL 4.3.59 Read aloud.

| Tyrol | [ti ˈroːl] |
| Zylinder | [tsi ˈlɪn dər] |

In these words, pronounce the letter *y* as [j].

LL 4.3.60 Read aloud.

| York | [jɔrk] |
| Yeoman | [ˈjo mən] |

German Consonants in Detail

The letter *b* has two pronunciations, voiced [b] and unvoiced [p].

When *b* is initial in a word or syllable, pronounce it as [b].

LL 4.4.01   Read aloud.

Bett	[bɛt]
Bibel	['biː bəl]
über	['yː bər]
lieben	['liː bən]
Ebbe	['ɛ bə]
Bube	['buː bə]

When *b* occurs before *s* or *t* or at the end of a word or word element, pronounce it as [p].

LL 4.4.02   Read aloud.

Knab'	[knaːp]
abnehmen	['ap neː mən]
Grabstein	['graːp ʃtaen]
gibt	[giːpt]
Herbst	[hɛrpst]
erbebt	[ɛr 'beːpt]

In German, the single letter *c* occurs only in words of foreign origin, where it usually retains the pronunciation used in the original language. The following rules generally apply.

When *c* occurs before *a, o, u,* or any *consonant* except *h,* pronounce it as [k].

LL 4.4.03   Read aloud.

Café	[ka 'feː]
Creme	[kreː m]

In words of Latin origin, German pronunciations follow the rules of classical Latin and pronounce *c* before *e, i, y, ae,* or *oe* as [ts].

Note: The rule for Latin diction in *Diction for Singers* follows the pronunciation of liturgical Latin, which uses [tʃ] as in the English word *chin*.

German

LL 4.4.04 Read aloud.

Cis (C-sharp)	[tsɪs]
Cäcilie	[tsɛ ˈtsi ljə]
Citrone	[tsi ˈtroː nə]
cito	[ˈtsiː to]
Cicero	[ˈtsiː tse ro]
Cäsar (Caesar)	[ˈtsɛː zar]

In many words of Italian origin, pronounce *c* before *e* or *i* as *ch* [tʃ].

LL 4.4.05 Read aloud.

Cembalo	[ˈtʃɛm ba lo]
Cello	[ˈtʃɛ lo]
Celesta	[tʃe ˈlɛ sta]

In a few words of French origin, pronounce *c* as [s].

LL 4.4.06 Read aloud.

Farce	[ˈfar sə]
Force	[ˈfɔr sə]
Cinemascope	[si ne ma ˈskoːp]

ck

Pronounce *ck* as [k].

The German [k] is pronounced with a sharper, more energized articulation than *ck* in English.

LL 4.4.07 Read aloud.

Ecke	[ˈɛ kə]
beglücken	[bə ˈglʏ kən]
Stück	[ʃtʏk]

ch

The two fricative sounds of *ch*, ichlaut [ç] and achlaut [x], are a special characteristic of the German language.

When *ch* follows a forward vowel, an umlauted vowel, a diphthong (except for *au*), or a consonant, pronounce it as ich-laut [ç].

Note:

Forward vowels:	*i, e*
Umlauted vowels	*ä, ö, ü*
Diphthongs	*äu, eu, ai, ei* (but not *au*)
Consonants	All consonants

Produce the ichlaut [ç] by forming your mouth for [j] as in *yes* and directing an energetic flow of air over the arch of your tongue.

Note: Ichlaut [ç], is an aspirated sound. Do not substitute the fricative [ʃ] or plosive [k]. Give special practice to the diminutive suffix *-chen* [çən], which must not slip to [ʃən] or [kən]. For a full discussion of the production of [ç], see page 184.

LL 4.4.08 Read aloud.

ichi	[içi]
eche	[eçe]
ächä	[ɛçɛ]
öchö	[øçø]
üchü	[yçy]

LL 4.4.09 Read aloud.

mich	[mɪç]
Milch	[mɪlç]
Bächlein	[ˈbɛç laen]
möchten	[ˈmø: çtən]
Bücher	[ˈby: çər]
leuchten	[ˈlɔyç tən]
Cherub	[ˈçe: rʊp]
Chemie	[çe ˈmi:]
Chirurg	[çi ˈrʊrk]
Mädchen	[ˈmɛːt çən]
Liedchen	[ˈliːt çən]
Kätzchen	[ˈkɛts çən]

Pronounce *ch* as achlaut [x] when *ch* follows a back vowel (the letters *a*, *o*, or *u*), or the diphthong *au*.

Produce the achlaut [x] by forming the mouth for [a] as in *ah* and directing an energetic flow of air over the arched back of your tongue. (For a full discussion of the production of [x], see page 184.)

German

Practice by reading aloud the achlaut sound.

LL 4.4.10   Read aloud.

acha	[axa]
ocho	[oxo]
uchu	[uxu]

LL 4.4.11   Read aloud.

hoch	[hoːx]
Buch	[buːx]
lachen	[ˈla xən]
auch	[aox]
Bruch	[brʊx]
Sprache	[ˈʃpraː xə]
Nacht	[naxt]
Loch	[lɔx]
jauchzet	[ˈjaox tsət]
taucht	[taoxt]

Note: Achlaut [x] is an aspirated sound. Do not substitute the plosive [k].

In words of Greek origin, usually pronounce *ch* as [k].

LL 4.4.12   Read aloud.

Chor	[koːr]
Christ	[krɪst]
Charakter	[ka ˈrak tər]

In words of French origin, pronounce *ch* as [ʃ].

LL 4.4.13   Read aloud.

Chef	[ʃɛf]
Chaise	[ˈʃɛː zə]
Chose	[ˈʃoː zə]
Chanson	[ʃã sõː]

German

chs

Pronounce *chs* as [ks] when it is an integral unit of a word stem.

LL 4.4.14   Read aloud.

sechs	[zɛks]
Ochse	[ˈɔ ksə]
Fuchs	[fʊks]
wachsen	[ˈva ksən]

When *ch* is followed by an *s* that begins a suffix, a verb ending, or a word that makes the whole a compound word, pronounce the combination of *chs* as [çs] or [xs].

LL 4.4.15   Read aloud.

s as part of a *suffix*		
höchstens höch I stens	[ˈhøːç stəns]	hoch + stens (adjective + suffix)
s as part of a *verb ending*		
lachst *lach I st	[laxst]	lach + st (verb + ending)
s as part of a *compound word*		
Sprechstimme Sprech I stimme	[ˈʃprɛç ʃtɪ mə]	Sprech + Stimme (compound word)

*(For details on *st*, see page 225.)

d

The letter *d* has two pronunciations, voiced [d] and unvoiced [t]. Pronounce the German [d] and [t] as dental consonants, with the tip of your tongue touching the gum line of your upper front teeth rather than against your teeth ridge as in English. In addition, these consonants are pronounced more crisply and with less escape of air than in English.

When *d* is initial in a word or syllable, pronounce it as [d].

LL 4.4.16   Read aloud.

Dank	[daŋk]
du	[duː]
dadurch	[da ˈdʊrç]
drei	[drae]

German

Räder	[ˈrɛː dər]
anders	[ˈan dərs]

When *d* occurs at the end of a word or syllable, or before *t* or *st*, pronounce it as [t].

LL 4.4.17   Read aloud.

Bild	[bɪlt]
Tod	[toːt]
Hand	[hant]
Stadt	[ʃtat]
Kindheit	[ˈkɪnt haet]
freundlich	[ˈfrɔynt lɪç]
sandte	[ˈzan tə]

f

Pronounce *f* as [f].

LL 4.4.18   Read aloud.

fein	[faen]
Ofen	[ˈoː fən]
offen	[ˈɔ fən]
Erfolg	[ɛr ˈfɔlk]
fünf	[fʏnf]
scharf	[ʃarf]

g

The letter *g* can be pronounced as voiced [g] or unvoiced [k]. The sound of [k] is pronounced more crisply and with less escape of air than in English.

When *g* is initial in a word or syllable, pronounce it as [g].

LL 4.4.19   Read aloud.

geben	[ˈgeː bən]
Geist	[gaest]
Gegend	[ˈgeː gənt]
obgleich	[ɔp ˈglaeç]
gnädige	[ˈgnɛː dɪ gə]
vergnügen	[fɛr ˈgnyː gən]

German

When *g* is final in a word or word element after any letter except *i* or *n*, pronounce it as [k].

LL 4.4.20 Read aloud.

Tag	[taːk]
genug	[gə ˈnuːk]
Lag' (lage)	[laːk]
täglich	[ˈtɛːk lɪç]
Siegfried	[ˈziːk friːt]

When the combinations *gd*, *gst*, or *gt* are final in a word or word element, pronounce *g* as [k].

LL 4.4.21 Read aloud.

Magd	[maːkt]
trägst	[trɛː kst]
birgt	[bɪrkt]

ng

When *g* follows *n* in the same syllable, pronounce the *-ng* as [ŋ].

Note: The combination [ŋg] as in the English word *hunger* [ˈhʌŋ gər] does not exist in German. (See page 220 for more information on *-ng*.)

LL 4.4.22 Read aloud.

Hoffnung	[ˈhɔf nʊŋ]
singen	[ˈzɪ ŋən]

ig

When the combination *ig* is final in a word or word element, pronounce it as [ɪç].

LL 4.4.23 Read aloud.

ewig	[ˈeː vɪç]
König	[ˈkøː nɪç]
eckig	[ˈɛk ɪç]
wichtig	[ˈvɪç tɪç]
Ewigkeit	[ˈeː vɪç kaet]
freudigste	[ˈfrɔy dɪç stə]

German

Exception: When the suffixes *-lich* or *-reich* are added to a word ending in *-ig,* pronounce *-ig* as [ɪk].

LL 4.4.24 Read aloud.

ewiglich	['eː vɪk lɪç]
wonniglich	['vɔ nɪk lɪç]
königlich	['køː nɪk lɪç]
Königreich	['køː nɪk raeç]

In words of French origin, usually pronounce *g* with its French sound [ʒ].

LL 4.4.25 Read aloud.

Genie	[ʒe 'niː]
Loge	['loː ʒə]
Gigue	['ʒiː gə]
Regisseur	[re ʒi 'søːr]

h

When *h* is initial in a word or word element, pronounce it with the aspirate [h] found in the English word *house*.

LL 4.4.26 Read aloud.

Hut	[huːt]
Himmel	['hɪ məl]
Hauch	[haox]
herzhaft	['hɛrts haft]
erhaben	[ɛr 'haː bən]
hierher	[hiːr 'heːr]
Haushalt	['haos ˌhalt]

When not initial in a syllable, *h* is silent.

When *h* follows a vowel and is not initial in a word or syllable, it is silent and serves as a sign that the preceding vowel is pronounced close and long.

LL 4.4.27 Read aloud.

ruhig	['ruː ɪç]
sehen	['zeː ən]
Ehe	['eː ə]
mühselig	['myː zeː lɪç]
frühe	['fryː ə]

j

Pronounce *j* as [j], as in the English word *yes*. Pronounce [j] energetically and move quickly to the following vowel.

LL 4.4.28   Read aloud.

ja	[jaː]
Jahr	[jaːr]
jeder	[ˈjeː dər]
Jüngling	[ˈjʏŋ lɪŋ]
jauchzen	[ˈjaox tsən]

In a few words of French origin, pronounce *j* with the soft sound of [ʒ].

LL 4.4.29   Read aloud.

Journal	[ʒʊr ˈnɑl]
Jury	[ʒy ˈriː]

k

Pronounce *k* as [k].

Pronounce [k] as a crisp, energized plosive with less escape of air than in English.

LL 4.4.30   Read aloud.

Kind	[kɪnt]
Kette	[ˈkɛ tə]
keine	[ˈkae nə]
Knospen	[ˈknɔs pən]
krumm	[krʊm]
Rock	[rɔk]
Kerker	[ˈkɛr kər]

l

Pronounce *l* as [l].

In German, *l* is a linguo-dental consonant. The tongue is placed more foward than in English, the tip just touching the gum line of your upper teeth rather than the teeth ridge as in the English word *wall*.

LL 4.4.31   Read aloud.

hell	[hɛl]
Felder	[ˈfɛl dər]

German

leben	['leː bən]
Moll	[mɔl]
allen	['a lən]
lieblich	['liːp lɪç]
lispeln	['lɪs pəln]
Huld	[hʊlt]

m

Pronounce *m* as [m].

LL 4.4.32 Read aloud.

Mann	[man]
Kummer	['kʊ mər]
manchmal	['manç mal]
Samt	[zamt]
Schmerz	[ʃmɛrts]
Kampf	[kampf]

n

Pronounce *n* as [n].

In German, *n* [n] is a linguo-dental consonant. The tongue is placed more forward than in English, the tip just touching your gum line rather than your teeth ridge as in the English word *north*.

LL 4.4.33 Read aloud.

nun	[nuːn]
Tannenbaum	['ta nən ˌbaom]
Sinn	[zɪn]
Wonnen	['vɔ nən]
unklar	['ʊn klaːr]
angenehm	['an gə neːm]
neben	['neː bən]

ng

When the letter combination *ng* is part of the same word element, pronounce it as [ŋ].

Note: In German, *ng* is pronounced [ŋk] only in dialect, and the combination [ŋg], as in the English word *hunger,* does not exist.

German

LL 4.4.34 Read aloud.

Hoffnung	[ˈhɔf nʊŋ]
singen	[ˈzɪ ŋən]
Finger	[ˈfɪ ŋər]
Wange	[ˈva ŋə]
England	[ˈɛŋ lant]
Angst	[aŋst]

When the combination of *ng* does not occur in the same word element, as when it is at the juncture of a compound word or at the combination of a prefix and a word, the letters retain their individual sounds [n] and [g].

LL 4.4.35 Read aloud.

angehen	[ˈan geː ən]
hingeben	[ˈhɪn geː bən]
Eingeweide	[ˈaen gə ˌvae də]

nk

When the letters *nk* are part of the same word element, pronounce them as [ŋk]

LL 4.4.36 Read aloud.

Dank	[daŋk]
links	[lɪŋks]
dunkel	[ˈdʊ ŋkəl]
wanken	[ˈva ŋkən]

When the combination of *nk* does not occur in the same word element, but occurs at the juncture of a compound word or at the combination of a prefix and word, the letters retain their original sounds [n] and [k].

LL 4.4.37 Read aloud.

unklar	[ˈʊn klaːr]
Einklang	[ˈaen klaŋ]
anklagen	[ˈan klaː gən]

German

p

Pronounce *p* as [p].

Give the German [p] a more sharply articulated sound, as in initial *p* of the English word *pepper*, but with less escape of air.

LL 4.4.38   Read aloud.

Papier	[pa ˈpiːr]
plötzlich	[ˈplœts lıç]
Knospe	[ˈknɔs pə]

pf

Connect the two consonants of the combination *pf* in a quick and energetic manner without an intervening schwa. It is most easily accomplished when the position for *p* is as close to that of *f* as possible. Practice *cupful*, with an exaggerated *pf*, gradually shortening and finally eliminating the first syllable.

LL 4.4.39   Read aloud.

Pfui!	[pfʊ i]
Pferd	[pfeːrt]
stumpf	[ʃtʊmpf]
Apfel	[ˈap fəl]

ph

In words of Greek origin, pronounce *ph* as [f].

LL 4.4.40   Read aloud.

Philosophie	[fi lo zo ˈfiː]
Physik	[fy ˈziːk]

q

Pronounce *qu* as [kv].

The letter *q* is found only in the combination *qu* with the [v] clearly voiced and without a trace of schwa between the two consonants.

LL 4.4.41   Read aloud.

Quelle	[ˈkvɛ lə]
quälen	[ˈkvɛː lən]

German

erquicken	[ɛr ˈkvɪ kən]
bequem	[bə ˈkveːm]

r

Pronounce *r* as flipped *r*.

In singing, use the flipped *r*. At the end of an unaccented syllable, give only one tap. Otherwise, give 2 to 3 flaps. The number of flaps and their intensity will vary with the emotional value of the word. Avoid the American *retroflex r* at all times when singing German!

LL 4.4.42   Read aloud.

Räder	[ˈrɛː dər]
Rhein	[raen]
Tür	[tyːr]
Garten	[ˈgar tən]
irrt	[ɪrt]
Werke	[ˈvɛr kə]
erreichen	[ɛrː ˈrae çən]

s

When *s* is initial in a word or syllable, pronounce it as [z].

LL 4.4.43   Read aloud.

sanft	[zanft]
Silber	[ˈzɪl bər]
sorgsam	[ˈzɔrk zaːm]

When *s* occurs between two vowels, pronounce it as [z].

LL 4.4.44   Read aloud.

Rose	[ˈroː zə]
lesen	[ˈleː zən]
Musik	[mu ˈziːk]
säuselt	[ˈzɔø zəlt]

Exception: When a suffix beginning with a vowel is added to a word ending in *s*, pronounce the *s* as [s].

LL 4.4.45   Read aloud.

Eis + -ig = eisig	[ˈae sɪç]

German

When *s* is final in a word or syllable, pronounce it as [s].

LL 4.4.46   Read aloud.

Haus	[haos]
als	[als]
dies	[diːs]
längs	[lɛŋs]

In each of the following words, *s* is final in a compound word. To determine which words are compound words and how they divide into syllables, you may need to consult a dictionary.

LL 4.4.47   Read aloud.

Liebespaar (Liebes-paar)	[ˈliː bəs ˌpaːr]
Frühlingstraum (Frühlings-traum)	[ˈfryː lɪŋs ˌtraom]
Waldeseinsamkeit (Waldes-ein-sam-keit)	[ˈval dəs ˌaen zaːm kaet]
Windesatmen (Windes-atmen)	[ˈvɪn dəs ˌat mən]

Pronounce the letters *ss* and *ß* as [s].

The letter *ß* is named *Eszett* [ɛs ˈtsɛt] and can be spelled as *ss*.

LL 4.4.48   Read aloud.

wissen	[ˈvɪ sən]
essen	[ˈɛ sən]
Fluß	[flʊs]
Straße	[ˈʃtraː sə]

sch

Pronounce the combination *sch* as [ʃ].

LL 4.4.49   Read aloud.

Initial:	Schall	[ʃal]
	schnell	[ʃnɛl]
Medial:	Asche	[ˈa ʃə]
	Abschluß	[ˈap ʃlʊs]
Final:	Bursch	[bʊrʃ]
	Mensch	[mɛnʃ]

German

sp & st

When the letters *sp* and *st* occur as initial letters in a word or syllable of primary or secondary stress, pronounce them as [ʃp] and [ʃt].

LL 4.4.50 Read aloud.

Initial in word:	
spielen	[ˈʃpiː lən]
spät	[ʃpɛːt]
Stein	[ʃtaen]
Stunde	[ˈʃtʊn də]
still	[ʃtɪl]

Initial in primary and secondary stressed syllables:	
Aus-sprache	[ˈaos ʃpra xə]
Früh-stück	[ˈfryː ʃtʏk]
Feld-stein	[ˈfɛlt ʃtaen]
Grab-stein	[ˈgraːp ʃtaen]
Lippen-stift	[ˈlɪ pən ʃtɪft]

When the letters *st* are final in a word, pronounce them as [st].

LL 4.4.51 Read aloud.

Last	[last]
Trost	[troːst]
zuerst	[tsu ǀ ˈeːrst]
meinst	[maenst]
weist	[vaest]
West	[vɛst]
fest	[fɛst]

When *sp* and *st* occur before an unstressed [ə], pronounce them as [sp] and [st].

Note: The *sp* and *st* do not need to be in the same syllable for this rule to apply, but they do need to occur before schwa [ə].

In adjectives, put the *st* and *sp* with the second syllable.

LL 4.4.52 Read aloud.

schönsten	schön-sten	[ˈʃøːn stən]	*loveliest*
tiefstem	tief-stem	[ˈtiːf stəm]	*deepest*
Liebste	Lieb-ste	[ˈliːp stə]	*dearest*

German

In nouns, adverbs, and verbs, divide the two consonants.

LL 4.4.53   Read aloud.

Nouns:			
Raste	Ras-te	['ras tə]	*rest, repose*
Knospe	Knos-pe	['knɔs pə]	*bud*
Espe	Es-pe	['ɛs pə]	*asp*
Meister	Meis-ter	['maes tər]	*master*
Adverbs:			
gestern	ges-tern	['gɛs tərn]	*yesterday*
meistens	meis-tens	['maes təns]	*most*
Verbs:			
lispeln	lis-peln	['lɪs pəln]	*to lisp*

t

In German, *t* is more dental and plosive than in English and is pronounced more crisply and with less escape of air.

Note: The archaic spelling of *th* for *t* is found in some song texts and in a few words in modern German. For example: *Mut* is sometimes spelled *Muth*; *Teil* is sometimes spelled *Theil*.

LL 4.4.54   Read aloud.

Tod	[toːt]
Mut	[muːt]
Gott	[gɔt]
Thron	[troːn]
Theater	[te 'aː tər]
Rath	[raːt]
Theil	[tael]

Exception: When *th* occurs at the juncture of two word elements, pronounce *t* and *h* as separate sounds.

Rat ǀ haus	['raːt ˌhaos]
mit ǀ hören	['mɪt høːrən]

-tion, -tient

In borrowed words ending in the suffixes *-tion* and *-tient*, pronounce the combination of *ti* as [tsj].

German

LL 4.4.55 Read aloud.

Nation	[na ˈtsjoːn]
Aktion	[ak ˈtsjoːn]
Funktion	[fʊŋk ˈtsjoːn]
Patient	[pa ˈtsjɛnt]

-tsch, -tz

When the combination *-tsch* occurs in the same word element, pronounce it as [tʃ].

LL 4.4.56 Read aloud.

deutsch	[dɔøtʃ]

Pronounce *-tz* as [ts].

LL 4.4.57 Read aloud.

Platz	[plats]
Schatz	[ʃats]
sitzen	[ˈzɪ tsən]

Note: When *t* ends one word element and *z* begin the next, prolong the sound of the *t*.

LL 4.4.58 Read aloud.

entzwei	[ɛntː ˈtsvae]
entzücken	[ɛntː ˈtsʏ kən]

V

Pronounce *v* as [f].

LL 4.4.59 Read aloud.

Vater	[ˈfaː tər]
vergessen	[fɛr ˈgɛ sən]
davon	[da ˈfɔn]
Volkslied	[ˈfɔlks ˌliːt]
Archiv	[ar ˈçiːf]
bravster	[ˈbraːf stər]

When *v* occurs in words of foreign origin, pronounce *v* as [v].

LL 4.4.60 Read aloud.

Vase	[ˈvaː zə]
Vokal	[vo ˈkaːl]
November	[no ˈvɛm bər]

German

Universität	[u ni vɛr zi 'teːt]
nervös	[nɛr 'vøːs]

W

Pronounce *w* as voiced [v].

The movement from unvoiced [f] to voiced [v] needs special practice.

LL 4.4.61 Compare and contrast.

auffinden	['aofː fɪn dən]	aufwinden	['aof vɪn dən]
auffallen	['aofː fa lən]	aufwallen	['aof va lən]

LL 4.4.62 Read aloud.

Wasser	['va sər]
Winter	['vɪn tər]
warum	[va 'rʊm]
Schwalbe	['ʃval bə]
Urwelt	['uːr vɛlt]
Schafwolle	['ʃaːf ˌvɔ lə]
Volkswagen	['fɔlks ˌvaː gən]
verwöhnen	[fɛr 'vøː nən]

X

Pronounce *x* as [ks].

Note: The letter *x* contains two consonant sounds and causes the preceding vowel to be open and short.

LL 4.4.63 Read aloud.

Hexe	['hɛ ksə]
Nixen	['nɪ ksən]
exakt	[ɛ 'ksakt]
Expreß	[ɛks 'prɛs]

Z

Pronounce *z* as a crisp [ts].

LL 4.4.64 Read aloud.

zart	[tsaːrt]
Schmerzen	['ʃmɛr tsən]
zwei	[tsvae]
zwischen	['tsvɪ ʃən]
Mozart	['moː tsart]

French

French Diction

In all languages, there is an academic approach to presenting the content of the language—syllabification, stressing, etc.—which is useful for organizing the information and returning to it later. This academic approach offers a whole picture, like a jigsaw puzzle, of how the language is put together. Yet, in French, perhaps a more useful way to begin is to pull out a few unusual pieces of the puzzle and become familiar with their distinctiveness before placing them into the whole picture.

One unusual "piece" of French diction is that several letters are often pronounced as a single sound, as in the word *beau* [bo], where the three letters *eau* are pronounced simply as [o], or the word *travailler* [tra va 'je] where the three letters *ill* are pronounced as the single sound [j].

Also, many letters in French words are silent, particularly final consonants, final mute *e*, mute *h*, and the *m* and *n* that follow nasal vowels. There are sounds in French that do not exist in English. These include mixed vowels, nasal vowels, the enya [ɲ], and the glide [ɥ]. And there is a stress pattern in French that differs from other languages. You will find all of these unusual "pieces" of French diction discussed in the "Special Features" section.

Your first challenge will be to learn how to group letters together. You will find the chart at the beginning of this chapter helpful because it displays the most common letter groupings. As you read through the text you will find exercises and word lists that repetitively illustrate those letter combinations. Finally, under the headings "French Vowels" and "French Consonants," you will find each spelling described in detail. By getting a handle on the letter groups, you will quickly become skilled with French spelling and pronunciation.

French

Chart of French Sounds

The following chart lists the most frequently used sounds of French in alphabetical order. Refer to this chart to quickly check the sound of a spelling. For special circumstances and exceptions to the sounds that cannot be presented easily in a simple chart, see the discussions of the individual sounds later in this chapter.

French Letter and Position in Word			IPA	Example and IPA		Page
a	a, à	usually	[a]	Paris, là	[pa ˈri] [la]	259
	a	before [s] and [z]	[ɑ]	extase	[ɛk ˈstɑ zə]	260
	a	before final silent *s* usually	[ɑ]	bas	[bɑ]	260
	â	usually	[ɑ]	âme	[ɑ mə]	
	ai, aî	usually	[ɛ]	mais	[mɛ]	260
				comparaître	[kɔ̃ pa ˈrɛ trə]	
	ai	final	[e]	gai	[ge]	261
	aient		[ɛ]	étaient	[e ˈtɛ]	261
	aim, ain*		[ɛ̃]	faim, ainsi	[fɛ̃] [ɛ̃ ˈsi]	245, 262
	am, an*		[ɑ̃]	champ	[ʃɑ̃]	245, 262
				fumant	[fy ˈmɑ̃]	
	au		[o]	chevaux	[ʃə ˈvo]	263
	au	before *r*	[ɔ]	Fauré	[fɔ ˈre]	263
	ay		[ɛj]	payer	[pɛ ˈje]	263
b	b		[b]	bois	[bwa]	286
	bb		[b]	abbesse	[a ˈbɛ sə]	286
	b	before *s* or *t*	[p]	absent	[ap ˈsɑ̃]	286
	b	final usually	[b]	snob	[snɔb]	286
	b	final after nasal consonant	silent	plomb	[plɔ̃]	286
c	c	before *a, o, u,* or a *consonant*	[k]	encore	[ɑ̃ ˈkɔ rə]	287
	cc	before *a, o, u,* or a *consonant*	[k]	succulent	[sy ky ˈlɑ̃]	287
	c	before *e, i,* or *y*	[s]	cède	[ˈsɛ də]	287
	cc	before *e, i,* or *y*	[ks]	accent	[ak ˈsɑ̃]	287
	ç		[s]	garçon	[gar ˈsɔ̃]	287
	c	final usually	[k]	avec	[a ˈvɛk]	287
	c	final after *n* usually	silent	blanc	[blɑ̃]	288
	ch	usually	[ʃ]	chemin	[ʃə ˈmɛ̃]	288
	cqu	usually	[k]	acquitter	[a ki ˈte]	289
	ct		silent	respect	[rɛs ˈpɛ]	289
		or	[kt]	direct	[di ˈrɛkt]	

This letter combination can be nasal or non-nasal. See "Nasal Vowels" on page 245 for details.

French

French Letter and Position in Word		IPA	Example and IPA		Page
d	d		[d]	diable	['dja blə]	290
	dd		[d]	addition	[a di 'sjõ]	289
	d	final	silent	grand	[grã]	289
	d	in liaison	[t]	quand‿un	[kã tœ̃]	289
e	é		[e]	été	[e 'te]	264
	è, ê, ë		[ɛ]	père forêts Noël	['pɛ rə] [fɔ 'rɛ] [nɔ 'ɛl]	264
	e	before a single consonant and a vowel	[ə]	cheval	[ʃə 'val]	265
	e	before two consonants	[ɛ]	elle	['ɛ lə]	265
	e	before final pronounced consonant	[ɛ]	fer	[fɛr]	266
	e	before final silent consonant (except *s* or *t*; see below)	[e]	pied	[pje]	266
	er	final sometimes	[ɛr]	hiver	[i 'vɛr]	267
	er	final in verb endings and some nouns and adjectives	[e]	parler boulanger	[par 'le] [bu lã 'ʒe]	267
	es	final	[ə]	parles	['par lə]	264
	es	final in monosyllables	[e]	des	[de]	268
	et	final	[ɛ]	filet	[fi 'lɛ]	268
	et	(meaning *and*)	[e]	et	[e]	268
	e	final	silent or [ə]	parle	[parl] ['par lə]	268
	e	final in monosyllable	[ə]	je	[ʒə]	268
	eau		[o]	beau	[bo]	269
	ei		[ɛ]	seize	['sɛ zə]	269
	eim, ein*		[ẽ]	plein	[plẽ]	245, 270
	em, en*		[ã]	ensemble	[ã 'sã blə]	245, 270
	en	after *i*	[ẽ]	combien	[kõ 'bjẽ]	245, 270
	ent	final in verb endings	[ə]	parlent	['par lə]	270
	ent	final otherwise	[ã]	firmament	[fir ma 'mã]	270
	eu	in the interior of a word	[œ]	heure	['œ rə]	240, 272
	eu	before [z]	[ø]	creuse	['krø zə]	240, 272
	eu	as final sound	[ø]	peu	[pø]	240, 272
f	f		[f]	foyer	[fwa 'je]	290
	ff		[f]	effort	[e 'fɔr]	290

* *This letter combination can be nasal or non-nasal. See "Nasal Vowels" on page 245 for details.*

French

232

French Letter and Position in Word			IPA	Example	and IPA	Page
f	f	final usually	[f]	soif	[swaf]	290
	f	in liaison	[v]	neuf_heures	[nœ 'vœ rə]	290
g	g	before *a, o, u*, or a *consonant*	[g]	gant	[gɑ̃]	290
	gg	before *a, o, u*, or a *consonant*	[g]	aggraver	[a gra 've]	292
	g	before *e, i*, or *y*	[ʒ]	genou	[ʒə 'nu]	291
	gg	before *e, i*, or *y*	[gʒ]	suggérer	[syg ʒe 're]	292
	g	final	*silent*	poing	[pwɛ̃]	291
	g	in liaison	[k]	sang_impur	[sɑ̃ kɛ̃ 'pyr]	291
	ge	before *u* or *o*	[ʒ]	bourgeois	[bur 'ʒwa]	291
	gn	usually	[ɲ]	compagnon	[kõ pa 'ɲõ]	292
	gt		*silent*	doigt	[dwa]	292
	gu	before a vowel	[g]	fatiguer	[fa ti 'ge]	292
h	h		*silent*	heure	['œ rə]	250, 292
i	î, i	final or before a consonant	[i]	île, finir	['i lə] [fi 'nir]	274
	i	before a "stressed" vowel usually	[j]	hier	[jer]	274
	i	before a mute *e*	[i] or [i ə]	partie	[par 'ti] [par 'ti ə]	274
	ien*		[jɛ̃]	bien	[bjɛ̃]	245, 274
	ient	final, verb ending	[i] or [i ə]	rient	[ri] or ['ri ə]	275
	il, ill	initial	[il]	illusion	[i ly 'zjõ]	275
	il, ill, ille	after a vowel** usually	[j] or [jə]	soleil détaillant abeille	[sɔ 'lej] [de ta 'jɑ̃] [a 'bɛ jə]	243, 275
	ill, ille	after a consonant usually	[ij] or [ijə]	brillant fille	[bri 'jɑ̃] ['fi jə]	276
	im, in*		[ɛ̃]	timbre	['tɛ̃ brə]	277
j	j		[ʒ]	Jean	[ʒɑ̃]	293
k	k		[k]	kilo	[ki 'lo]	293

* *This letter combination can be nasal or non-nasal. See page 245 for full explanation.*
***See page 275 for a full explanation of these letter combinations, including exceptions for final* il, ile, *and the words* mille, tranquille, ville.

French

French Letter and Position in Word			IPA	Example	and IPA	Page
l	l		[l]	larme	['lar mə]	294
	l	final	[l]	appel	[a 'pɛl]	294
	ll		[l]	belle	['bɛ lə]	294
	ll	after *i* (see *ill* above)				
m	m		[m]	marche	['mar ʃə]	295
	m	final or after a nasal vowel	silent	parfum combat	[par 'fœ̃] [kɔ̃ 'ba]	295
	mm		[m]	comme	['kɔ mə]	295
n	n		[n]	nous	[nu]	296
	n	final or after a nasal vowel	silent	non montre	[nɔ̃] ['mɔ̃ trə]	296
	ng	final	silent	poing	[pwɛ̃]	296
	nn		[n]	donne	['dɔ nə]	296
o	o	usually	[ɔ]	fort	[fɔr]	277
	o	before [z]	[o]	chose	['ʃo zə]	278
	o	as final sound	[o]	galop	[ga 'lo]	278
	ô		[o]	vôtre	['vo trə]	278
	oeu		[œ]	coeur	[kœr]	240, 279
	oi		[wa]	vois	[vwa]	243, 279
	oin*		[wɛ̃]	loin	[lwɛ̃]	243, 280
	om, on*		[ɔ̃]	rond	[rɔ̃]	245, 280
	ou, où, oû		[u]	fou	[fu]	280
	ou	before a "stressed" vowel	[w]	oui	[wi]	243, 280
	ou	before mute *e*	[u] or [u ə]	dénouement	[de nu 'mɑ̃] [de nu ə 'mɑ̃]	243, 280
	oy		[waj]	royal	[rwa 'jal]	243, 281
p	p		[p]	pas	[pɑ]	296
	pp		[p]	application	[a pli ka 'sjɔ̃]	297
	p	final	silent	trop	[tro]	296
	ph		[f]	morphine	[mɔr 'fi nə]	297
q	q	final	[k]	coq	[kɔk]	297
	qu		[k]	quand	[kɑ̃]	297
r	r	flipped	[r]	ronde	['rɔ̃ də]	298
	rr	flipped or rolled	[r]	terre	['tɛ rə]	298

This letter combination can be nasal or non-nasal. See "Nasal Vowels" on page 245 for details.

French

234

French Letter and Position in Word			IPA	Example and IPA		Page
r	r	final usually	[r]	amour, professeur	[a 'mur] [prɔ fɛ 'sœr]	298
	r	as final -er in verb endings	silent	parler	[par 'le]	299
	r	as final -er, -ier, -yer in some nouns and adjectives usually or sometimes	silent [ɛr]	boulanger hiver	[bu lɑ̃ 'ʒe] [i 'vɛr]	299
s	s	usually	[s]	sport	[spɔr]	299
	ss		[s]	tasse	['tɑ sə]	299
	s	between vowels	[z]	maison	[mɛ 'zɔ̃]	300
	s	final	silent	repos	[rə 'po]	300
	s	in liaison	[z]	puis_il	[pɥi zil]	300
	sc	before a, o, u, or consonant	[sk]	scandale	[skɑ̃ 'da lə]	300
	sc	before e or i	[s]	sceptre	['sɛp trə]	301
	sch	usually	[ʃ]	schéma	['ʃe ma]	301
t	t		[t]	total	[tɔ 'tal]	301
	tt		[t]	quitter	[ki 'te]	301
	t	final	silent	saint	[sɛ̃]	301
	th		[t]	théâtre	[te 'ɑ trə]	302
	ti	in suffixes -tion, -tience	[sj]	élection	[e lɛk 'sjɔ̃]	302
	tie	final	[ti] or [ti ə]	sortie	[sɔr 'ti] [sɔr 'ti ə]	302
u	u, û		[y]	une	['y nə]	240, 282
	u	final or before a consonant	[y]	subito, tu	[sy bi 'to], [ty]	240, 282
	u	before a "stressed" vowel	[ɥ]	nuit	[nɥi]	240, 283
	u	before final mute e	[y] or [y ə]	revue	[rə 'vy] [rə 'vy ə]	240, 283
	u	after g and before a *vowel*	silent	guitare	[gi 'ta rə]	240, 283
	ue	before il, ill, ille	[œ]	cercueil	[sɛr 'kœj]	240, 283
	um, un*		[œ̃]	parfum chacun	[par 'fœ̃] [ʃa 'kœ̃]	245, 284
v	v		[v]	violon	[vjɔ 'lɔ̃]	302
w	w	usually	[v]	wagon	[va 'gɔ̃]	302

French

French Letter and Position in Word			IPA	Example and IPA		Page
x	x	before a consonant	[ks]	texte	['tɛk stə]	303
	x	before a *vowel* or *h* usually	[gz]	exile	[ɛg 'zi lə]	303
	x	final usually	*silent*	doux	[du]	303
	x	in liaison	[z]	deux‿amis	[dø za 'mi]	303
y	y	initial	[j]	yeux	[jø]	284
	y	before or after a consonant	[i]	lyre	['li rə]	284
	y	between two vowels = *ii*	[ij]	rayon	[rɛ 'jõ]	285
	ym, yn*		[ẽ]	thym	[tẽ]	245, 285
z	z		[z]	Ézéchiel	[e ze 'kjɛl]	304
	z	final	*silent*	allez	[a 'le]	304

French

Special Features of French

Syllabification

French is a language of long vowels! That is, when you are pronouncing correctly, you elongate the French vowel to the greatest extent and then articulate the following consonant only at the beginning of the next note or the release of the note. Neither emphasize nor elongate a consonant in French, even when the consonant is doubled. This differs from English, Italian, and German where you give considerable emphasis and prolongation to consonants.

The way a printed French word looks may not match the way it is pronounced. For example, in the text of a song, the word *connais* may be printed as *con-nais*; the first syllable is shown ending with *n*, ostensibly making it a closed syllable. The closed syllable implies that the first vowel has a short duration followed by a prolonged [n] in the same syllable. When singing, however, you pronounce the word as *co-nnais* [kɔ ˈnɛ], giving the first vowel long duration and putting the consonant [n] on the beginning of the second syllable.

In this text, we've divided syllables as they are printed in songs to keep the visual representation of words consistent with what you normally see. The IPA transcriptions also follow that same syllable division to avoid confusion. You must remember, therefore, that *regardless of the printed syllabification, you must pronounce the vowels long and the consonants short*. The rhythm and flow of the French language depends upon keeping French a language of long vowels!

Many French words end with the letter *e*, which is silent in speech, and is referred to as the *mute e*. Composers often give a note to a mute *e*, which is then sung as schwa [ə]. The final mute *e* is so frequently sung in French songs that in this text we treat it as a separate final syllable. For example, in this line it appears in all but one word.

LL 5.2.01	Read aloud.
Tout*e* fleuri*e* sembl*e* ma destiné*e*	[ˈtutə flœˈriə ˈsɑ̄blə ma dɛsti ˈneə]

From "Depuis le jour," *Louise* (Charpentier)

The rules on the following pages govern the division of French words into syllables.

Single Consonant Between Vowels

When a single consonant stands between two vowel sounds, put the consonant with the second vowel sound.

French

LL 5.2.02 Read aloud.

ré-vé-ler	[re ve 'le]
pi-co-ter	[pi kɔ 'te]
plai-sir	[plɛ 'zir]
na-tal	[na 'tal]
je-ter	[ʒə 'te]
fau-ves	['fo və]

Exception: When *x* occurs between two vowels, put it with the first vowel sound.

LL 5.2.03 Read aloud.

ex-a-gé-rer	[ɛg za ʒe 're]

Two Consecutive Consonants

Divide double consonants.

LL 5.2.04 Read aloud.

con-nais	[kɔ 'nɛ]
glis-sant	[gli 'sɑ̃]
ver-meil-les	[vɛr 'mɛ jə]
ap-pel-lent	[a 'pɛ lə]
hom-mes	['ɔ mə]
sug-gé-rer	[syg ʒe 're]
ac-ci-dent	[ak si 'dɑ̃]
im-men-se	[i 'mɑ̃ sə]

Usually divide two different consonants.

LL 5.2.05 Read aloud.

ber-ceau	[bɛr 'so]
en-fant	[ɑ̃ 'fɑ̃]
tan-te	['tɑ̃ tə]
im-por-te	[ɛ̃ 'pɔr tə]
ver-se	['vɛr sə]
an-ge	['ɑ̃ ʒə]

When a consonant is followed by *l* or *r*, put both consonants with the second syllable.

LL 5.2.06 Read aloud.

in-té-grant	[ɛ̃ te 'grɑ̃]
é-tran-gler	[e trɑ̃ 'gle]

French

ta-bleau	[ta ˈblo]
rou-vrent	[ˈru vrə]
dé-bris	[de ˈbri]
dé-clas-ser	[de klɑ ˈse]

Exception: Divide the combination of *r* and *l* as in *parler* [par ˈle].

When two consonants form a digraph, put them with the second syllable.

Note: Two consonants with a *single phonetic sound* (such as *ch*, *th*, *ph*, and *gn*) are called *digraphs*. They are treated as single consonants and join the second syllable.

LL 5.2.07   Read aloud.

ch:	cher-cher	[ʃɛr ˈʃe]
ph:	sy-phi-lis	[si fi ˈlis]
th:	mé-tho-de	[me ˈtɔ də]
gn:	mi-gnon	[mi ˈɲõ]

Three Consecutive Consonants

Usually divide three consonants between the first and second letters.

LL 5.2.08   Read aloud.

souf-fler	[su ˈfle]
morphine	[mɔr ˈfi nə]
en-clave	[ɑ̃ ˈkla və]
con-sti-tu-tion	[kõ sti ty ˈsjõ]

Consecutive Vowels

Each syllable in French contains one, and only one, vowel sound. However, a single vowel sound may be indicated by multiple orthographic letters. In the word beauté [boˈte], *for example, the three letters* eau *stand for the single vowel sound* [o].

A syllable may contain a glide and a vowel, as in bien [bjɛ̃]. *A glide alone, however, cannot constitute a syllable. There are three glides in French:* [j], [w], *and* [ɥ].

When consecutive vowels are pronounced as a *single vowel sound*, put them in the same syllable.

LL 5.2.09   Read aloud.

beau-coup	[bo ˈku]
vais-seaux	[vɛ ˈso]
de-main	[də ˈmɛ̃]
crain-dre	[ˈkrɛ̃ drə]
a-mour	[a ˈmur]
cou-leur	[ku ˈlœr]
tau-reau	[tɔ ˈro]
re-viens	[rə ˈvjɛ̃]

French

When one of two consecutive vowels appears under a dieresis [daɪ 'ɛ rə sɪs] (two dots), divide the two vowels into two syllables.

LL 5.2.10 Read aloud.

Noël	No-ël	[nɔ 'ɛl]
haïr	ha-ïr	[a 'ir]
Thaïs	Tha-ïs	[ta 'is]

Exception:

LL 5.2.11 Read aloud.

| Saint-Saëns | [sɛ̃ 'sɑ̃s] |

Occasionally divide two consecutive vowels into two syllables. Check a dictionary.

LL 5.2.12 Read aloud.

cruel	cru-el	[kry 'ɛl]
travailler	tra-va-iller	[tra va 'je]
saillir	sa-illir	[sa 'jir]
théâtre	thé-â-tre	[te 'ɑ trə]

Stress

In English, Italian, and German, you create strong and weak stress patterns in words by changing loudness and pitch of different syllables. Do not carry this practice into French, however; pronounce all syllables with almost equal emphasis. To pronounce a tonic syllable in French, give it a *longer duration* than the other syllables.

In French, the last syllable of a word is usually the tonic syllable. The only exception occurs in words ending with mute *e*, when the second-to-last (penultimate) syllable is the tonic syllable. This pattern is so regular that some texts do not even indicate the tonic syllable in IPA transcriptions.

To become more accustomed to this unfamiliar pattern of stress, listen to recordings of outstanding singers and speakers. Before you begin to sing a song, read the lyrics aloud to establish the pattern of stress.

The special rhythm of the French language is achieved by the prolonged tonic syllables. This feature has considerable impact upon the melodic line of songs.

> Exercise: In the following list of words, the final syllable is the tonic syllable. Read these words aloud, prolonging the final syllable.

The syllable that has the primary stress in a word is called the tonic syllable.

Final e is usually silent in French and is called mute e.

French

LL 5.2.13 Read aloud.

perdu	[pɛr ˈdy]
liberté	[li bɛr ˈte]
pensif	[pã ˈsif]
occasion	[ɔ kɑ ˈzjõ]
toujours	[tu ˈʒur]
wagon	[va ˈgõ]
parler	[par ˈle]

In the two columns below, all of the words end with mute *e*, so the tonic syllable is the next-to-last syllable (the penultimate syllable). Pronounce the words in the first column of IPA transcriptions, omitting the final mute *e* as in spoken French. Then pronounce the words in the second column, voicing the mute *e* as you would in singing. In both columns, as you pronounce the words, prolong the tonic syllable.

LL 5.2.14 Read aloud.

carte	[kart]	[ˈkar tə]
charme	[ʃarm]	[ˈʃar mə]
quatre	[katr]	[ˈka trə]
école	[e ˈkɔl]	[e ˈkɔ lə]
flèche	[flɛʃ]	[ˈflɛ ʃə]
écoute	[e ˈkut]	[e ˈku tə]
théâtre	[te ˈɑtr]	[te ˈɑ trə]
impossible	[ɛ̃ pɔ ˈsibl]	[ɛ̃ pɔ ˈsi blə]

In short phrases, the primary stress, or longer duration, is reserved for the last tonic syllable of the *phrase*. This gives French a very smooth rhythm. Read the following short phrases aloud and prolong the last syllable of the *phrase*.

LL 5.2.15 Read aloud.

de ta pensée	[də ta pã ˈse ə]
au cri doux	[o kri ˈdu]
la vie importune	[la vi ɛ̃ pɔr ˈty nə]

Features of French Pronunciation

The Mixed Vowels

Mixed vowels are those that combine, or mix, the articulation shape of the lips for a back vowel with the articulation shape of the tongue for a forward vowel. For example, round your lips to the position of *oo* [u] as in b*oo*t, and then, *without moving your lips*, move your tongue to the forward arched position for *ee* [i] as in b*ee*t. Add voice and you will hear the close mixed vowel sound [y], a blending of the back sound of [u] and the forward sound of [i].

Of the four mixed vowels, only three are found in French. (All four are found in German.)

The lip and tongue positions for the three French mixed vowels are indicated on the following chart. For each mixed vowel, start with the rounded lip position suggested by [u], [o], or [ɔ]. Then, *without moving your lips*, move your tongue to the high, forward positions suggested by [i], [e] or [ɛ]. Notice that to produce the mixed vowel, you do not glide from the back vowel to the forward vowel. Instead, you produce both vowels *simultaneously*. By combining the two sounds into a unified single vowel sound, you produce the mixed vowel.

Mixed vowels are not found in English, but the sound of reversed epsilon [ɜ] as in the word bird *when spoken with a dropped r as in a British accent,* [bɜd], *is very similar to open* [œ]. *For* [œ], *the lips are more rounded and the jaw more dropped.*

LL 5.2.16   Read aloud.

Chart of Lip and Tongue Positions for the Mixed Vowels					
Lip Position		Tongue Position		Mixed Vowel	
[u]	+	[i]	=	[y]	Close ü
[o]	+	[e]	=	[ø]	Close ö
[ɔ]	+	[ɛ]	=	[œ]	Open ö

Those familiar with German often choose to refer to the mixed vowels as close umlaut ü [y], *close umlaut ö* [ø], *and* open *umlaut ö* [œ].

When reading IPA transcriptions aloud, refer to the mixed vowels by their sounds, or call them *close* [y], *close* [ø], and *open* [œ] to identify their method of production (from the most close to most open).

These are the usual spellings for [y]:

û and *u* when final, or before a consonant or a mute *e*

LL 5.2.17   Read aloud.

revue	[rə 'vy ə]
salut	[sa 'ly]
une	['y nə]
studio	[sty 'djo]
dû	[dy]
purée	[py 're ə]

In certain tenses of the verb avoir, eu *and* eû *are irregularly pronounced as* [y]: eu, eus, eûmes, eûtes, eurent, eusse, eusses, eût, eussions, eussiez, eussent.

These are the usual spellings for [ø]:

eu or *oeu* as the final sound of a word (not necessarily the final letters of the word)

LL 5.2.18   Read aloud.

peu	[pø]
veut	[vø]
dieu	[djø]
peut	[pø]

eu before [z]

LL 5.2.19　　Read aloud.

creuse	[ˈkrø zə]
chanteuse	[ʃɑ̃ ˈtø zə]

eû

LL 5.2.20　　Read aloud.

jeûne	[ˈʒø nə]

These are the usual spellings for [œ]:

eu or *oeu* when in the interior of a word

LL 5.2.21　　Read aloud.

heure	[ˈœ rə]
malheur	[ma ˈlœr]
peuple	[ˈpœ plə]
coeur	[kœr]

ue when followed by *il* or *ill*

LL 5.2.22　　Read aloud.

orgueil	[ɔr ˈgœj]
écueil	[e ˈkœj]

To familiarize yourself with the various spellings of [ø] and [œ], read the following lists of words. Recall the rule that governs the pronunciation of the underlined vowels.

Close [ø]	Open [œ]
bl<u>eu</u>	s<u>eu</u>l
harmoni<u>eux</u>	h<u>eu</u>re
j<u>eû</u>ne	j<u>eu</u>nesse
mystéri<u>eux</u>	dem<u>eu</u>re
ci<u>eux</u>	fl<u>eu</u>rs
mi<u>eux</u>	pl<u>eu</u>rent
malheur<u>eu</u>se	malh<u>eu</u>reuse
amour<u>eu</u>se	b<u>oe</u>uf

To familiarize yourself with the spellings of the mixed vowel [y], read through the following words. Recall the rule that governs the pronunciation of *u* as [y].

<u>u</u>ne	f<u>u</u>mée
rev<u>ue</u>	l<u>u</u>ne
t<u>u</u>	perd<u>u</u>

importune	plus
ramures	pure
sur	vue
connu	salut

Glides

A glide is a speech sound characterized by a movement of the articulators from one position to another. Glides are classified as consonants, not vowels, because they do not form the core of a syllable. The glides in French, [j], [w], and [ɥ], are described below.

Glides are sometimes referred to as semi-vowels or semi-consonants.

The glide [j], called *jot* [jɔt], is the sound of *y* in the English word *you* [ju].

Pronounce [j] by moving the blade of your tongue to a high, arched position close to your hard palate, similar to the vowel [i], then quickly shifting to the vowel that follows.

Below are the usual spellings of [j].

i before a stressed vowel is [j]:

LL 5.2.23 Read aloud.

dieu	[djø]
nation	[nɑ ˈsjɔ̃]
bien	[bjɛ̃]
premier	[prə ˈmje]

il, *ill*, and *ille* are pronounced as [j] or [jə]:

LL 5.2.24 Read aloud.

soleil	[sɔ ˈlɛj]
famille	[fa ˈmi jə]

(For details on these letter groups, see "il, ill, ille" on page 275.)

y is pronounced as [j]:

LL 5.2.25 Read aloud.

yeux	[jø]
payer	[pɛ ˈje]
rayon	[rɛ ˈjɔ̃]
ayant	[ɛ ˈjɑ̃]

(For details on these letter groups, see "The Letter y" on page 284.)

French

The glide [w] is the sound of *w* in the English word *wear*.

Pronounce the [w] sound by rounding your lips and raising the back of your tongue as if saying the vowel [u]. Then quickly shift to the vowel that follows.

Below are the usual spellings of [w].

oi is [wa]:

LL 5.2.26   Read aloud.

| moi | [mwa] |
| voix | [vwa] |

oin is [wẽ]:

LL 5.2.27   Read aloud.

| loin | [lwẽ] |
| poindre | ['pwẽ drə] |

oy is [waj] (see page 281):

LL 5.2.28   Read aloud.

| royal | [rwa 'jal] |
| soyeux | [swa 'jø] |

ou is [w] when before a stressed vowel (a vowel other than mute *e*):

LL 5.2.29   Read aloud.

| oui | [wi] |
| ouest | [wɛst] |

When ou *occurs before* mute e, *it is pronounced* [u] *(See page 281).*

Note: In singing, if two notes are provided for a one syllable word like *jouer* [ʒwe], the *ou* becomes [uw]: [ʒu 'we].

The glide [ɥ] has no equivalent sound in English. It is the gliding articulation of the mixed vowel [y]. The symbol [ɥ] is called by its sound.

[ɥ] must not sound like [w]. Your tongue should be more forward and your lips more tensely rounded for [ɥ].

Exercise: Discover the sound of the glide [ɥ] by first sustaining the mixed vowel [y]. Then speak the word *puis* [pɥi], shortening the duration of the first vowel until it becomes the glide [ɥ], a sound that is not sustained but rather moves quickly from one position to another.

The usual spelling of [ɥ] is *u* when before any vowel except mute *e*:

LL 5.2.30   Read aloud.

lui	[lɥi]
nuage	['nɥa ʒə]
suis	[sɥi]

French

depuis	[də ˈpɥi]
pluie	[ˈplɥi ə]
suave	[ˈsɥa və]

To familiarize yourself with the spellings of the glide [ɥ], read through this list. Recall the rule that governs the pronunciation of the underlined vowel.

nu_it	l_ui_sant
br_u_it	l_ue_tte
c_ui_vre	enf_ui_r
cond_u_it	s_ui_vi
fr_u_its	br_ui_ssant

When u occurs before a mute e, it is pronounced [ɥ]. (See page 241.)

Nasal Vowels

The following chart describes the four nasal vowels of French.

LL 5.2.31   Read aloud.

The Four French Nasal Vowels
The nasal vowel [ɛ̃] is nasalized *eh* as in *bet* [ɛ].
The nasal vowel [ɑ̃] is nasalized *ah* as in *father* [ɑ].
The nasal vowel [õ] is nasalized *o* as in *pole* [o].
The nasal vowel [œ̃] is nasalized *oeu* as in *coeur* [œ].

Produce the nasal vowels by slightly lowering your soft palate (velum) and permitting air to enter your nose. You must watch that the nasal vowels do not become so nasal as to be sharply twangy. Listen to French singers to hear how beautifully these vowel sounds can be sung.

In IPA transcriptions, the diacritical mark [~], called a tilde, *indicates that the vowel is nasalized.*

Notice how the nasal vowels are ordered in the chart to help you identify the sounds. The order [ɛ̃], [ɑ̃], [õ], [œ̃] indicates how the lips gradually increase their rounding and the jaw drops.

A vowel becomes nasalized in French under the following two conditions.

1. When a vowel precedes a final *m* or *n*, as in the word *son* [sõ], the letters *on* form a unit that you pronounce as a single sound: the nasal vowel [õ]. Do not pronounce the *n*; it is silent.

2. When a vowel precedes an *m* or *n* that is followed by another consonant other than *m* or *n*, as in the word *songer* [sõ ˈʒe], the letters *on* form a unit that you pronounce as [õ]. Do not pronounce the *n*; it is silent.

These are the usual spellings of the nasal vowel [ɛ̃].

   aim or *ain*

LL 5.2.32   Read aloud.

faim	[fɛ̃]
main	[mɛ̃]

For clarification of the nasal sounds, you can refer to them as:

1st position   [ɛ̃]
2nd position   [ɑ̃]
3rd position   [õ]
4th position   [œ̃]

French

sainte	[ˈsɛ̃ tə]
daim	[dɛ̃]

eim or *ein*

LL 5.2.33   Read aloud.

Reims	[rɛ̃s]
teint	[tɛ̃]

im or *in*

LL 5.2.34   Read aloud.

simple	[ˈsɛ̃ plə]
matin	[ma ˈtɛ̃]

ym or *yn*

LL 5.2.35   Read aloud.

thym	[tɛ̃]
syndicat	[sɛ̃ di ˈka]

en after *i*

LL 5.2.36   Read aloud.

bien	[bjɛ̃]
reviens	[rə ˈvjɛ̃]

These are the usual spellings of the nasal vowel [ã].

am or *an*

LL 5.2.37   Read aloud.

champ	[ʃã]
dans	[dã]
grands	[grã]
devant	[də ˈvã]

em or *en*

LL 5.2.38   Read aloud.

temps	[tã]
ensemble	[ã ˈsã blə]
encor	[ã ˈkɔr]
prendre	[ˈprã drə]

These are the usual spellings of the nasal vowel [õ].

om and *on*

LL 5.2.39 Read aloud.

tombeau	[tõ 'bo]
son	[sõ]
ombre	['õ brə]
mon	[mõ]

Dictionaries often transcribe this nasal vowel as open [ɔ̃]. This sound is currently being identified in French speech as close [õ].

These are the usual spellings of the nasal vowel [œ̃].

um and *un*

LL 5.2.40 Read aloud.

parfum	[par 'fœ̃]
humble	['œ̃ blə]
un	[œ̃]
lundi	[lœ̃ 'di]

Do not nasalize a vowel followed by *m* or *n* under the following two conditions.

1. If a vowel precedes an *m* or *n* that is followed by another *m* or *n*, do not nasalize it.

   LL 5.2.41 Read aloud.

comme	['kɔ mə]
donne	['dɔ nə]
tienne	['tjɛ nə]
connaître	[kɔ 'nɛ trə]
sonnée	[sɔ 'ne ə]
homme	['ɔ mə]

2. If a vowel precedes an *m* or *n* that is followed by a vowel, do not nasalize it.

   LL 5.2.42 Read aloud.

émule	[e 'my lə]
timonier	[ti mɔ 'nje]
domaine	[dɔ 'mɛ nə]
image	[i 'ma ʒə]
sonore	[sɔ 'nɔ rə]
funeste	[fy 'nɛ stə]

French

For a full discussion of liaison, see page 256.

In liaison, when you connect a normally silent final consonant to the initial vowel sound of the next word, pronounce the otherwise silent final *m* and *n*. The vowel retains its nasalization and you attach the final *m* or *n* to the initial vowel of the following word.

LL 5.2.43   Read aloud.

en‿est fanée	[ã nɛ fa 'ne ə]
qu'on‿aime	[kõ 'nɛ mə]
mon‿amour	[mõ na 'mur]

To familiarize yourself with the spellings of the nasal vowel [ɛ̃], read through this list. Recall the rule that governs the pronunciation of the underlined letters.

soud<u>ain</u>	chem<u>in</u>
th<u>ym</u>	s<u>ein</u>
v<u>ien</u>dra	m<u>ain</u>
<u>in</u>visible	cr<u>ains</u>
ch<u>ien</u>	pl<u>ein</u>
rev<u>iens</u>	v<u>ain</u>queur
v<u>in</u>gt	mat<u>in</u>
pr<u>in</u>temps	s<u>ain</u>te

To familiarize yourself with the various spellings of the nasal vowel [ã], read through this list. Recall the rules that govern the pronunciation of the underlined letters.

qu<u>an</u>d	gr<u>an</u>d
fl<u>am</u>ber	élég<u>an</u>ce
h<u>an</u>che	bl<u>an</u>che
rép<u>an</u>d	r<u>en</u>ds
sil<u>en</u>ce	v<u>en</u>t
ch<u>am</u>ps	ch<u>am</u>ps
s<u>en</u>tier	naiss<u>an</u>t
couch<u>an</u>ts	t<u>em</u>ps
<u>em</u>brasse	dev<u>an</u>t
t<u>an</u>t	phal<u>an</u>ge
s<u>an</u>tal	charm<u>an</u>ts

To familiarize yourself with the various spellings of the nasal vowel [õ], read through this list. Recall the rules that govern the pronunciation of the underlined letters.

s<u>on</u>	m<u>on</u>
t<u>om</u>be	m<u>on</u>ter

French

on	profonde
ombre	souffrons
horizons	venions
monceau	monde
ombrages	ombreuse

To familiarize yourself with the various spellings of the nasal vowel [œ̃], read through this list. Recall the rules that govern the pronunciation of the underlined letters.

parfums
un
humble

Final mute e

In spoken French, the final *e* in a word is silent ("mute"), unless marked with an accent (é). However, musical notation often requires the mute *e* to be sung; when this occurs, mute *e* is pronounced as schwa [ə].

The French schwa [ə] is a more forward and rounded sound than the schwa [ə] of English. It is more like the sound of the mixed vowel [ø] than that of the weakened, neutral vowel *uh* as in *about* [ə 'baʊt]. You must bring your lips forward into a more rounded position to achieve the French schwa.

French uses these accents:

acute (é)
grave (è)
circumflex (ê)

Exercise: Read these words aloud to contrast the pronunciation of final mute *e* and the accented *é*.

LL 5.2.44   Read aloud.

Final mute e		Final accented é	
marque	['mar kə]	marqué	[mar 'ke]
locale	[lɔ 'ka lə]	localité	[lɔ ka li 'te]
personne	[pɛr 'sɔ nə]	personnalité	[pɛr sɔ na li 'te]

The Pure Vowels [e] and [o]

The vowels [e] and [o] are pure vowels in French, so you must never turn them into diphthongs as in the English words *bait* [beɪt] and *boat* [boʊt]. Because American speakers consistently use the diphthongal forms of these vowels, you must be careful to identify and produce the pure vowel sounds that occur in French. In English, these pure vowels can only be found in a few unstressed syllables, as in some pronunciations of [e] in *chaotic* [ke 'ɑ tɪk] and [o] in *obey* [o 'beɪ].

The French [e] is unlike English in a second way. In the French [e] the high point of the arch of the tongue is more forward and close to the

French

alveolar ridge than in English. To American ears, the resulting [e] sounds almost like the [i] in b<u>ee</u>t.

The alveolar ridge, *also called the teeth ridge, is the hard gum ridge behind the upper front teeth.*

Read these words aloud using a pure [e].

LL 5.2.45   Read aloud.

fréter	[fre 'te]
fumer	[fy 'me]
détacher	[de ta 'ʃe]
manger	[mã 'ʒe]
et	[e]
détirer	[de ti 're]

Read these words aloud using a pure [o].

LL 5.2.46   Read aloud.

faux	[fo]
baume	['bo mə]
chauffe	['ʃo fə]
repos	[rə 'po]
faute	['fo tə]
beau	[bo]

Mute and Aspirate h

The two kinds of *h* in French are mute and aspirate. Both are silent. The term *aspirate* indicates a special speech classification in French; it does not indicate that any air escapes, as it does with the *h* in English words <u>h</u>eat or <u>h</u>ome.

Liaison is the linking of a normally silent final consonant to the initial vowel of the following word.

Elision is the omission of a sound, such as the dropping of the final mute e.

French pronunciation forbids the linking of words through liaison or elision with any word that begins with the initial aspirate *h*, while permitting the linking with a word with an initial mute *h* (see page 292). You should check the words in a dictionary to know whether a word begins with an aspirate or mute *h*. Often the dictionary will employ an asterisk (*h) before the aspirate *h*.

Examples:

Mute *h*: linking of words is permitted.

LL 5.2.47   Read aloud.

heure	['œ rə]	quelle_heure	[kɛ 'lœ rə]
herbe	['ɛr bə]	une_herbe	[y 'nɛr bə]

French

Aspirate *h*: linking of words is forbidden.

LL 5.2.48   Read aloud.

*haute	['o tə]	voix haute	[vwa 'o tə]
*haine	['ɛ nə]	en haine	[ã 'ɛ nə]

The Enya

The sound of enya [ɲ], as in *bagne,* is not found in English. It resembles the sound of [nj] in *onion,* but you form it with a single articulatory motion. You make [ɲ] by touching the tip of your tongue to the back of your lower teeth while simultaneously arching the *blade* of your tongue upward to touch your alveolar ridge. Enya is a humming type of sound similar to [n].

cognac	[kɔ 'ɲak]
poignet	[pwa 'ɲɛ]

Pronounced and Silent Consonants

Consonants in the interior of a word (called *medial consonants*) are usually pronounced.

LL 5.2.49   Read aloud.

venais	[və 'nɛ]
exalter	[ɛg zal 'te]
jardin	[ʒar 'dɛ̃]
gala	[ga 'la]

Note: Consonants before a final mute *e* are classified as medial in a word even when the mute *e* is silent and the consonant is the final sound.

LL 5.2.50   Read aloud.

pose	['po zə]	or	[poz]
envoles	[ã 'vɔ lə]	or	[ã 'vɔl]
lèvres	['lɛ vrə]	or	[lɛvr]
sonores	[sɔ 'nɔ rə]	or	[sɔ 'nɔr]
blanche	['blã ʃə]	or	[blãʃ]

Medial *m* and *n* after a nasal vowel are silent.

LL 5.2.51   Read aloud.

monter	[mɔ̃ 'te]
timbre	['tɛ̃ brə]

French

There is an old saying that the only final consonants which are pronounced in French are the letters in the word careful. *Final b and q are rarer.*

The final consonants *c, r, f, l, b* and *q* are usually pronounced.

Final *c* is usually pronounced:

LL 5.2.52　　　Read aloud.

avec	[a 'vɛk]
lac	[lak]
parc	[park]

Note: Final *c* is sometimes silent (see page 287).

Final *r* is usually pronounced:

LL 5.2.53　　　Read aloud.

professeur	[prɔ fɛ 'sœr]
secteur	[sɛk 'tœr]
servir	[sɛr 'vir]
voir	[vwar]
soupir	[su 'pir]
tour	[tur]
hiver	[i 'vɛr]
car	[kar]

In spoken French, the uvular r [ʀ] *is commonly used in Paris and the Île de France. However, in singing, always use the tongue point* r, *either with a single flip—particularly between vowels—or a rolled* r *(two or three flaps).*

Note: Final *r* is sometimes silent as explained later in this section and under "The single letter e" on page 264.

Final *f* is usually pronounced:

LL 5.2.54　　　Read aloud.

sauf	[sof]
vif	[vif]

Final *l* is usually pronounced:

LL 5.2.55　　　Read aloud.

idéal	[i de 'al]
racinal	[ra si 'nal]
vol	[vɔl]
bal	[bal]

Final *b* is usually pronounced:

LL 5.2.56　　　Read aloud.

Jacob	[ʒa 'kob]
snob	[snɔb]

French

Note: Final *b* is silent after *m*:

LL 5.2.57   Read aloud.

| plomb | [plõ] |

Final *q* is pronounced:

LL 5.2.58   Read aloud.

| coq | [kɔk] |

Otherwise, final consonants are usually silent.

Final *d* is silent:

LL 5.2.59   Read aloud.

regard	[rə 'gar]
pied	[pje]
pillard	[pi 'jar]

Final *g* is silent:

LL 5.2.60   Read aloud.

| sang | [sɑ̃] |
| poing | [pwɛ̃] |

Final *m* is silent:

LL 5.2.61   Read aloud.

| parfum | [par 'fœ̃] |

Final *n* is silent:

LL 5.2.62   Read aloud.

chemin	[ʃə 'mɛ̃]
canon	[ka 'nɔ̃]
refrain	[rə 'frɛ̃]

Final *p* is silent:

LL 5.2.63   Read aloud.

| camp | [kɑ̃] |
| galop | [ga 'lo] |

Final *r* is sometimes silent when following the letter *e*.

Final *r* is silent in verb endings *-er* (first conjugation infinitives):

LL 5.2.64   Read aloud.

| changer | [ʃɑ̃ 'ʒe] |
| chanter | [ʃɑ̃ 'te] |

For more information about final letters see "The letter c", "The letter r", "The letter f", and "The letter l", under French Consonants in Detail.

When r *precedes a final silent consonant, as in the word* regard [rə 'gar], *where the final* d *is silent, pronounce the* r.

French

abuser	[a by ˈze]
regarder	[rə gar ˈde]

Final *r* is usually silent in nouns and adjectives ending in *-er*, *-ier*, and *-yer* (See "The single letter e" on page 264.)

LL 5.2.65   Read aloud.

boulanger	[bu lɑ̃ ˈʒe]
épicier	[e pi ˈsje]
baiser (noun)	[be ˈze]
danger	[dɑ̃ ˈʒe]
foyer	[fwa ˈje]
premier	[prə ˈmje]

There are a few common words in which the final s is pronounced: bis, hélas, Saint-Saëns *and* lis.

Final *s* is silent:

LL 5.2.66   Read aloud.

après	[a ˈprɛ]
bas	[bɑ]
mais	[mɛ]
pas	[pɑ]

Note: The addition of a final *s* for pluralization does not alter the pronunciation of the word. Treat the letter before the *s* as a final letter. The following examples show the identical pronunciations of the singular and plural forms of words.

LL 5.2.67   Read aloud.

baiser	[be ˈze]
baisers	[be ˈze]
noire	[ˈnwa rə]
noires	[ˈnwa rə]
branche	[ˈbrɑ̃ ʃə]
branches	[ˈbrɑ̃ ʃə]

Final *t* is silent:

LL 5.2.68   Read aloud.

bouquet	[bu ˈkɛ]
tout	[tu]
secret	[sə ˈkrɛ]
port	[pɔr]
parlent	[ˈpar lə]
firmament	[fir ma ˈmɑ̃]

French

Final *t* frequently combines with other consonants:

Final *ct*: Sometimes both are silent, sometimes pronounced. Refer to a dictionary.

LL 5.2.69   Read aloud.

Silent:	aspect	[as ˈpɛ]
Pronounced:	direct	[di ˈrɛkt]

Final *st*: Sometimes both are silent, sometimes pronounced. Refer to a dictionary.

LL 5.2.70   Read aloud.

Silent:	est (*is*)	[ɛ]
Pronounced:	est (*east*)	[ɛst]

In final *gt*, *lt*, and *pt*, both letters are usually silent:

LL 5.2.71   Read aloud.

doigt	[dwa]
prompt	[prɔ̃]

Final *x* is silent:

LL 5.2.72   Read aloud.

doux	[du]
prix	[pri]

Final *z* is silent:

LL 5.2.73   Read aloud.

allez	[a ˈle]
souffrez	[su ˈfre]

Final silent consonants are often pronounced in liaison. (See "Liaison and Elision" in the next section):

LL 5.2.74   Read aloud.

pas	[pɑ]	=	pas à pas	[pɑ za ˈpɑ]
est	[ɛ]	=	est un	[ɛ ˈtœ̃]
faut	[fo]	=	faut il	[fo ˈtil]
suis	[sɥi]	=	suis heureuse	[sɥi zœ ˈrø zə]
leurs	[lœr]	=	leurs ébats	[lœr ze ˈba]
sentais	[sɑ̃ ˈtɛ]	=	sentais en	[sɑ̃ te ˈzɑ̃]

French

Liaison and Elision

French is a legato language. Its smooth flow results from the generous linking of words.

The linking of most concern to you is that which is done through liaison and elision. The terms *liaison* and *elision* have been poorly defined in some diction texts, and are often mistakenly used interchangeably. *Liaison* [ljɛ 'zõ] is the pronunciation of a normally silent final consonant at the end of a word to link with the next word beginning with a vowel, a glide, or mute *h*. *Elision* [e li 'zjõ] is the omission of a final mute *e* in a word that is followed by a word beginning with a vowel or mute *h*.

Exercise: Read these words aloud, linking the normally silent consonant to the initial vowel of the next word. This liaison is indicated by the curved line between the words.

LL 5.2.75   Read aloud.

après un	[a prɛ 'zœ̃]
revient un	[rə vjɛ̃ 'tœ̃]
des oiseaux	[de zwa 'zo]
ton âme	[tõ 'nɑ mə]

Exercise: Read aloud these words that elide the mute *e*. Link the preceding consonant to the initial vowel of the next word.

LL 5.2.76   Read aloud.

âme en	[ɑ 'mɑ̃]
rose et	[ro 'ze]
notre amour	[nɔ tra 'mur]

Rules for Liaison and Elision

Liaison and elision occur more frequently in singing than in speech. Deciding which words to connect in singing is a somewhat complex subject that requires understanding of the grammatical structure of the language: there are times when linking is compulsory, when it is optional, and when it is forbidden. Listening to recordings of leading French singers can help you build good discernment about the principles of liaison and elision. Meanwhile, these simplified rules can guide you into reasonable choices.

You may link a word ending in a normally silent final consonant sound to a following word beginning with a vowel, a glide, or a mute *h*. The words should be closely connected (as an article connects to an adjective or noun, an adjective to a noun, or a personal pronoun to a verb).

For further study of liaison see The Interpretation of French Song, Singing in French, *and* Phonetic Readings of Songs and Arias, *which are listed in the bibliography.*

French

LL 5.2.77 Read aloud.

un enfant	[œ̃ nɑ̃ 'fɑ̃]
un ami	[œ̃ na 'mi]
bien-aimée	[bjɛ̃ nɛ 'me ə]
puis il revient	[pɥi zil rə 'vjɛ̃]

Some consonants take on a different sound in liaison.

s will sound like [z]:

LL 5.2.78 Read aloud.

| dans un sommeil | [dɑ̃ zœ̃ sɔ 'mɛj] |
| de tes traitres yeux | [də te trɛ trə 'zjø] |

x will sound like [z]:

LL 5.2.79 Read aloud.

| deux amis | [dø za 'mi] |
| aux aurores | [o zɔ 'rɔ rə] |

d will sound like [t]:

LL 5.2.80 Read aloud.

| de pied en cap | [də pje tɑ̃ 'kap] |
| grand arbre | [grɑ̃ 'tar brə] |

g will sound like [k]:

LL 5.2.81 Read aloud.

| long hiver | [lõ ki 'vɛr] |

You may elide the final mute *e* to permit the preceding consonant to be linked to the next word.

LL 5.2.82 Read aloud.

l'herbe agitée	[lɛr ba ʒi 'te ə]
Je rêve aux baisers	[ʒə rɛ vo be 'ze]
la fille en rose	[la fi jɑ̃ 'ro zə]

Do not link in these situations:

Do not link words where a separation is needed to support the meaning of the text.

LL 5.2.83 Read aloud.

Tu m'appelais, ǀ et je quittais la terre	[ty ma pə 'lɛ e ʒə ki tɛ la 'tɛ rə]
si tu le veux, ǀ ô mon amour	[si ty lə 'vø o mõ na 'mur]
mais, ǀ ô mon bien-aimée....	[mɛ o mõ bjɛ̃ nɛ 'me ə]

French

After the word est (is), you do link the final t to the next word. By linking the t of est, you help the listener understand that you mean is and not and.

In many dictionaries an aspirate h is indicated by an asterisk : *haies

Do not link the word *et* (*and*) to the next word.

LL 5.2.84   Read aloud.

| et alors | [e a 'lɔr] |
| et aussi | [e o 'si] |

Do not link a final consonant to a word that begins with an aspirate *h*.

LL 5.2.85   Read aloud.

| des *haies | [de 'ɛ] |
| des *hérauts | [de e 'ro] |

Do not link into *oui* (*yes*).

LL 5.2.86   Read aloud.

| mais oui | [mɛ 'wi] |

In words ending with *rd*, *rs*, or *rt*, usually link the *r* instead of the final silent consonant.

LL 5.2.87   Read aloud.

sur le bord arrivée	[syr lə bɔ ra ri 've ə]
mort exquise	[mɔ rɛk 'ski zə]
me penchant vers elle	[mə pɑ̃ ʃɑ̃ vɛ 'rɛ lə]

Exception: When final *-rs* indicates pluralization, link the *s*.

LL 5.2.88   Read aloud.

| Si mes vers avaient des ailes | [si me vɛr za vɛ de 'zɛ lə] |

Nouns in the plural may be linked: les nuits enivrées [le nɥi za ni 'vre ə], aux jardins ombreux [o ʒar dɛ̃ zõ 'brø].

Do not link after a noun in the singular.

LL 5.2.89   Read aloud.

| la nuit ǀ immense | [la nɥi i 'mɑ̃ sə] |
| le printemps ǀ est venu | [lə prɛ̃ tɑ̃ ɛ və 'ny] |

Exceptions: Some singular nouns have become part of a frequently-used expression. Linking may be made.

LL 5.2.90   Read aloud.

| nuit et jour | [nɥi te 'ʒur] |
| un fait accompli | [œ̃ fɛ ta kõ 'pli] |

French

§ French Vowels in Detail

The letter *a* in French has a variety of pronunciations, depending upon the following qualifiers. To determine the pronunciation of *a*, ask yourself these four questions.

1. Is there a diacritical mark over the *a*?
2. What letters follow the *a*?
3. Is the letter *a* found as a single letter, or is it part of a letter group?
4. What is the position of *a* in the word? Is it initial, medial, or final?

The pronunciation rules below will help you determine the answers to these questions.

The letter

a

The single letter a

The letter *a* in French is frequently pronounced as [a]. And when *à* has a grave accent, it is *always* [a].

> Note: Bright [a] is more frequently used in French than dark [ɑ] (as in the English word *father*). In English, bright [a] is not used in isolation, but can be heard in the first part of the diphthong in the words *I* [aɪ], *by* [baɪ], and *might* [maɪt], or as Bostonians say, *"pahk the cah" (park the car)*. Bright [a] is a more forward vowel than dark [ɑ]. On the vowel chart it is found between [ɑ] and [æ] as in *cat*. Americans must be careful not to produce the bright [a] as [æ].

LL 5.3.01   Read aloud.

Paris	[pa ˈri]
chapelle	[ʃa ˈpɛ lə]
chalet	[ʃa ˈlɛ]
nativité	[na ti vi ˈte]
pardon	[par dō]
caviar	[ka ˈvjar]
harpe	[ˈar pə]
dame	[ˈda mə]
là	[la]
voilà	[vwa ˈla]
ami	[a ˈmi]
bagatelle	[ba ga ˈtɛ lə]

The following spellings are exceptions to the above rule.

1. The letter *a* before the sound [s] or [z] is sometimes [ɑ].

   Note: The *sound* [s] or [z] can be spelled by several orthographic letters; for example in *lacer*, the letter *c* is pronounced [s].

   LL 5.3.02   Read aloud.

passer	[pɑ 'se]
occasion	[ɔ kɑ 'zjõ]
lacer	[lɑ 'se]
extase	[ɛk 'stɑ zə]
rasade	[rɑ 'za də]
raser	[rɑ 'ze]

2. The letter *a* before final silent *s* is usually [ɑ].

   LL 5.3.03   Read aloud.

pas	[pɑ]
trépas	[tre 'pɑ]
las	[lɑ]
bas	[bɑ]

3. The letter *â* is almost always [ɑ].

   LL 5.3.04   Read aloud.

âge	['ɑ ʒə]
âme	['ɑ mə]
pâle	['pɑ lə]
mâle	['mɑ lə]

4. The letter *a* in a few other words is pronounced as [ɑ]. Refer to a dictionary.

   LL 5.3.05   Read aloud.

crabe	['krɑ bə]
sable	[sɑ blə]
flamme	['flɑ mə]
proclamer	[prɔ klɑ 'me]
diable	['djɑ blə]

ai

When *ai* is in the interior of a word, the letters are usually pronounced [ɛ].

> Note: The spellings *aî*, *aie*, *ais*, *ait*, *aient* are also pronounced [ɛ].
>
> LL 5.3.06   Read aloud.
>
> | mais | [mɛ] |
> |---|---|
> | étaient | [e 'tɛ] |
> | serait | [sə 'rɛ] |
> | plaît | [plɛ] |
> | faite | ['fɛ tə] |
> | comparaître | [kõ pa 'rɛ trə] |

> Exceptions: *ai* is irregularly pronounced as schwa [ə] in some forms of the verb *faire* [fɛ rə] (*to do*).
>
> LL 5.3.07
>
> | faisais | [fə 'zɛ] |
> |---|---|
> | faisant | [fə 'zã] |

> When *ai* is before [z], it may be pronounced as [e] when followed by a stressed [e] sound.
>
> LL 5.3.08   Read aloud.
>
> | baiser | [be 'ze] |
> |---|---|

When *ai* is final in a word, pronounce the letters as [e].

> Note: To be pronounced as [e], *ai* must be the final *letters* of the word, as in the following words. (However, when a silent consonant follows *ai*, as in the word *mais*, *ai* is pronounced with the open vowel [ɛ].)
>
> LL 5.3.09   Read aloud.
>
> | gai | [ge] |
> |---|---|
> | serai | [sə 're] |

The letters *ail* and *aill* are pronounced [aj].

> Note: The letters *ail* and *aill* are composed of the single letter *a* followed by the digraphs *il* and *ill*, which are pronounced as [j]. In the word *travail*, *ai* appears to form the vowel unit, but it doesn't: the *il* actually forms the unit—pronounced as [j]—and the *a* is separate. The word *travail* is therefore pronounced as [tra 'vaj]. (See "il, ill, ille" on page 275 for more examples.)

French

LL 5.3.10   Read aloud.

corail	[kɔ ˈraj]
cailloux	[ka ˈju]

aim, ain

When the letters *aim* or *ain* are final or before another consonant, pronounce them as the nasal vowel [ɛ̃]. Do not pronounce the *m* and *n* consonants unless in liaison.

LL 5.3.11   Read aloud.

faim	[fɛ̃]
ainsi	[ɛ̃ ˈsi]
daim	[dɛ̃]
grain	[grɛ̃]

When the letters *aim* or *ain* are followed by a vowel or another *m* or *n*, do not nasalize them, but pronounce them as [ɛm] and [ɛn].

LL 5.3.12   Read aloud.

haine	[ˈɛ nə]
plaine	[ˈplɛ nə]
je t'aime	[ʒə ˈtɛ mə]
graine	[ˈgrɛ nə]

am, an

When the letters *am* or *an* are final or before another consonant, pronounce them as the nasal vowel [ɑ̃]. Do not pronounce the *m* and *n* consonants unless in liaison.

LL 5.3.13   Read aloud.

champ	[ʃɑ̃]
grand	[grɑ̃]
chantant	[ʃɑ̃ ˈtɑ̃]
cependant	[sə pɑ̃ ˈdɑ̃]
secouant	[sə ku ˈɑ̃]
ambigu	[ɑ̃ bi ˈgy]
galant	[ga ˈlɑ̃]
an	[ɑ̃]

When the letters *am* or *an* are followed by a vowel or another *m* or *n*, do not nasalize them, but pronounce them as [am] and [an].

LL 5.3.14   Read aloud.

tamis	[ta ˈmi]
manifeste	[ma ni ˈfɛ stə]
animer	[a ni ˈme]

au

The letters *au* and *aux* are usually pronounced as close [o].

LL 5.3.15   Read aloud.

au	[o]
Renault	[rə ˈno]
chevaux	[ʃə ˈvo]
sauve	[ˈso və]

There are several exceptions to this rule.

au before *r* is open [ɔ]:

LL 5.3.16   Read aloud.

Fauré	[fɔ ˈre]
aurai	[ɔ ˈre]
restaurant	[re stɔ ˈrɑ̃]

Other exceptional words are:

LL 5.3.17   Read aloud.

automne	[ɔ ˈtɔ nə]
mauvais	[mɔ ˈvɛ]
Paul	[pɔl]

ay

The letters *ay* are usually pronounced as [ɛj]. The sound of [ɛj] is similar to the sound of the letters *ay* in the English word *say* [seɪ].

LL 5.3.18   Read aloud.

payer	[pɛ ˈje]
rayon	[rɛ ˈjɔ̃]

French

Note: Exceptions to this rule are:

LL 5.3.19   Read aloud.

pays	[pe ˈi]
bayadère	[ba ja ˈdɛ rə]
Lafayette	[la fa ˈje tə]

The letter e

The letter *e* in French has a variety of pronunciations, depending upon the following qualifiers. To determine the pronunciation of *e*, ask yourself these four questions.

1. Is there a diacritical mark over the *e*?

2. What letters follow the *e*?

3. Is the letter *e* found as a single letter, or is it part of a letter group?

4. What is the position of *e* in the word? Is it initial, medial, or final?

The pronunciation rules below will help you determine the answers to these questions.

The single letter e

Pronounce *é* as [e].

LL 5.3.20   Read aloud.

été	[e ˈte]
défaut	[de ˈfo]
dictée	[dik ˈte ə]
élément	[e le ˈmã]

Pronounce *è*, *ê*, and *ë* as [ɛ].

LL 5.3.21   Read aloud.

père	[ˈpɛ rə]
forêts	[fɔ ˈrɛ]
sortilège	[sɔr ti ˈlɛ ʒə]
après	[a ˈprɛ]
Noël	[nɔ ˈɛl]
rêver	[rɛ ˈve]

Exception:

LL 5.3.22   Read aloud.

Saint-Saëns	[sẽ ˈsãs]

When *e* occurs before a single consonant followed by a vowel, it is pronounced as [ə].

LL 5.3.23 Read aloud.

cheval	[ʃə 'val]
banderilles	[bɑ̃ də 'ri jə]
premier	[prə 'mje]
venez	[və 'ne]
demain	[də 'mɛ̃]
cheveux	[ʃə 'vø]
jeter	[ʒə 'te]
rayonnement	[rɛ jɔ nə 'mɑ̃]

Note: *e* after another vowel or glide is usually silent.

LL 5.3.24 Read aloud.

gaiement	[gɛ 'mɑ̃]
payement	[pɛj 'mɑ̃]

When *e* occurs before two or more consonants, it is pronounced as [ɛ]. (Note: *e* is pronounced as [ɛ] before the letter *x* which has two *phonetic* consonant sounds, [ks] or [gz].)

LL 5.3.25 Read aloud.

esprit	[ɛs 'pri]
permettre	[pɛr 'mɛ trə]
elle	['ɛ lə]
nerveux	[nɛr 'vø]
est	[ɛ]
servir	[sɛr 'vir]
esclave	[ɛs 'kla və]
verse	['vɛr sə]
exile	[ɛg 'zi lə]
geste	['ʒɛs tə]
expert	[ɛk 'spɛr]
soutanelle	[su ta 'nɛ lə]

French

There are three exceptions to this rule:

1. *e* in initial *ess* or *eff* is close [e].

    LL 5.3.26   Read aloud.

essor	[e 'sɔr]
effort	[e 'fɔr]

2. *e* in the prefix *re-* before two or more consonants is schwa [ə].

    LL 5.3.27   Read aloud.

refrain	[rə 'frɛ̃]
reflux	[rə 'fly]

3. *e* when followed by *m* or *n* and another consonant is [ɑ̃]. (See "em, en" on page 270.)

    LL 5.3.28   Read aloud.

emporte	[ɑ̃ 'pɔr tə]
enrobe	[ɑ̃ 'rɔ bə]

When *e* occurs before a final pronounced consonant, it is pronounced as [ɛ].

LL 5.3.29   Read aloud.

avec	[a 'vɛk]
hôtel	[ɔ 'tɛl]
chef	[ʃɛf]
rappel	[ra 'pɛl]

Note: Usually *r* is a final pronounced consonant. However, after *e*, it is sometimes pronounced, sometimes not. You may need to consult a dictionary. There is only one clear and easy rule: when *er* is a verb ending, pronounce it as [e].

These are examples of words ending in final pronounced *r*. (See next page for discussion of final *er* in nouns and adjectives.)

LL 5.3.30   Read aloud.

hiver	[i 'vɛr]
cher	[ʃɛr]
mer	[mɛr]
ver	[vɛr]

When *e* occurs before a final silent consonant, it is [e], [ɛ], [ə], or silent. (See also "Pronounced and Silent Consonants" on page 251.)

1. When *e* occurs before a final silent consonant, it is usually [e].

    LL 5.3.31   Read aloud.

    | pied | [pje] |
    | allez | [a 'le] |

    Note: It is helpful to think of final *er*, *es*, and *et* as units by themselves.

2. Final *er*

    Pronounce *er* in verb endings (first conjugation infinitives) as [e].

    LL 5.3.32   Read aloud.

    | chanter | [ʃã 'te] |
    | chercher | [ʃɛr 'ʃe] |
    | importer | [ɛ̃ pɔr 'te] |
    | donner | [dɔ 'ne] |
    | rêver | [rɛ 've] |
    | danser | [dã 'se] |
    | monter | [mõ 'te] |
    | refuser | [rə fy 'ze] |
    | aller | [a 'le] |
    | écouter | [e ku 'te] |
    | poser | [po 'ze] |
    | bouler | [bu 'le] |
    | doubler | [du 'ble] |
    | charger | [ʃar 'ʒe] |

    When final *er* occurs in nouns and adjectives, it is sometimes [ɛr] but usually [e]. In endings *-ier* and *-yer*, the *er* is pronounced as [e].

    LL 5.3.33   Read aloud.

    | guerrier | [gɛ 'rje] |
    | danger | [dã 'ʒe] |
    | premier | [prə 'mje] |
    | léger | [le 'ʒe] |
    | berger | [bɛr 'ʒe] |
    | foyer | [fwa 'je] |
    | étranger | [e trã 'ʒe] |
    | portier | [pɔr 'tje] |

boulanger	[bu lɑ ˈʒe]
épicier	[e pi ˈsje]

3. Final *es*

Final *es* in a polysyllable word is silent or schwa [ə], depending on the number of notes provided in the melody. Final *es* as a pluralization occurs frequently in French.

LL 5.3.34   Read aloud.

parles	[ˈpar lə]
elles	[ˈɛ lə]
lettres	[ˈlɛ trə]
belles	[ˈbɛ lə]
écloses	[e ˈklo zə]
noires	[ˈnwa rə]

Final *es* in a monosyllable word is pronounced [e].

LL 5.3.35   Read aloud.

des	[de]
les	[le]
tes	[te]
mes	[me]

Note: Some diction books transcribe final *es* in monosyllables as [e], others as [ɛ]. Actually the vowel sound in these monosyllables might be described as a sound *between* the very close French [e] and the open [ɛ].

4. Final *et*

Final *et* is pronounced [ɛ].

LL 5.3.36   Read aloud.

goulet	[gu ˈlɛ]
filet	[fi ˈlɛ]
flanchet	[flɑ ˈʃɛ]
bouquet	[bu ˈkɛ]

Exception: The monosyllable *et*, meaning *and*, is pronounced close [e].

Final *e* without an accent is silent or schwa [ə]. Final *e* in monosyllables is schwa [ə].

Note: Final *e* in polysyllables, normally silent in spoken French, is pronounced as schwa [ə] in singing when a note in the music is provided. See also "Liaison and Elision" on page 256.

Remember that in French, schwa [ə] is more forward and rounded than the schwa [ə] of English.

LL 5.3.37 Read aloud.

le	[lə]
parle	['par lə]
je	[ʒə]
image	[i 'ma ʒə]
fumée	[fy 'me ə]
embrumée	[ɑ̃ bry 'me ə]

eau

Pronounce *eau* (or *eaux*) as [o].

LL 5.3.38 Read aloud.

beau	[bo]
beaux	[bo]
l'eau	[lo]
ruisseaux	[rɥi 'so]
tombeau	[tõ 'bo]
nouveau	[nu 'vo]

ei

Pronounce *ei* as [ɛ].

LL 5.3.39 Read aloud.

seine	['sɛ nə]
geignard	[ʒɛ 'ɲar]
seize	['sɛ zə]
cheik	[ʃɛk]

Pronounce *eil* and *eill* as [ɛj].

The letters *eil* and *eill*, are composed of the single letter *e* followed by the digraphs *il* and *ill*, which are pronounced as [j]. When *e* is before these letters, it is pronounced as open [ɛ]. The symbols [ɛj] sound very similar to the *ay* in the English word *say* [seɪ].

French

LL 5.3.40   Read aloud.

soleil	[sɔ 'lɛj]
appareilles	[a pa 'rɛ jə]
vermeil	[vɛr 'mɛj]
meilleur	[mɛ 'jœr]
veille	['vɛ jə]
sommeil	[sɔ 'mɛj]

eim, ein

When the letters *eim* or *ein* are final or before another consonant, pronounce them as the nasal vowel [ẽ]. Do not pronounce the *m* and *n* consonants unless in liaison.

LL 5.3.41   Read aloud.

Reims	[rẽs]
plein	[plẽ]
teint	[tẽ]
peindre	['pẽ drə]

When the letters *eim* or *ein* are followed by a vowel or another *m* or *n*, do not nasalize them, but pronounce them as [ɛm] and [ɛn].

LL 5.3.42   Read aloud.

reine	['rɛ nə]
seine	['sɛ nə]

em, en

When the letters *em* or *en* are final or before another consonant, pronounce them as the nasal vowel [ã]. Do not pronounce the *m* and *n* consonants unless in liaison.

LL 5.3.43   Read aloud.

temps	[tã]
enfant	[ã 'fã]
ensemble	[ã 'sã blə]
encor	[ã 'kɔr]

The letters *en* after *i* are pronounced as [ẽ]. Do not pronounce the *n* unless in liaison.

LL 5.3.44   Read aloud.

bien	[bjẽ]
combien	[kõ 'bjẽ]
rien	[rjẽ]
reviens	[rə 'vjẽ]

When the letters *em* or *en* are followed by a vowel or another *m* or *n*, do not nasalize them.

LL 5.3.45   Read aloud.

émission	[e mi 'sjõ]
émule	[e 'my lə]
énervant	[e nɛr 'vɑ̃]
Cène	['sɛ nə]
tenir	[tə 'nir]
tennis	[tɛ 'nis]

Exception: Initial *emm* is nasalized:

LL 5.3.46   Read aloud.

emmancher	[ɑ̃ mɑ̃ 'ʃe]
emmêler	[ɑ̃ mɛ 'le]

LL 5.3.47   Note this word, however:

femme	['fa mə]

The final letters *ent* are pronounced in various ways.

Final *ent* in verbs (third person plural) is silent or schwa [ə], depending on the number of notes in the music.

LL 5.3.48   Read aloud.

parlent	['par lə]
semblent	['sɑ̃ blə]
donnent	['dɔ nə]
envolent	[ɑ̃ 'vɔ lə]
songent	['sõ ʒə]
plaignent	['plɛ ɲə]
tournent	['tur nə]
échangent	[e 'ʃɑ̃ ʒə]

French

tombent	['tõ bə]
disent	['di zə]

Otherwise *ent* in nouns and adjectives is pronounced as [ã].

LL 5.3.49 Read aloud.

firmament	[fir ma 'mã]
patient	[pa 'sjã]
excellent	[ɛk sɛ 'lã]
emplacement	[ã plas 'mã]

eu

When the letters *eu* are in the interior of a word, they are usually pronounced as [œ].

LL 5.3.50 Read aloud.

peuple	['pœ plə]
jeune	[ʒœ 'nə]
heure	['œ rə]
malheur	[ma 'lœr]
seigneur	[sɛ 'ɲœr]
monseigneur	[mõ sɛ 'ɲœr]

There are several exceptions to this rule.

eu before the sound of [z] is [ø].

LL 5.3.51 Read aloud.

creuset	[krø 'zɛ]
malheureuse	[ma lœ 'rø zə]

eû is [ø].

LL 5.3.52 Read aloud.

jeûner	[ʒø 'ne]

Note: *eu* and *eû* in certain tenses of the verb *avoir* are [y]: *eu* [y], *eût* [y], *eusse* ['y sə].

Other exceptions are:

LL 5.3.53 Read aloud.

jeudi	[ʒø 'di]
Europe	[ø 'rɔp]
Euridice	[ø ri 'di sə]

When *eu* is the final sound of the word (not necessarily the final letters), pronounce it as [ø].

LL 5.3.54   Read aloud.

peu	[pø]
honteux	[õ 'tø]
veut	[vø]
malheureux	[ma lœ 'rø]
jeu	[ʒø]
joyeux	[ʒwa 'jø]
queue	[kø] or [kø ə]
bleu, bleue, bleues	[blø] or [blø ə]

Note: Final *-r* and *-rs* are silent in these two words:

LL 5.3.55   Read aloud.

monsieur (singular)	[mɔ 'sjø]
messieurs (plural)	[mɛ 'sjø]

Note: When the normally silent final consonant is pronounced in liaison, it does not change the preceding vowel sound.

LL 5.3.56   Read aloud.

peut-être	[pø 'tɛ trə]

The letter *i* in French has a variety of pronunciations, depending upon the following qualifiers. To determine the pronunciation of *i*, ask yourself these four questions.

1. Is there a diacritical mark over the *i*?

2. What letters follow the *i*?

3. Is the letter *i* found as a single letter, or is it part of a letter group?

4. What is the position of *i* in the word? Is it initial, medial, or final?

The pronunciation rules below will help you determine the answers to these questions.

The letter

i

French

The single letter i

When the single letter *î* or *i* is final or before a consonant, it is pronounced [i].

Note: The letter *i* has two pronunciations in French: as [i] in *beet* [bit] and as [j] in *you* [ju]. The French letter *i* is never pronounced as Americans say *ih* [ɪ] as in *bit* [bɪt].

LL 5.3.57   Read aloud.

dîner	[di 'ne]
île	['i lə]
ici	[i 'si]
divisible	[di vi 'zi blə]
finir	[fi 'nir]
puisque	['pɥis kə]

When *i* precedes a "stressed" vowel (a vowel in the same syllable other than mute *e*), it is pronounced as the glide [j].

LL 5.3.58   Read aloud.

ie:	hier	[jer]
	pieds	[pje]
	Charpentier	[ʃar pɑ̃ 'tje]
ieu:	dieu	[djø]
	cieux	[sjø]
ien:	bien	[bjẽ]
	vient	[vjẽ]
	rien	[rjẽ]
	reviens	[rə 'vjẽ]
ion:	nation	[nɑ 'sjõ]

There is one exception to this rule: When *i* follows *l* or *r*, pronounce it as [ij].

LL 5.3.59   Read aloud.

oublions	[u bli 'jõ]
prier	[pri 'je]

When the single letter *i* precedes mute *e*, it is pronounced as [i].

> Note: French speakers rarely pronounce the mute *e*. Singers, however, pronounce mute *e* as schwa [ə] when there is a note provided in the melody.

1. When *ie* or *ies* is final in a word or syllable, pronounce these letter groups as [i] or [i ə] depending on the number of notes.

    LL 5.3.60   Read aloud.

sortie	[sɔr ˈti ə]
partie	[par ˈti ə]
Italie	[i ta ˈli ə]
philosophie	[fi lɔ zɔ ˈfi ə]
raniement	[ra ni (ə) ˈmã]
vie, vies	[ˈvi ə]

2. When *ient* is final in third person plural verb endings, pronounce it as [i] or [i ə], again depending upon the number of notes.

    LL 5.3.61   Read aloud.

rient	[ri] or [ˈri ə]

    > Note: Final *-aient* is pronounced [ɛ].

il, ill, ille

There are several pronunciations for the letter groups *il*, *ill*, and *ille*. The most common spelling and pronunciation is described under Rule 1.

1. In French, final *il* and medial *ill* are digraphs, pronounced as the single sound [j]. These letters normally follow another vowel as in the word *aille*, where *ille* follows the letter *a*.

    > Note: When *il* follows a vowel in a word, as in *travail*, the vowels *ai* do not pair up to form a unit. Instead, the *il* forms a unit and *a* is by itself, resulting in the sound of [a] followed by the glide [j].

    LL 5.3.62   Read aloud.

travail	[tra ˈvaj]

    In each of the following words, *il* and *ill* are pronounced as [j] following the underlined vowel.

    LL 5.3.63   Read aloud.

deuil	[dœj]
corail	[kɔ ˈraj]

French

détaillant	[de ta ˈjã]
travailler	[tra va ˈje]
abeille	[a ˈbɛ jə]
grenouille	[grə ˈnu jə]
cailloux	[ka ˈju]

Note: Final -*ile* is not included in this rule. The word *aile* forms two syllables.

LL 5.3.64   Read aloud.

ai-le	[ˈɛ lə]

2. When medial *ill* follows a consonant, pronounce it as [ij].

LL 5.3.65   Read aloud.

gentille	[ʒã ˈti jə]
grilles	[ˈgri jə]
charmille	[ʃar ˈmi jə]
brillant	[bri ˈjã]
brille	[ˈbri jə]
fille	[ˈfi jə]
papillons	[pa pi ˈjõ]
famille	[fa ˈmi jə]

Note: Final -*il* is not included in this rule.

LL 5.3.66   Read aloud.

profil	[prɔ ˈfil]

Note this irregular pronunciation.

LL 5.3.67   Read aloud.

fils	[fis]

3. In the three words *mille*, *tranquille*, and *ville*, and their derivatives, the letter groups *ill* and *ille* are pronounced as [il]. A memory "tickler" is to recall the phrase "a million tranquil villages."

LL 5.3.68   Read aloud.

ville	[ˈvi lə]
village	[vi ˈla ʒə]
villa	[vi ˈla]
mille	[ˈmi lə]
tranquille	[trã ˈki lə]
million	[mi ˈljõ]

4. When *il* or *ill* is initial in the word, it is pronounced as [il].

LL 5.3.69 Read aloud.

illusion	[i ly 'zjõ]
ils	[il]
illicite	[i li 'si tə]
il	[il]

im, in

When the letters *im* or *in* are final or before another consonant, pronounce them as the nasal vowel [ɛ̃]. Do not pronounce the *m* and *n* consonants unless in liaison.

LL 5.3.70 Read aloud.

importune	[ɛ̃ pɔr 'ty nə]
vin	[vɛ̃]
timbre	['tɛ̃ brə]
inviter	[ɛ̃ vi 'te]

When the letters *im* or *in* are followed by a vowel sound or another *m* or *n*, do not nasalize them. Pronounce them as [im] and [in].

LL 5.3.71 Read aloud.

timonier	[ti mɔ 'nje]
tinette	[ti 'nɛ tə]
inhabité	[i na bi 'te]
innocent	[in ɔ 'sã]
inimitable	[i ni mi 'ta blə]
immobile	[im mɔ 'bi lə]

The letter O

The letter *o* in French has a variety of pronunciations, depending upon the following qualifiers. To determine the pronunciation of *o*, ask yourself these four questions.

1. Is there a diacritical mark over the *o*?

2. What letters follow the *o*?

3. Is the letter *o* found as a single letter, or is it part of a letter group?

4. What is the position of *o* in the word? Is it initial, medial, or final?

The pronunciation rules below will help you determine the answers to these questions.

French

The single letter o

The letter *o* is usually pronounced [ɔ].

LL 5.3.72 Read aloud.

comme	['kɔ mə]
cloches	['klɔ ʃə]
bonne	['bɔ nə]
gorge	['gɔr ʒə]
potager	[pɔ ta 'ʒe]
fort	[fɔr]
soleil	[sɔ 'lɛj]
toréador	[tɔ re a 'dɔr]

There are three major exceptions to this rule:

1. *o* before [z] is close [o].

LL 5.3.73 Read aloud.

rose	['ro zə]
poser	[po 'ze]
chose	['ʃo zə]

2. *o* as the final sound of a word is close [o].

LL 5.3.74 Read aloud.

galop	[ga 'lo]
écho	[e 'ko]
sanglot	[sɑ̃ 'glo]
pierrot	[pjɛ 'ro]
kilo	[ki 'lo]
flot	[flo]

Note these pronunciations:

LL 5.3.75 Read aloud.

l'os (the bone)	[lɔs]
les os (the bones)	[le zo]

3. *ô* is pronounced as close [o].

LL 5.3.76 Read aloud.

tôt	[to]
nôtre	['no trə]

| drôle | ['dro lə] |
| vôtre | ['vo trə] |

One exception:

LL 5.3.77   Read aloud.

| hôtel | [ɔ 'tɛl] |

oeu

The letters *oeu* in the interior of a word are usually pronounced [œ].

LL 5.3.78   Read aloud.

coeur	[kœr]
boeuf	[bœf]
oeuf	[œf]

The letters *oeu* as the final sound of a word (not necessarily the final letters) are usually pronounced [ø].

LL 5.3.79   Read aloud.

| boeufs | [bø] |
| voeux | [vø] |

oi

The letters *oi* are usually pronounced [wa].

LL 5.3.80   Read aloud.

toi	[twa]
droit	[drwa]
noir	[nwar]
crois	[krwa]
voici	[vwa 'si]
doigts	[dwa]
vois	[vwa]
voix	[vwa]

Exception:

LL 5.3.81   Read aloud.

| trois | [twɑ] |

oin

When the letters *oin* are final or before another consonant, pronounce them as [wẽ]. Do not pronounce the *n* unless in liaison.

LL 5.3.82 Read aloud.

loin	[lwẽ]
besoin	[bə 'zwẽ]

om, on

When the letters *om* or *on* are final or before another consonant, pronounce them as [õ]. Do not pronounce the *m* and *n* consonants unless in liaison.

LL 5.3.83 Read aloud.

gondole	[gõ 'dɔ lə]
donc	[dõ] or [dõk]
maison	[mɛ 'zõ]
rond	[rõ]
pompe	['põ pə]
nom	[nõ]

Exceptions:

monsieur	[mə 'sjø]
bonheur	[bɔ 'nœr]

When the letters *om* and *on* are followed by a vowel or another *m* or *n*, do not nasalize them, but pronounce them as [ɔm] and [ɔn].

LL 5.3.84 Read aloud.

homme	['ɔ mə]
honorer	[ɔ nɔ 're]
donne	['dɔ nə]
domaine	[dɔ 'mɛ nə]
madone	[ma 'dɔ nə]
automne	[ɔ 'tɔ nə]

ou

The letters *ou*, *où*, and *oû* are usually pronounced [u].

LL 5.3.85   Read aloud.

où	[u]
goût	[gu]
fou	[fu]
loup	[lu]
doux	[du]
tout	[tu]
coup	[ku]
nouvelle	[nu 'vɛ lə]
pour	[pur]
court	[kur]
sourd	[sur]
toujours	[tu 'ʒur]
amour	[a 'mur]
sourire	[su 'ri rə]

When the letters *ou* occur before a "stressed" vowel (a vowel in the same syllable other than mute *e*), they are usually pronounced as the glide [w] as in the word *oui* [wi] (*yes*).

LL 5.3.86   Read aloud.

oui	[wi]
ouest	[wɛst]

When the letters *ou* occur before a mute *e*, they are pronounced as [u] or [u ə] depending on the number of notes.

LL 5.3.87   Read aloud.

dénouement	[de nu ə 'mā]

oy

The letters *oy* are pronounced [waj].

Note: For a full discussion of *y* occuring between two vowels see "The Single Letter *y*" on page 285.

LL 5.3.88   Read aloud.

noyée	[nwa 'je ə]
royal	[rwa 'jal]
foyer	[fwa 'je]

French

The letter u

The letter *u* in French has a variety of pronunciations, depending upon the following qualifiers. To determine the pronunciation of *u*, ask yourself these four questions.

1. Is there a diacritical mark over the *u*?
2. What letters follow the *u*?
3. Is the letter *u* found as a single letter, or is it part of a letter group?
4. What is the position of *u* in the word? Is it initial, medial, or final?

The pronunciation rules below will help you determine the answers to these questions.

The single letter u

The French letter *u* is pronounced as the mixed vowel [y]. It is never pronounced [u] as in the English word *boot* nor [ju] as in the word *use*. The letter *u* in French is often used in the vowel combinations of *eu*, *oeu*, *ou*, and *ue*, each of which has its own pronunciation. See the alphabetical listings for combined spellings with *u*.

Note: See "The Mixed Vowels" on page 240 for a full description of the sound [y], which is formed with the lips in the [u] position and the tongue in [i] position.

The letter *û* is pronounced [y].

LL 5.3.89   Read aloud.

| dû | [dy] |

When the letter *u* is final or before a consonant, it is pronounced [y].

LL 5.3.90   Read aloud.

une	['y nə]
inutile	[i ny 'ti lə]
salut	[sa 'ly]
connu	[kɔ 'ny]
murmure	[myr 'my rə]
union	[y 'njõ]
sud	[syd]
studio	[sty 'djɔ]

French

The letter *u* before a "stressed" vowel (a vowel in the same syllable other than mute *e*) is usually the glide [ɥ].

> Note: See "Glides" on page 243 for a full description of the sound [ɥ] which you produce by quickly moving through the pronunciation of [y].
>
> LL 5.3.91   Read aloud.
>
> | nuit | [nɥi] |
> |---------|------------|
> | puisque | ['pɥis kə] |
> | suave | ['sɥa və] |
> | bruit | [brɥi] |
> | lueur | [lɥœr] |
> | suis | [sɥi] |
>
> Exception: Some words are pronounced as two syllables:
>
> LL 5.3.92   Read aloud.
>
> | cruelle | [kry 'ɛl] |
> |---------|------------|
> | fluide | [fly 'i də] |

The letter *u* before a final mute *e* is usually pronounced [y]. (See also "The letter group ue" below.)

LL 5.3.93   Read aloud.

revue	[rə 'vy ə]
vue	['vy ə]

The letter *u* after *g* and before a vowel is silent.

LL 5.3.94   Read aloud.

guitare	[gi 'ta rə]
guet	[gɛ]

ue

When the letters *ue* are followed by *il, ill,* or *ille,* they are pronounced as open [œ]. (See "The Mixed Vowels" on page 240, for a description of the sound [œ].)

LL 5.3.95   Read aloud.

cercueil	[sɛr 'kœj]
orgueil	[ɔr 'gœj]

French

um, un

When the letters *um* or *un* are final or before another consonant, pronounce them as [œ̃]. Do not pronounce the *m* and *n* consonants unless in liaison.

LL 5.3.96   Read aloud.

parfum	[par 'fœ̃]
chacun	[ʃa 'kœ̃]
humble	['œ̃ blə]
un	[œ̃]

When the letters *um* and *un* are followed by a vowel or another *m* or *n*, do no nasalize them, but pronounce them as [ym] and [yn].

LL 5.3.97   Read aloud.

une	['y nə]
plume	['ply mə]

The letter y

The letter *y* in French has a variety of pronunciations, depending upon the following qualifiers. To determine the pronunciation of *y*, ask yourself these three questions.

1. What letters follow the *y*?

2. Is the letter *y* found as a single letter, or is it part of a letter group?

3. What is the position of *y* in the word? Is it initial, medial, or final?

The pronunciation rules below will help you determine the answers to these questions.

The single letter y

When the letter *y* is initial in a word, it is pronounced as [j].

LL 5.3.98   Read aloud.

yeux	[jø]
yeuse	['jø zə]

When the letter *y* occurs before or after a consonant, it is pronounced as [i].

LL 5.3.99   Read aloud.

lyre	['li rə]

martyr	[mar 'tir]
style	['sti lə]
lycée	[li 'se ə]

When the letter *y* occurs between two vowels, think of it as representing the letter group *ii*. The first *i* combines with the preceding vowels and the second *i* combines with the next syllable, becoming the vowel sound [j]. In the word *rayon*, for example, after mentally substituting *ii* for *y*, the syllables would be spelled *rai-ion* [rɛ jõ].

LL 5.3.100   Read aloud.

royal	=	roi-ial	[rwa 'jal]
fuyard	=	fui-iard	[fɥi 'jar]

ym, yn

When the letters *ym* or *yn* are final or followed by another consonant, pronounce them as the nasal vowel [ɛ̃]. Do not pronounce the *m* and *n* consonants unless in liaison.

LL 5.3.101   Read aloud.

thym	[tɛ̃]
syndicat	[sɛ̃ di 'ka]
symbole	[sɛ̃ 'bɔ lə]
symphonie	[sɛ̃ fɔ 'ni ə]
synthèse	[sɛ̃ 'tɛ zə]

When the letters *ym* and *yn* are followed by a vowel or another *m* or *n*, do not nasalize them, but pronounce them as [im] and [in].

LL 5.3.102   Read aloud.

hymne	[imn] or ['im nə]

French

§ French Consonants in Detail

b

Pronounce the letters *b* or *bb* as [b].

LL 5.4.01   Read aloud.

beau	[bo]
ballades	[ba ˈla də]
blanc	[blɑ̃]
oublier	[u bli ˈje]
baiser	[be ˈze]
arbres	[ˈar brə]
belles	[ˈbɛ lə]
double	[ˈdu blə]
abbesse	[a ˈbɛ sə]
gabbro	[ga ˈbro]

When *b* is final, it is sometimes pronounced as [b].

LL 5.4.02   Read aloud.

club	[klyb]
snob	[snɔb]
Jacob	[ʒa ˈkob]
nabab	[na ˈbab]

When *b* is final and follows a nasal consonant, do not pronounce it. It is silent.

LL 5.4.03   Read aloud.

plomb	[plõ]

When *b* is before *s* or *t*, pronounce it as unvoiced [p].

LL 5.4.04   Read aloud.

absent	[ap ˈsɑ̃]
obtus	[ɔp ˈty]
absorber	[ap sɔr ˈbe]
obtenir	[ɔp tə ˈnir]

French

C

When *c* is followed by *a, o, u,* or a *consonant*, pronounce it as [k].

LL 5.4.05 Read aloud.

académie	[a ka de 'mi ə]
composer	[kõ po 'ze]
cause	['ko zə]
encore	[ã 'kɔ rə]
catholique	[ka tɔ 'li kə]
conduit	[kõ 'dɥi]
captivité	[kap ti vi 'te]
cuisine	[kɥi 'zi nə]
âcre	['ɑ krə]
cueillir	[kœ 'jir]
action	[ak 'sjõ]
sacre	['sa krə]
contacteur	[kõ tak 'tœr]
octavo	[ɔk ta 'vo]

When *c* is followed by *e, i,* or *y*, pronounce it as [s].

LL 5.4.06 Read aloud.

cède	['sɛ də]
pièce	['pjɛ sə]
cieux	[sjø]
licence	[li 'sã sə]
ciel	[sjɛl]
facile	[fa 'si lə]
cigarette	[si ga 'rɛ tə]
cygne	['si ɲə]
concierge	[kõ 'sjɛr ʒə]
radiance	[ra 'djã sə]

When *c* is final, it is usually pronounced as [k].

LL 5.4.07 Read aloud.

parc	[park]
lac	[lak]
avec	[a 'vɛk]
Poulenc	[pu 'lẽk]

Exception: final *c* is silent in *estomac, tabac, croc, escroc.*

When *c* is final and follows *n*, it is usually silent. Read aloud.

LL 5.4.08 Read aloud.

jonc	[ʒō]
blanc	[blā]
donc	[dō]

Note: When spoken with emphasis, the final *c* is pronounced in this word.

LL 5.4.09 Read aloud.

donc	[dōk]

When *cc* is followed by *a, o, u,* or a *consonant,* pronounce it as [k].

LL 5.4.10 Read aloud.

succulent	[sy ky 'lā]
accaparant	[a ka pa 'rā]

When *cc* is followed by *e, i,* or *y,* pronounce it as [ks].

LL 5.4.11 Read aloud.

succès	[syk 'sɛ]
accent	[ak 'sā]
accélérer	[ak se le 're]
accident	[ak si 'dā]

Pronounce *ç* as [s].

The hooked diacritical mark under the *c* is called a *cédille* [se 'di jə].

LL 5.4.12 Read aloud.

suçon	[sy 'sō]
deçà	[də 'sa]
garçon	[gar 'sō]
façon	[fa 'sō]

Pronounce *ch* as [ʃ].

The IPA symbol [ʃ] is the sound of *sh* as in *she.* It is called *esh.*

LL 5.4.13 Read aloud.

chose	['ʃo zə]
floche	['flɔ ʃə]
échotier	[e ʃɔ 'tje]
faucher	[fo 'ʃe]

chemin	[ʃə 'mẽ]
chacun	[ʃa 'kœ̃]

Exception: In a few words of Greek derivation, *ch* is [k].

LL 5.4.14   Read aloud.

Christ	[krist]
orchestre	[ɔr 'kɛs trə]
écho	[e 'ko]
chœur	[kœr]

Pronounce *cqu* as [k].

LL 5.4.15   Read aloud.

acquisition	[a ki zi 'sjõ]
acquérir	[a ke 'rir]
acquitter	[a ki 'te]

When *ct* is final, pronounce it as [kt] or silent. Refer to a dictionary for the pronunciation of final *ct*.

LL 5.4.16   Read aloud.

[kt]		silent	
direct	[di 'rɛkt]	respect	[rɛs 'pɛ]
infect	[ẽ 'fɛkt]	aspect	[as 'pɛ]
		instinct	[ẽ 'stẽ]

Pronounce *d* or *dd* as [d].

LL 5.4.17   Read aloud.

diable	['dja blə]
admirable	[ad mi 'ra blə]
désoler	[de zɔ 'le]
addition	[a di 'sjõ]

When *d* is final, it is usually silent.

LL 5.4.18   Read aloud.

pied	[pje]
pillard	[pi 'jar]
grand	[grã]
quand	[kã]

French

When *d* is in liaison, pronounce it as [t].

LL 5.4.19   Read aloud.

| grand‿arbre | [grɑ̃ tar brə] |

f

Pronounce *f* or *ff* as [f].

LL 5.4.20   Read aloud.

foyer	[fwa 'je]
enfant	[ɑ̃ 'fɑ̃]
flambeau	[flɑ̃ 'bo]
référence	[re fe 'rɑ̃ sə]
officier	[ɔ fi 'sje]
affection	[a fɛk 'sjɔ̃]

Note: *e* before *ff* is pronounced close [e].

LL 5.4.21   Read aloud.

| effort | [e 'fɔr] |
| effroi | [e 'frwa] |

When *f* is final, usually pronounce it as [f].

LL 5.4.22   Read aloud.

soif	[swaf]
chef	[ʃɛf]
neuf	[nœf]
subjectif	[syb ʒɛk 'tif]
décisif	[de si 'zif]
comparatif	[kɔ̃ pa ra 'tif]

When *f* is in liaison, pronounce it as [v].

LL 5.4.23   Read aloud.

| neuf‿heures | [nœ 'vœ rə] |

g

When *g* is followed by *a, o, u,* or a *consonant,* pronounce it as [g].

Note: *g* pronounced as [g] is called *hard g*.

LL 5.4.24   Read aloud.

| goût | [gu] |
| grève | ['grɛ və] |

gant	[gã]
glotte	['glɔ tə]
guerre	['gɛ rə]
navigateur	[na vi ga 'tœr]

When *g* is followed by *e, i,* or *y*, pronounce it as [ʒ].

> Note: *g* pronounced as [ʒ] is called *soft g*. The symbol [ʒ] represents the sound in the English words *vision* ['vɪ ʒən] and *azure* ['æ ʒʊr].

LL 5.4.25 Read aloud.

gentille	[ʒã 'ti jə]
gypse	['ʒip sə]
girafe	[ʒi 'ra fə]
geste	['ʒɛs tə]
courage	[ku 'ra ʒə]
partage	[par 'ta ʒə]
sabotage	[sa bɔ 'ta ʒə]
énergie	[e nɛr 'ʒi ə]

When *g* is final, it is usually silent.

LL 5.4.26 Read aloud.

sang	[sã]
long	[lõ]
poing	[pwẽ]
seing	[sẽ]

When *g* is in liaison, pronounce it as [k].

LL 5.4.27 Read aloud.

suer sang‿et eau (*to sweat blood*)	[sɥe sã ke 'o]

When *ge* is followed by *a* or *o*, pronounce it as [ʒ].

LL 5.4.28 Read aloud.

pigeon	[pi 'ʒõ]
nageoire	[na 'ʒwa rə]
égrugeoir	[e gry 'ʒwar]
bourgeois	[bur 'ʒwa]

French

When *gg* is followed by *a, o, u,* or a *consonant,* pronounce it as [g].

LL 5.4.29   Read aloud.

| aggraver | [a gra 've] |

When *gg* is followed by *e, i,* or *y,* pronounce it as [gʒ].

LL 5.4.30   Read aloud.

| suggérer | [syg ʒe 're] |
| suggestion | [syg ʒɛs 'tjõ] |

Pronounce *gn* as [ɲ].

The sound of enya [ɲ] does not exist in English. It is similar to the [nj] in the English word *onion*. See "The Enya" on page 251 for a full discussion of this sound.

LL 5.4.31   Read aloud.

consigner	[kõ si 'ɲe]
peigner	[pɛ 'ɲe]
compagnon	[kõ pa 'ɲõ]
montagne	[mõ 'ta ɲə]

The letters *gt* are silent.

LL 5.4.32   Read aloud.

| doigt | [dwa] |

When *gu* is followed by a *vowel,* pronounce it as [g].

LL 5.4.33   Read aloud.

| gigue | ['ʒi gə] |
| fatiguer | [fa ti 'ge] |

Exception: In the word *aiguille* and its derivatives, *gu* is pronounced [gɥ]: [e 'gɥi jə].

h

In French there are two classifications of *h,* mute and aspirate. Both classifications are silent, except during expressions of great intensity.

The mute *h* and aspirate *h* classifications become significant when words are linked: liaison and elision are permitted with mute *h,* but forbidden with aspirate *h.*

To identify aspirate *h,* refer to a dictionary, where you will find it indicated by a diacritical mark, usually an asterisk (*).

French

LL 5.4.34   Read aloud.

Mute h		*Aspirate h	
hélas	[e 'lɑs]	*haut	[o]
heure	['œ rə]	*habler	[ɑ 'ble]
herbe	['ɛr bə]	*halte	['al tə]
inhabité	[i na bi 'te]	*hideuse	[i 'dø zə]

Note: In words such as *inhabité*, the *in* before *h* is not nasalized.

Read aloud and link words with initial mute *h*.

LL 5.4.35   Read aloud.

des‿hirondelles	[de zi rõ 'dɛ lə]
votre‿horizon	[vɔ trɔ ri 'zõ]
la gerbe‿hélas	[la ʒɛr be 'lɑs]

Read aloud and do not link words with initial aspirate *h*.

LL 5.4.36   Read aloud.

les hautes-contre	[le o tə 'kõ trə]

j

Pronounce *j* as [ʒ].

LL 5.4.37   Read aloud.

jouer	[ʒu 'e]
jouir	[ʒu 'ir]
jeune	['ʒœ nə]
jet	[ʒɛ]
je	[ʒə]
joie	['ʒwa ə]
Jean	[ʒɑ̃]
jardin	[ʒar 'dɛ̃]

k

Pronounce *k* as [k].

LL 5.4.38   Read aloud.

kimono	[ki mɔ 'no]
kiosque	['kjɔs kə]
kilo	[ki 'lo]
kaki	[ka 'ki]

French

1

Pronounce *l* as [l].

LL 5.4.39   Read aloud.

larme	[ˈlar mə]
lecture	[lɛk ˈty rə]
Napoléon	[na pɔ le ˈō]
nominal	[nɔ mi ˈnal]

When *l* is final, usually pronounce it as [l].

LL 5.4.40   Read aloud.

idéal	[i de ˈal]
mal	[mal]
nominal	[nɔ mi ˈnal]
appel	[a ˈpɛl]
fil	[fil]
profil	[prɔ ˈfil]

Pronounce *ll* as [l].

LL 5.4.41   Read aloud.

pelle	[ˈpɛ lə]
follet	[fɔ ˈlɛ]
ballet	[ba ˈlɛ]
tulle	[ˈty lə]
calleuse	[ka ˈlø zə]
selle	[ˈsɛ lə]

Exceptions: When *il* or *ill* follows a vowel (*corail*), the combination is pronounced [j]. When *ill* follows a consonant sound (*gentille, fille*), it is usually pronounced [ij].

LL 5.4.42   Read aloud.

corail	[kɔ ˈraj]
gentille	[ʒɑ̃ ˈti jə]
fille	[ˈfi jə]

(See "il, ill, ille" on page 275.)

However, in the three words *mille, tranquille,* and *ville,* and their derivatives, the letter group *ill* is pronounced as [il]. A memory "tickler" is to recall the phrase "a million tranquil villages."

French

LL 5.4.43 Read aloud.

mille	['mi lə]
ville	['vi lə]
tranquille	[trɑ̃ 'ki lə]
village	[vi 'la ʒə]

Pronounce *m* as [m].

LL 5.4.44 Read aloud.

malheur	[ma 'lœr]
estime	[ɛs 'ti mə]
moduler	[mɔ 'dy lə]
limite	[li 'mi tə]
timide	[ti 'mi də]
gémir	[ʒe 'mir]

Pronounce *mm* as [m].

LL 5.4.45 Read aloud.

comme	['kɔ mə]
commerce	[kɔ 'mɛr sə]
nommer	[nɔ 'me]

When *m* is combined with a nasal vowel, it is silent. (See "Nasal Vowels" on page 245 for details.)

LL 5.4.46 Read aloud.

parfum	[par 'fœ̃]
timbre	['tɛ̃ brə]
combat	[kɔ̃ 'ba]
humble	['œ̃ blə]
impayable	[ɛ̃ pɛ 'ja blə]
champs	[ʃɑ̃]

When a silent *m* that follows a nasal vowel is pronounced in liaison, pronounce the *m* as [m].

LL 5.4.47 Read aloud.

nom‿à tiroirs	[nɔ̃ ma ti 'rwar]

n

Pronounce *n* as [n].

LL 5.4.48 Read aloud.

neige	[ˈnɛ ʒə]
nez	[nɛ]
raffine	[ra ˈfi nə]
nombre	[ˈnõ brə]

Pronounce *nn* as [n].

LL 5.4.49 Read aloud.

donne	[ˈdɔ nə]
abonne	[a ˈbɔ nə]

When *n* is combined with a nasal vowel, it is silent. (See "Nasal Vowels" on page 245 for details.)

LL 5.4.50 Read aloud.

non	[nõ]
bon	[bõ]
craindre	[ˈkrɛ̃ drə]
grand	[grã]
ensemble	[ã ˈsã blə]
montre	[ˈmõ trə]

When a silent *n* that follows a nasal vowel is pronounced in liaison, pronounce the *n* as [n].

LL 5.4.51 Read aloud.

en‿aimant	[ã nɛ ˈmã]
son‿âme	[sõ ˈnɑ mə]

When *ng* is final, it is silent.

LL 5.4.52 Read aloud.

poing	[pwɛ̃]

p

Pronounce *p* as [p].

LL 5.4.53 Read aloud.

père	[ˈpɛ rə]
impression	[ɛ̃ prɛ ˈsjõ]

French

pas	[pɑ]
spirituelle	[spi ri 'tyɛ lə]
couple	['ku plə]
plain	[plẽ]

When *p* is final, it is usually silent.

LL 5.4.54   Read aloud.

trop	[tro]
beaucoup	[bo 'ku]
corps	[kɔr]
loup	[lu]

The *p* in the letter group *mpt* is silent.

LL 5.4.55   Read aloud.

compter	[kõ 'te]
compte	[kõ 'tə]
escompte	[ɛs 'kõ tə]
exempt	[eg 'zã]

Pronounce *ph* as [f].

LL 5.4.56   Read aloud.

Joseph	[ʒɔ 'zɛf]
morphine	[mɔr 'fi nə]
phrase	['frɑ zə]
colophane	[kɔ lɔ 'fa nə]

Pronounce *pp* as [p].

LL 5.4.57   Read aloud.

application	[a pli ka 'sjõ]
support	[sy 'pɔr]

Pronounce *qu* as [k].

LL 5.4.58   Read aloud.

quand	[kã]
qualité	[ka li 'te]
liqueur	[li 'kœr]
musique	[my 'zi kə]

q

French

que	[kə]
lorsque	[ˈlɔr skə]
croquet	[krɔ ˈkɛ]
acquis	[a ˈki]

Exception: In a few words, *qu* is pronounced [kw].

LL 5.4.59   Read aloud.

quarterne	[kwa ˈtɛr nə]
quatuor	[kwa ˈtɥɔr]
quadruple	[kwa ˈdry plə]

When *q* is final, pronounce it as [k].

LL 5.4.60   Read aloud.

coq	[kɔk]
cinq	[sẽk]

r

Pronounce *r* as flipped [r].

LL 5.4.61   Read aloud.

regard	[rə ˈgar]
régale	[re ˈga lə]
refuser	[rə fy ˈze]
ronde	[ˈrõ də]
tremble	[ˈtrã blə]
timbre	[ˈtẽ brə]

Pronounce *rr* as flipped [r].

LL 5.4.62   Read aloud.

terre	[ˈtɛ rə]
terrible	[tɛ ˈri blə]

When *r* is final, usually pronounce it as flipped [r].

LL 5.4.63   Read aloud.

espoir	[ɛs ˈpwar]
pour	[pur]
miroir	[mi ˈrwar]
coeur	[kœr]
enfer	[ã ˈfɛr]

When singing French, pronounce the letter r as a flipped [r] or trilled [r̄]. Although in speaking French, you may use a uvular [ʀ], which is a standard pronunciation in the vicinity of Paris, do not use a uvular [ʀ] in singing. A single flip or two or three flaps of the tip of the tongue is preferable. This chapter uses the symbol [r] to represent the tongue tip r.

amour	[a 'mur]
or	[ɔr]
hiver	[i 'vɛr]

When *r* is in final *er, ier,* or *yer* in some nouns and adjectives, it is usually silent.

LL 5.4.64 Read aloud.

routier	[ru 'tje]
communier	[kɔ my 'nje]
foyer	[fwa 'je]
léger	[le 'ʒe]

Note: Final *-r* and *-rs* are silent in these words:

LL 5.4.65 Read aloud.

monsieur	[mə 'sjø]
messieurs	[mɛ 'sjø]

When *r* is in final *er* in verbs, it is silent.

LL 5.4.66 Read aloud.

chanter	[ʃɑ̃ 'te]
baiser	[be 'ze]
parler	[par 'le]
manger	[mɑ̃ 'ʒe]

S

Usually pronounce *s* as [s].

LL 5.4.67 Read aloud.

saucée	[so 'se ə]
séance	[se 'ɑ̃ sə]
sport	[spɔr]
sensualité	[sɑ̃ sɥa li 'te]
posture	[pɔs 'ty rə]
escorte	[ɛs 'kɔr tə]

Pronounce *ss* as [s].

LL 5.4.68 Read aloud.

défausser	[de fo 'se]
florissant	[flɔ ri 'sɑ̃]

French

tasse	[ˈtɑ sə]
assimiler	[a si mi ˈle]

When *s* occurs between vowels, pronounce it as [z].

LL 5.4.69 Read aloud.

malheureuse	[ma lœ ˈrø zə]
honteuse	[õ ˈtø zə]
fusant	[fy ˈzɑ̃]
maison	[mɛ ˈzõ]

When *s* is final, it is usually silent.

LL 5.4.70 Read aloud.

tous	[tu]
las	[la]
repos	[rə ˈpo]
des	[de]
pas	[pɑ]
déclos	[de ˈklo]

Note: There are a few common words in which the final *s* is pronounced: *bis, hélas, Saint-Saëns,* and *lis*.

An *s* may be added to a word for pluralization, as in English, but it is silent and does not change the pronunciation of the word.

LL 5.4.71 Read aloud.

belle	[ˈbɛ lə]	belles	[ˈbɛ lə]

When *s* is in liaison, pronounce it as [z].

LL 5.4.72 Read aloud.

sans‿amour	[sɑ̃ za ˈmur]
prends‿un	[prɑ̃ ˈzœ̃]

When *sc* is followed by *a, o, u,* or a *consonant,* pronounce it as [sk].

LL 5.4.73 Read aloud.

scandale	[skɑ̃ ˈda lə]
scolastique	[skɔ lɑs ˈti kə]
sculpture	[skyl ˈty rə]
scruter	[skry ˈte]

French

When *sc* is followed by *e* or *i*, pronounce it as [s].

LL 5.4.74   Read aloud.

sciant	[sjɑ̃]
sceptre	['sɛp trə]
science	['sjɑ̃ sə]
adolescent	[a dɔ lɛ 'sɑ̃]
scintillant	[sɛ̃ ti 'jɑ̃]
scion	[sjɔ̃]
sceau	[so]
descendre	[de 'sɑ̃ drə]

Usually pronounce *sch* as [ʃ].

The symbol *esh* [ʃ] represents the sound of *sh* as in *she*.

LL 5.4.75   Read aloud.

schéma	['ʃe ma]
schisme	['ʃis mə]

Pronounce *t* as [t].

LL 5.4.76   Read aloud.

tous	[tu]
spectacle	[spɛk 'ta klə]
total	[tɔ 'tal]
tension	[tɑ̃ 'sjɔ̃]
tendre	['tɑ̃ drə]
compte	['kɔ̃ tə]

Pronounce *tt* as [t].

LL 5.4.77   Read aloud.

quitter	[ki 'te]
flottille	[flɔ 'ti jə]

When *t* is final, it is silent.

LL 5.4.78   Read aloud.

et	[e]
esprit	[ɛs 'pri]
saint	[sɛ̃]
enfant	[ɑ̃ 'fɑ̃]

French

| trait | [trɛ] |
| complet | [kõ ˈplɛ] |

Pronounce *th* as [t].

LL 5.4.79 Read aloud.

| théâtre | [te ˈɑ trə] |
| éthéré | [e te ˈre] |

When *ti* occurs in the noun endings *-tion* or *-tience*, pronounce it as [sj].

LL 5.4.80 Read aloud.

traction	[trak ˈsjõ]
élection	[e lɛk ˈsjõ]
location	[lɔ ka ˈsjõ]
conviction	[kõ vik ˈsjõ]
patience	[pa ˈsjã sə]

When *tie* is final, pronounce it as [ti ə].

LL 5.4.81 Read aloud.

| sortie | [sɔr ˈti ə] |
| partie | [par ˈti ə] |

V

Pronounce *v* as [v].

LL 5.4.82 Read aloud.

vie	[ˈvi ə]
esclave	[ɛs ˈkla və]
vieux	[vjø]
livre	[ˈli vrə]
vingt	[vẽ]
souvenir	[su və ˈnir]
violon	[vjɔ ˈlõ]
voix	[vwa]

W

Usually pronounce *w* as [v].

LL 5.4.83 Read aloud.

| Wagnérien | [vag ne ˈrjẽ] |
| wagon | [va ˈgõ] |

French

X

When *x* is followed by a consonant, pronounce it as [ks].

LL 5.4.84 Read aloud.

texte	[ˈtɛk stə]
expose	[ɛk ˈspo zə]
externe	[ɛk ˈstɛr nə]
extra	[ɛk ˈstra]
extase	[ɛk ˈsta zə]
expansif	[ɛk spɑ̃ ˈsif]

When *x* is followed by a vowel or *h*, pronounce it as [gz].

LL 5.4.85 Read aloud.

exhibition	[ɛg zi bi ˈsjɔ̃]
exilé	[ɛg zi ˈle]
exulter	[ɛg zyl ˈte]
exode	[ɛg ˈzɔ də]
exaspérer	[ɛg zɑs pe ˈre]
exemple	[ɛg ˈzɑ̃ plə]

Exception:

LL 5.4.86 Read aloud.

luxe	[ˈlyk sə]

Exceptions: *x* in these words is pronounced [z].

LL 5.4.87 Read aloud.

deuxième	[dø ˈzjɛ mə]
sixième	[si ˈzjɛ mə]
dixième	[di ˈzjɛ mə]

When *x* is final, it is usually silent.

LL 5.4.88 Read aloud.

deux	[dø]
prix	[pri]
croix	[krwa]
voix	[vwa]

When *x* is in liaison, pronounce it as [z].

LL 5.4.89 Read aloud.

deux‿enfants	[dø zɑ̃ ˈfɑ̃]

Z

Pronounce z as [z].

LL 5.4.90   Read aloud.

| Ézéchiel | [e ze 'kjɛl] |
| seizième | [sɛ 'zjɛ mə] |

When z is final, it is usually silent.

LL 5.4.91   Read aloud.

allez	[a 'le]
dépêchez	[de pe 'ʃe]
chez	[ʃe]
dormez	[dɔr 'me]

Exceptions:

| gaz | [gɑz] |
| Berlioz | [bɛr 'ljɔz] |

Spanish

Spanish Diction

As a singer, you need to include Spanish in your arsenal of pronunciation skills. During the last twenty years, songs from Spain and Latin America have become standard vocal literature.

You will encounter several new ideas as you learn to pronounce Spanish, particularly the *breath phrase*: between breaths, all words are run together and pronounced as a stream of equal-length syllables. You will hear the word boundaries disappear within the breath phrase, which essentially causes the words to sound like one long word. You will also find that consonants are pronounced differently depending on their position in a word or breath phrase. You will see how vowels change at word boundaries. And finally, you will encounter the special way Spanish syllables are stressed, which, together with the other features mentioned above, gives Spanish its distinct staccato character.

Depending on the literature you sing, you will use either Latin American Spanish or Castillian Spanish. This chapter generally presents Latin American pronunciation first, and then identifies Castillian alternatives.

Spanish

Chart of Spanish Sounds

The following chart lists the sounds of Spanish in alphabetical order. Refer to this chart to quickly check the sound of a spelling. For special circumstances and exceptions to the sounds that cannot be presented easily in a simple chart, see the discussions of the individual sounds later in this chapter.

Spanish Letter and Position in Word		IPA	Example and	IPA	Page
a	a	[ɑ]	atrás, mano	[ɑ tɾɑs] [mɑ no]	329
	ay	syllable final	[ɑi]	hay, ay	[ɑi] [ɑi]	329
	ai	syllable final	[ɑi]	paila, vainita	[pɑi lɑ] [bɑi ni tɑ]	329
	aí		[ɑ i]	país, raíz	[pɑ is] [rɑ is]	329
	au	syllable final	[ɑu]	causa, jaula	[kɑu sɑ] [xɑu lɑ]	330
b	b	syllable initial	[b]	bala, bono	[bɑ lɑ] [bo no]	337
		between vowels	[β]	tubo, haba	[tu βo] [ɑ βɑ]	337
		following s, r	[β]	esbelto, hierba	[ez βel to] [jeɾ βɑ]	337
		syllable final	[β]	submarino	[suβ mɑ ɾi no]	337
		before r, l	[β]	hablar, sobra	[ɑ βlaɾ] [so βɾɑ]	338
c	c	before a, o, u	[k]	casa, cosa	[kɑ sɑ] [ko sɑ]	338
		before e, i	[s] or [θ]*	cesar, cima	[se saɾ] [si mɑ]	338
	cc	across syllables	[ks]	acción, ficción	[ɑk sjon] [fik sjon]	338
	ch	syllable initial	[tʃ]	choza, mucho	[tʃo sɑ] [mu tʃo]	339
d	d	syllable initial	[d]	danza	[dɑn sɑ]	339
		between vowels	[ð]	hada, mido	[ɑ ðɑ] [mi ðo]	339
		after s, r	[ð]	desde	[dez ðe]	339
		syllable final	[ð]	verdad, usted	[beɾ ðɑð] [us teð]	339
e	e		[e]	elegante, gente	[e le ɣɑn te] [xen te]	330
	ey	syllable final	[ei]	rey	[r̄ei]	331
	ei	syllable final	[ei]	reina, peine	[r̄ei nɑ] [pei ne]	331
	eu	syllable final	[eu]	deuda, feudal	[deu ðɑ] [feu ðɑl]	331
f	f	syllable initial	[f]	fácil, afanar	[fɑ sil] [ɑ fɑ naɾ]	341
g	g	before a, o, u	[g]	gato, gota	[gɑ to] [go tɑ]	341
		before e, i	[x]	gente, gimnasia	[xen te] [xim nɑ sjɑ]	341
		between vowels	[ɣ]	haga, miga	[ɑ ɣɑ] [mi ɣɑ]	341
		after s or z	[ɣ]	desgana	[dez ɣɑ nɑ]	342
	gua	word initial	[gwɑ]	guarnir	[gwaɾ niɾ]	342
		after a vowel	[ɣwɑ]	fraguar	[frɑ ɣwaɾ]*	342

*Castilllian Spanish.
**These g's are pronounced {V} because they are between vowels.

Spanish

Spanish Letter and Position in Word			IPA	Example and	IPA	Page
g	gue	word initial	[ge]	guerrero	[ge r̄e ɾo]	342
		after a vowel	[ɣe]	la guerra	[la ɣe r̄a]	342
	gui	word initial	[gi]	guía	[gi a]	342
		after a vowel	[ɣi]	la guija	[la ɣi xa]	342
	güe	word initial	[gwe]	güepil	[gwe pil]	342
	güi	syllable initial	[gwi]	lingüística	[liŋ gwis ti ka]	342
h	h	syllable initial	silent	hogar, ahorrar	[o ɣaɾ] [a o r̄aɾ]	343
				hielo, huerta	[ie lo] [ueɾ ta]	
i	i		[i]	imagen, isla	[i ma xen] [iz la]	332
				mi, mil	[mi] [mil]	332
	ia	syllable final	[ja]	hacia, piano	[a sja] [pja no]	332
	ie	syllable final	[je]	tiene, viene	[tje ne] [bje ne]	332
	iu	syllable final	[ju]	viuda, ciudad	[bju ða] [sju ðað]	332
	io	syllable final	[jo]	adiós, amplio	[a ðjos] [am pljo]	332
j	j	syllable initial	[x]	joven	[xo βen]	343
				jaula	[xau la]	
				ajustar	[a xus taɾ]	
k	k	syllable initial	[k]	kilogramo	[ki lo gra mo]	343
				kibutz	[ki βuts]	
l	l	syllable initial	[l]	litro, palo	[li tɾo] [pa lo]	344
		syllable final	[l]	mil, vil, alto	[mil] [bil] [al to]	344
	ll	syllable initial	[ʎ] or [j]	lleno, cabello	[ʎe no] [ka βe ʎo]	344
m	m	syllable initial	[m]	mano, amasar	[ma no] [a ma saɾ]	345
n	n	syllable initial	[n]	nene, nido	[ne ne] [ni ðo]	345
		before [m], [b], [p]	[m:]	inmenso	[i m:en so]	345
		before [k], [g], [x]	[ŋ]	incubar	[iŋ ku βaɾ]	345
				ingrato	[iŋ gra to]	
				ingenio	[iŋ xe njo]	
	ñ	syllable initial	[ɲ]	ñato, puño	[ɲa to] [pu ɲo]	346
o	o		[o]	oro, canción	[o ɾo] [kan sjon]	333
	oi	syllable final	[oi]	heroico	[e ɾoi ko]	334
	oí	across syllables	[oi]	egoísta, boína	[e ɣo is ta] [bo i na]	334
	oy	syllable final	[o i]	voy, hoy	[boi] [oi]	334

*These g's are pronounced {V} because they occur between vowels.
**When a written accent is placed over the i, the i is no longer a glide and the two vowels are pronounced in separate syllables. (See page 321.)

Spanish

Spanish Letter and Position in Word		IPA	Example and	IPA	Page
p	syllable initial	[p]	peso, apostar	[pe so] [a pos taɾ]	346
	syllable final	[p]	optar, captar	[op taɾ] [kap taɾ]	346
qu		[k]	queso	[ke so]	346
			quitar	[ki taɾ]	346
r	word initial	[r̄]	rosa, rana	[r̄o sa] [r̄a na]	347
	syllable initial	[ɾ]	pero, apuro	[pe ɾo] [a pu ɾo]	347
	syllable final	[ɾ] or [r̄]	ir, cesar	[iɾ] [se saɾ]	347
	after s, n	[r̄]	Israel, enredar	[iz r̄a el] [en r̄e ðaɾ]	348
rr	between vowels	[r̄]	perro, carro	[pe r̄o] [ka r̄o]	348
s	syllable initial	[s]	sala, aseo	[sa la] [a se o]	348
	between vowels	[s]	oso, pasa	[o so] [pa sa]	348
	before voiced consonants	[z]	desde, musgo	[dez ðe] [muz ɣo]	348
	syllable final	[s]	los, niños	[los] [ni ɲos]	348
t	syllable initial	[t]	tina, untar	[ti na] [un taɾ]	350
	syllable final	[t]	atmósfera	[at mos fe ɾa]	350
u		[u]	uso, nuca	[u so] [nu ca]	334
ua	syllable final	[wa]	suave, cuarto	[swa βe] [kwaɾ to]	335
ue	syllable final	[we]	cuerda, puesta	[kweɾ ða] [pwes ta]	335
ui	syllable final	[wi]	cuidar, buitre	[kwi ðaɾ] [bwi tɾe]	335
uo	syllable final	[wo]	cuota	[kwo ta]	335
uy	syllable final	[wi]	muy	[mwi]	335
v	syllable initial	[b]	vaca, vengo	[ba ka] [beŋ go]	350
	between vowels	[β]	uva, tuvo	[u βa] [tu βo]	350
	following s or r	[β]	intervalo	[in ter βa lo]	350
w	syllable initial	[w]	whisky	[wis ki]	350
x	word initial	[s]	xenofobia	[se no fo βja]	351
	syllable initial	[ks]	exámen	[ek sa men]	351
			exoneración	[ek so ne ɾa sjon]	
y	syllable initial, followed by a vowel	[j]	yeso	[je so]	336
y	followed by a consonant	[i]	y bailar	[i bai lar]	336
z	syllable initial	[s] or [θ]**	zapato, zar	[sa pa to] [saɾ]	351
	syllable final	[s] or [θ]**	tez, nariz	[tes] [na ɾis]	351
	before a voiced consonant	[z] or [θ]**	hazlo	[az lo]	351

*Not a letter of the Spanish alphabet; only appears in borrowed words.
**Castillian Spanish.

Spanish

Special Features of Spanish

In contrast to English, Spanish is virtually pronounced as it is written. The alphabet-sound correspondences charted in the previous section hold true in all instances.

Syllabification

The division of Spanish words into syllables is straightforward and follows clear rules. The correct division is important since it often determines how a sound is pronounced: certain consonants (for example *b* and *d*) are pronounced differently depending on their location in a syllable. (For more information, see page 337, "Spanish Consonants in Detail.")

LL 6.2.01   Examples:

<u>cac</u>-tus:	*c* initial	[k]
	c final	[ɣ]
<u>den</u>só	*d* initial	[d]
verd<u>ad</u>:	*d* final	[ð]

See page 312 for a description of the fricative g [ɣ].

Single Consonant Between Vowels

A single consonant starts a new syllable when it occurs between vowels.

LL 6.2.02

ma-ma	[mɑ mɑ]
ca-sa	[kɑ sɑ]
to-ma	[to mɑ]

The letters *ch*, *ll*, and *rr* each represent one sound. Because each letter combination is treated as a single consonant, it is not divided.

LL 6.2.03

mu-cho	[mu tʃo]
ca-lle	[kɑ ʎe]
pe-rro	[pe r̄o]

Two Consecutive Consonants

Two consecutive consonants together may or may not be divided.

Note: A rule of thumb is that if the two consonants *can* occur at the beginning of a word, they form a cluster and will always be in the same syllable.

Spanish

LL 6.2.04

blanco	blan-co
ablandar	a-blan-dar

(*bl* can occur at the beginning of a word.)

LL 6.2.05

calma	cal-ma

(*lm cannot* occur at the beginning of a word, so you must divide it into separate syllables.)

There are twelve clusters that are always in the same syllable. They are:

LL 6.2.06

bl	br	cl	cr	dr	fl	fr
gl	gr	pl	pr	tr		

Three Consecutive Consonants

Three consonants are always divided. If the last two consonants form one of the twelve indivisible clusters just mentioned, you must keep them in the same syllable.

LL 6.2.07

siem-pre
hom-bre
am-pliar

However, if the last two consonants are not one of the twelve clusters, divide syllables between the second and third consonant.

LL 6.2.08

ins-pi-rar
cons-tar

Four Consecutive Consonants

Four consecutive consonants are rare. When they do occur, place two consonants in one syllable and two consonants in the next syllable.

LL 6.2.09

obs-truc-ción

Two Consecutive Vowels

Two consecutive vowels can be divided in two ways. If one of the vowels is an unstressed *i* or *u*, the two vowels occur in the same syllable.

LL 6.2.10

cau-sa
cai-go
cie-lo
pies

In all other cases, two consecutive vowels are divided into separate syllables.

LL 6.2.11

le-ón
ca-er
le-er
ra-íz
ba-úl

A written accent mark over a vowel means that it is stressed. The accent over the i *in the word* raíz, *for example, means that the* i *is stressed.*

Exercise: Divide the words into syllables:

LL 6.2.12

quieto	poeta	caído
allá	pasillo	carro
exponer	deuda	subyacente
paisaje	airoso	isla
hombre	dialecto	transportar

Features of Spanish Pronunciation

Breath Phrases

Word boundaries are, for the most part, ignored in spoken Spanish. Between breath pauses, words are run together and pronounced as one word. The phrase *Tómas anduvo con Ana* (Thomas walked with Ann) would be pronounced [to ma san du βo ko na na]. This long "word" is divided into syllables following the rules above.

Note that any word's final consonant that occurs between vowels begins the following syllable:

LL 6.2.13

con Ana	[ko na na]

When a consonant's position is referred to as "within a word," it can also mean "within a breath phrase," which is like one long word made up of several words run together. See "Breath Phrases" on the previous page.

Spanish

A zarzuela is a short drama with incidental music, similiar to an operetta or musical comedy. Taken from the Palace of La Zarzuela near Madrid, where festive dramas were presented.

Note also that when a consonant ends a word and the same consonant begins the next word, pronounce the two consonants as one:

LL 6.2.14

| los santos | [lo santos] |

Exercise: Divide the following lines from the chorus of the sailors in the zarzuela *La Gran Via*, Act 1.

LL 6.2.15

| Cuando los vientos cual furias se agitan, |
| cuando las olas se encrespan e irritan. |

b, v, d, g: Pronunciation and Word Position

The pronunciation of *b, v, d,* or *g* depends on the letter's location in a word or breath phrase. Regardless of the letter's position in a syllable, you use one pronunciation for the letter when it occurs at the beginning of a word and another if it occurs in the middle of a word or breath phrase. Remember that *b* and *v* are pronounced the same. (See page 337 for details.)

To produce the fricative *b* sound, [β], put your lips together lightly and blow so that the air flows through your lips. Be sure to voice the sound. You will feel your lips vibrate. Articulating this sound is similar to articulating [b], except that your lips do not completely stop the air flow.

The fricative *g* sound, [ɣ], is articulated the same way as the German ach-laut [x], except that it is voiced. To produce the [ɣ], raise your tongue as you would for a [k], but don't let your tongue completely touch your soft palate. Let air flow through the small opening between your soft palate and your tongue; then voice the sound. You will feel your tongue and soft palate vibrate.

LL 6.2.16 Examples:

be-be	*b* word initial	[b]
be-be	*b* between vowels	[β]
ven	*v* word initial	[b]
u-va	*v* between vowels	[β]
de-do	*d* word initial	[d]
de-do	*d* between vowels	[ð]
ga-to	*g* word initial	[g]
Hu-go	*g* between vowels	[ɣ]

Spanish

Exercise: Look at these lines from the *La Gran Via*. Write the IPA symbol for the underlined consonant. Watch out for those sounds that begin a word, but occur between vowels within the phrase:

LL 6.2.17

| Ya nuestro <u>b</u>arco cual rau<u>d</u>a ga<u>v</u>iota |
| Las alas <u>v</u>an rompien<u>d</u>o nuestra |
| suerte en pos.¡Hip! ¡A <u>b</u>ogar! ¡Hip! ¡A bogar! |
| ¡Qué hermosa es esta <u>v</u>ida <u>d</u>e la mar! |

Lack of Aspiration in [p], [t], [k]

In English, the consonants [p], [t], and [k] are pronounced with a puff of air if they occur before a stressed vowel (*Peter, appeal, king*). Spanish has no such aspiration. Pronounce these sounds like the non-aspirated English sounds following an *s*, as in *spill, still,* and *skill*.

Practice saying these pairs of words in English to feel the difference in the aspiration/non-aspiration.

LL 6.2.18

peak	speak
till	still
kill	skill
pill	spill
teal	steal
key	ski
punk	spunk
ton	stun
Kate	skate

Now, practice these Spanish words, being careful not to aspirate.

LL 6.2.19

Pablo	[pɑ blo]
taza	[tɑ sɑ]
casa	[kɑ sɑ]
peso	[pe so]
tengo	[teŋ go]
queso	[ke so]
pino	[pi no]
tino	[ti no]
quiso	[ki so]

Spanish

pongo	[poŋ go]
topo	[to po]
cosa	[ko sɑ]
puso	[pu so]
tuna	[tu nɑ]
cuna	[ku nɑ]

Note: Remember that the [t] is dental. (See page 350.)

Practice the *p*'s and *t*'s in these lines from *La Gran Via*.

LL 6.2.20

Y allá en la playa que lejos se divisa	[jɑ jɑen lɑ plɑ jɑ ke le xo se ði βi sɑ]
pañuelos que se agitan sin cesar	[pɑ ɲwe los ke seɑ xi tɑn sin se sɑɾ]
nos llaman con amor	[nos jɑ mɑn ko nɑ moɾ]
¡Oh! ¡Mágico placer! ¡Oh! ¡Dicha singular!	[o mɑ xi ko plɑ seɾ o di t͡ʃɑ siŋ gu lɑɾ]

See page 324 for an explanation of vowels across word boundaries.

Assimilation of [s]

Assimilation is the alteration of a speech sound influenced by a neighboring sound, which makes it more like the neighboring sound.

The rules for the pronunciation of *s* and *z* are the same. The letters are pronounced as [s] or [z] depending on the consonant sound that follows.

If the next consonant is voiceless, pronounce the *s* or *z* as a voiceless [s].

LL 6.2.21

rascar	[r̄as kaɾ]
haztu	[as tu]

If the next consonant is voiced, pronounce the *s* or *z* as [z].

LL 6.2.22

rasgar	[r̄az ɣaɾ]
hazlo	[az lo]

Note: Pronounce *s* or *z* between *vowels* as [s].

Exercise: Decide if the underlined *s* should be pronounced as [s] or [z].

LL 6.2.23

más angosto	las mismas
presente	dices
pesas	musgo

este	be<u>s</u>os
lo<u>s</u> año<u>s</u>	<u>s</u>igno

Exercise: Remembering that the letter z follows the same pronunciation rules as the letter s, decide how you would pronounce the following z's.

LL 6.2.24

ca<u>z</u>ar	<u>z</u>apato
ta<u>z</u>a	chori<u>z</u>o
esbo<u>z</u>o	pa<u>z</u>
ve<u>z</u>	<u>z</u>orro
una ve<u>z</u> más	halla<u>z</u>go

Assimilation of [n]

The letter *n* is pronounced at the same point of articulation as the sound that follows it.

1. *n* is pronounced as an alveolar [n] in most cases:

   LL 6.2.25

nena	[ne na]
un cielo	[un sje lo]

   An alveolar sound is formed by bringing the tip of the tongue near or against the alveolar ridge.

2. When *n* precedes a bilabial sound ([m], [b], [p]), it is pronounced as [m:]:

   LL 6.2.26

un peso	[um: pe so]
un beso	[um: be so]
inmejorable	[i m:e xo ɾa ble]

   Bilabial - *Formed by both lips.*

3. When *n* precedes a velar sound ([g], [k], [x]) it is pronounced as [ŋ]

   LL 6.2.27

inglés	[iŋ gles]
incubar	[iŋ ku βaɾ]
un gato	[uŋ ga to]
un caso	[uŋ ka so]
ingenio	[iŋ xe njo]

   Velar - *Pronounced with the back of the tongue raised toward or against the soft palate.*

(See page 345 for a more detailed discussion of *n* and more exercises.)

Spanish

Consonants Sounds Not Found in English

1. *ll* [ʎ]

    The *ll* has two acceptable pronunciations, [ʎ] (called elye) and [j]; both are widely used in parts of Spain and parts of South America.

    The [ʎ] does not exist in English. It is similar to the [lj] in *million*. Put the tip of your tongue behind your bottom front teeth and arch your tongue so that the arch touches the front of your hard palate. Add voice and let the air exit over the sides of your tongue.

    LL 6.2.28

calle	[ka ʎe]	or	[ka je]
llamar	[ʎa mar]	or	[ja mar]

    (See page 344 for exercises.)

2. *ñ* [ɲ]

    The letter *ñ* is pronounced [ɲ], called *enya*. It is similar to the *n* in the English word *canyon*.

    LL 6.2.29

niño	[ni ɲo]
paño	[pa ɲo]

    (See "Enya [ɲ] and Elya [ʎ]" on page 66)

3. *j* [x]

    The [x] is similar to the German ach-laut [x]. Put the back of your tongue close to the roof of your mouth, in the same position that you would use for a [k]. Be sure not to touch your soft palate. Feel the air rush through the narrow opening.

    LL 6.2.30

joven	[xo βen]
enojo	[e no xo]

    (See page 343 for a more detailed discussion and exercises.)

4. Dental *t* and *d*

    In English, [d] and [t] are alveolar. They are pronounced with the tip of the tongue touching the alveolar ridge. In Spanish, pronounce them dentally with the tip of your tongue touching the back of your upper front teeth.

LL 6.2.31

tengo	[teŋ go]
tuna	[tu na]

Exercise: Pronounce the following words.

LL 6.2.32

tengo	[teŋ go]
danza	[dan sa]
taza	[ta sa]
desde	[dez ðe]
todo	[to ðo]
dama	[da ma]
tuna	[tu na]
duque	[du ke]
tieso	[tje so]
dulce	[dul se]

5) [ɾ] and [r̄]

There are two Spanish *r* sounds. The first sound, [ɾ], is called *flipped r*. To produce it, flip the top of your tongue against your alveolar ridge once. The sound is similar to the English *t* or *d* that usually occurs between vowels, as in the words *Betty, city, Adam*. Pronounce these words and feel how your tongue flaps against the alveolar ridge. Now try the Spanish words *pero, pura, cera*.

Pronounce these words.

LL 6.2.33

cerámica	[se ɾa mi ka]
árbol	[aɾ βol]
brazo	[bɾa so]
otro	[o tɾo]
fruta	[fɾu ta]
madre	[ma ðɾe]
largo	[laɾ ɣo]
criatura	[kɾja tu ɾa]
verde	[beɾ ðe]
cortar	[koɾ taɾ]

Spanish

There is no comparable sound in American English for the [r̄] called *trilled r*. To approximate the sound, flip your tongue tip several times in rapid succession against your alveolar ridge.

LL 6.2.34

perro	[pe r̄o]
arroyo	[a r̄o jo]
forro	[fo r̄o]

In word initial position (even within a breath phrase), a single *r* is pronounced as trilled [r̄]. This is an exception where the spelling of single *r* does not reflect the simple alphabet-sound correspondence of Spanish.

LL 6.2.35

rosa	[r̄o sa]
rojo	[r̄o xo]
resto	[r̄es to]

(See page 348 for a more detailed discussion of how these sounds are spelled.)

Pure, Simple Vowels

As in the other languages, [e] and [o] are pronounced without the diphthongal off-glide that you would use in English. See "The Italian Vowels e and o" on page 64.

In Spanish, vowels have the same length, regardless of whether they occur in a stressed or unstressed syllable. They are never lengthened as they sometimes are in English.

LL 6.2.36

English	Spanish
ma	ma
me	mi
may	me
low	lo
too	tu

Practice saying the following words. Be careful not to turn the vowels into English dpihthongs.

LL 6.2.37

masa	[ma sa]
mesa	[me sa]
misa	[mi sa]
moza	[mo sa]
musa	[mu sa]
lama	[la ma]

Spanish

lema	[le mɑ]
lima	[li mɑ]
loma	[lo mɑ]
luna	[lu nɑ]
paso	[pɑ so]
peso	[pe so]
piso	[pi so]
pozo	[po so]
puso	[pu so]

(See "Spanish Vowels in Detail," page 329, for a more detailed discussion of the individual vowels and exercises.)

Strong Vowels

Spanish vowels are pronounced the same in stressed and unstressed syllables. Unstressed vowels are not reduced to a *schwa* [ə].

LL 6.2.38

English		Spanish	
productive	[prə 'dʌk tɪv]	productivo	[pro duk 'ti βo]
legitimate	[lə 'dʒɪ tɪ mət]	legítimo	[le 'xi ti mo]

Be careful to differentiate between the unstressed vowels in these syllables as you pronounce these pairs.

LL 6.2.39

bueno	['bwe no]	buena	['bwe nɑ]
comieron	[ko 'mje ɾon]	comieran	[ko 'mje ɾɑn]

Read aloud. Pronounce vowels in the stressed and unstressed syllables the same.

LL 6.2.40

extranjero	[eks tɾɑŋ 'xe ɾo]
desgracia	[dez 'ɣɾɑ sjɑ]
preposición	[pre po si 'sjon]
momento	[mo 'men to]
mañana	[mɑ 'ɲɑ nɑ]
francamente	[fɾɑŋ kɑ 'men te]
estatua	[es 'tɑ twɑ]
ahogado	[ɑ o 'ɣɑ ðo]
ambicioso	[ɑm bi 'sjo so]
inaplicables	[i nɑ pli 'kɑ bles]

Spanish

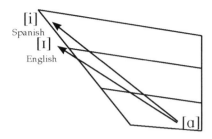

This vowel chart illustrates the tighter closure of the Spanish diphthong [ai] compared to English [aɪ].

Spanish also has a fourth diphthong eu, but its occurrence is rare.

Examples: Eugenia, Europa

Diphthongs

Spanish off-glide diphthongs end with vowels that are more closed than vowels in English diphthongs. In addition, you must close the vowels more quickly.

LL 6.2.41

English	[aɪ]	[ɔɪ]	[aʊ]	[eɪ]
Spanish	[ai]	[oi]	[au]	[ei]

LL 6.2.42

English		Spanish	
ray	[reɪ]	rey	[r̄ei]
I	[aɪ]	hay	[ai]
boy	[bɔɪ]	voy	[boi]
cow	[kaʊ]	causa	[kau sa]

Pronounce the following words.

LL 6.2.43

peine	[pei ne]
deuda	[deu ða]
reina	[r̄ei na]
caucho	[kau t͡ʃo]
baile	[bai le]
causa	[kau sa]
naipe	[nai pe]
jaula	[xau la]
Jaime	[xai me]
pauta	[pau ta]

Glides

Spanish has eight vowel combinations that form glides. Be careful not to break these sounds into two syllables.

LL 6.2.44

ia	hacia	[a sja]
ua	cuarto	[kwaɾ to]
ie	tierra	[tje r̄a]
ue	cuerda	[kweɾ ða]
io	adiós	[a ðjos]
uo	cuota	[kwo ta]

Spanish

iu	viuda	[bju ða]
ui	cuidar	[kwi ðaɾ]

LL 6.2.45   Read aloud.

fuera	[fwe ɾa]
piano	[pja no]
ruana	[r̄wa na]
piojo	[pjo xo]
suave	[swa βe]
patio	[pa tjo]
mueca	[mwe ka]
riego	[r̄je ɣo]
hueso	[we so]
fiel	[fjel]

Note: If an accent mark is written over an *i*, the *i* and the following vowel are pronounced as two separate syllables.

Stress

There are several aspects of Spanish stress that differ from English stress.

Predictable Patterns

Spanish word stress follows simple rules.

Words ending with a vowel, or the consonant *n* or *s* are stressed on the next-to-last (penultimate) syllable:

LL 6.2.46

hablo	['a blo]
imagen	[i 'ma ɣen]
esta	['es ta]
visitarnos	[bi si 'taɾ nos]

Words ending in other consonants are stressed on the last syllable:

LL 6.2.47

comer	[ko 'meɾ]
principal	[pɾin si 'pal]
verdad	[beɾ 'ðað]
capaz	[ka 'pas]

Spanish

All exceptions to these two rules carry a written accent:

LL 6.2.48

está	[es 'ta]
imán	[i 'man]
atrás	[a tras]
habló	[a 'blo]
rápido	[ra pi ðo]
impídemelo	[im 'pi ðe me lo]

Vowels in combination with *i* or *u* form diphthongs, unless a written accent is found on the *i* or *u*; in this case, the two vowels occur in separate syllables.

LL 6.2.49

paisano	[pai sa no]
país	[pa is]
tiara	[tja ra]
tía	[ti a]
miope	[mjo pe]
mío	[mi o]
actuación	[ak twa sjon]
actúa	[ak tu a]

Exercise: Where would you stress the following words?

LL 6.2.50

limosna	lavar	éstas
pañal	perrito	hable
lesión	estás	animal
lápices	dígamelo	periodo
rápido	parar	lentamente

Syllable Length

Although Spanish stressed syllables are louder, they are not longer. Every Spanish syllable is pronounced in the same amount of time.

LL 6.2.51

English	Spanish
industry	industria
magnificent	magnífico
industrial	industrial

Spanish

Exercise: Pronounce the following words. Keep all syllables of equal length; remember that the vowels in unstressed syllables do not reduce to [ə].

LL 6.2.52

ho-me-na-je	ex-tra-or-di-na-rio
es-pon-ta-nei-dad	a-gra-da-ble
mo-men-ta-rio	de-sas-tro-so
va-rie-dad	re-co-men-da-ble
ha-bi-ta-ción	psi-co-lo-gí-a

Lack of Secondary Stress

Spanish does not have secondary stress. Long words are not broken up into primary-secondary patterns as they are in English. Words have several weak stresses and one primary stress. Together with similar syllable length, this feature of Spanish stress creates the familiar staccato character of this language.

English	Spanish
\ . . / .	. . . . /
ad - min - is - tra- tion	ad - mi - nis - tra - cion
\ . / . .	. . . . /
na - tion - al - i - ty	na - cio - na - li - dad
. / . .	. . . / .
ge - og - ra - phy	ge - o - gra - fí - a
\ . / .	. . . /
ed - u - ca - tion	e - du - ca - cion

Pronounce the following Spanish words. The stress patterns are marked for you.

```
   .    .   .   .   /              .    .    .   .   .  .   /
cla - si - fi - ca - ción       i - rre - spon - sa - bi - li - dad

   .    .   .   /                 .    .    .   .   .  /
con - ti - nua - ción           in - com - pa - ti - bi - li - dad

   .    .   .   /                 .    .   .   /
cal - cu - la - ción             in - ca - pa - ci - dad

   .    .   .   /                 .    .   /   .
re - ve - la - ción              ca - ni - ba - lis - mo

   .    .   .   .   /              .    .   .   /   .
con - si - de - ra - ción        sen - ti - men - ta - lis - mo
```

Cognate Words

Many words in Spanish and English have similar Latin roots. Their meanings and spellings are similar; however, watch out for different stress patterns! As in the exercises above, the majority of cognates have different stress patterns.

Exercise: What are the English cognates for the following words? Are the stress patterns the same or different?

Spanish

LL 6.2.53

entusiástico	individual
examinación	vocabulario
curiosidad	rapidamente
metabolismo	departamental
comunicativo	inevitable

Stress Timing

Spanish rhythm is very different from English rhythm. Whereas English rhythm is determined by the number of stresses, Spanish rhythm is determined by the number of syllables. In other words, the syllable length varies in English according to the stress system, but in Spanish, syllable length stays the same. In poetry, and songs, the number of syllables gives the "beat."

See page 324 for vowel changes across word boundaries.

Rosita, in *Luisa Fernanda*, Act 1

LL 6.2.54

La zurcidora buena	[la sur si ðo ra βwe na]	7 syllables
sabe de sobra	[sa βe ðe so βra]	5 syllables
que a quien mucho le zurce	[kea kjen mu tʃo le sur se]	7 syllables
poco le cobra	[po ko le ko βra]	5 syllables
Y es que el bolsillo	[jes kel bol si ʎo]	5 syllables
también necesitaba	[tam bje ne se si ta βa]	7 syllables
buen zurcidillo	[bwen sur si ði ʎo]	5 syllables

Guardias, in *La Gran Via*, Act 2

LL 6.2.55

Caiga la trampa	[kai ɣa la tram pa]	5 syllables
con precaución	[kon pre kau sjon]	4 syllables
que ya tenemos	[ke ja te ne mos]	5 syllables
dentru* el raton	[den trwel ra ton]	4 syllables

*u instead of *o* (adentro) shows a dialect variation.

Due to the strong-weak stress patterns in English, an English speaker will tend to shorten and lengthen syllables when phrasing a musical line, even when the note values are the same. Do not carry this tendency into Spanish. Base the stress pattern on number of syllables when phrasing a musical line in Spanish.

Vowel Changes Across Word Boundaries

As mentioned earlier (see "Breath Phrases" on page 311), Spanish words run together within a breath phrase. When two vowels come together at the word boundaries several interesting changes occur.

When two identical vowels occur at a word boundary, the two vowels combine into one vowel. This is called *vowel deletion*. In rapid speech, this vowel is not even lengthened.

LL 6.2.56

aa	tierra árida	[tje ra ri ða]
oo	aire entró	[ai ren tro]
oo	cuatro ojos	[kwa tro xos]

When a more open vowel (that is, a vowel pronounced with the jaw lower) is followed by a more close vowel, the first vowel disappears.

LL 6.2.57

a + e	la esposa	[les po sa]
a + o	la hora	[lo ra]
a + i	la isla	[liz la]
a + u	la única	[lu ni ka]
e + i	me imagino	[mi ma xi no]
o + u	lo único	[lu ni ko]

Exception: This does not usually happen with the combinations *e + u* or *o + i*.

LL 6.2.58

| le utilizo | [le u ti li so] |
| lo informo | [lo in for mo] |

When *e* and *o* come into contact with each other, the first vowel "relaxes" and almost turns the two vowels into a glide. (This probably happens because they both involve the same degree of jaw lowering.) The two vowels are then part of the same syllable.

LL 6.2.59

| e + o | este otro | [es teo tro] |
| o + e | este o este | [es te oes te] |

This also occurs when *e* or *o* comes into contact with *a*.

LL 6.2.60

e + a	este alma	[es teal ma]
	me hablo	[mea βlo]
o + a	todo aquello	[to ðoa ke ʎo]
	pudo hacer	[pu ðoa ser]

Spanish

Vowel deletion and relaxation are both very important in singing. Separate vowels combine into one syllable. This allows Spanish rhythm to be maintained.

Notice the word boundaries of these lines from *Luisa Fernanda*.

LL 6.2.61

En mi tierra‿extremeña	[en mi tje r̄eks tre me ɲa]
tengo‿un nido de‿amores	[teŋ gu ni ðo ðea mo res]
entre‿encinas bizarras	[en tren si nɑs βi sɑ rɑs]
y castaños y robles	[i kɑs tɑ ɲo si r̄o βles]
donde‿el pájaro quiere	[don del pɑ xɑ ro kje re]
que‿una pájara venga	[keu nɑ pɑ xɑ rɑ βeŋ gɑ]
para ser soberana	[pɑ rɑ ser so βe rɑ nɑ]
de mi casa labriega.	[de mi kɑ sɑ lɑ βrje ɣɑ]

Exercise: Divide the following lines into syllables. (From the Chorus in *La Gran Via*, Act 1.)

LL 6.2.62

Porque es el caso, que según dicen
doña Municipalidad
va a dar a luz una Gran Via
que de fijo no ha tenido igual.

Triphthongs

Three vowels together occur only in the Castillian verb forms used with the pronoun *vosotros*. (Note that pronouns in Spanish are often deleted from the sentence. For example, *vosotros cambiáis* becomes simply *cambiáis*.)

The three vowels together are pronounced as a glide-vowel-glide, all in the same syllable.

LL 6.2.63

cambiáis	[kɑm bjɑis]
estudiáis	[es tu djɑis]
continuáis	[kon ti nwɑis]

Tripthongs also occur with some frequency at word boundaries.

LL 6.2.64

justicia humana	[xus ti sjɑu mɑ nɑ]
estatua importante	[es tɑ twɑim por tɑn te]

Spanish

negocio importante	[ne ɣo sjoim por tan te]
estudió historia	[es tu djois to rja]

Note: Neither of the glides carries a written accent. If either glide has a written stress, it will belong to a separate syllable.

LL 6.2.65

negocio ímprobo	[ne ɣo sjo im pro βo]
negocio único	[ne ɣo sjo u ni ko]

Dialectal Variations

English dialects differ because of vowel variations. Spanish dialects, on the other hand, differ because of consonant variations. Castillian Spanish and Latin American Spanish are the two main dialect groups. However, within these main groups, there are several regional dialect groups. The most salient differences are listed below.

Accepted Pronunciation

Letter	Example	Castillian	Latin American	Argentina
c before e or i		[θ]	[s]	
	cancion	[kan θjon]	[kan sjon]	
z, syllable initial or final		[θ]	[s]	
	caza	[ka θa]	[ka sa]	
z before voiced consonant		[θ]	[z]	
	hazlo	[aθ lo]	[az lo]	
ll		[ʎ]	[j]	[ʒ]
	calle	[ka ʎe]	[ka je]	[ka ʒe]
s (in syllable final)		[s]	[s], [h], or silent	
	los ríos	[los r̄ios]	[los r̄i os]	
			[lo r̄i o]	
			[loh r̄i oh]	

In addition, the sound [s] is pronounced [s̩] in spoken Castillian Spanish. Called the *apico dorsal fricative*, it is produced as an [s] with the tongue tip slightly curled toward the alveolar ridge. This sound is not used in singing, however.

You will also hear numerous variations of the consonants *p, t, k, b, d,* and *g* in syllable-final and word-final position. These variations are not only general dialectal patterns: even within a single dialectal region, an

Spanish

individual's pronunciation of these consonants may vary. The variations are numerous. For simplicity's sake, only the most common variations have been chosen to include in the text. A few examples are given below.

LL 6.2.66

	Variations
obtener	[op te ner]
	[o te ner]
	[oβ te ner]
	[ok te ner]
verdad	[beɾ ðɑt]
	[beɾ ðɑθ]
	[beɾ ðɑ]
	[beɾ ðɑð]

Spanish Vowels in Detail

The letter a

Always pronounce the letter *a* as [ɑ]. It is the same sound as the *a* in the English word *father*.

LL 6.3.01   Read aloud.

alma	[ɑl mɑ]
ala	[ɑ lɑ]
faltar	[fɑl tɑr]
mano	[mɑ no]
pasa	[pɑ sɑ]
rosa	[ro sɑ]

ay, ai

Pronounce the letter group *ay* or *ai* as the diphthong [ɑi].

LL 6.3.02   Read Aloud.

ay	[ɑi]
hay	[ɑi]
laico	[lɑi ko]
baile	[bɑi le]
Jaime	[xɑi me]
taita	[tɑi tɑ]

Note: This sound is similar to the diphthong in the English words *pie, sky*. Notice that in English your tongue closes toward the roof of your mouth as you pronounce the English [ɑɪ], gliding upward and toward the front. When you pronounce the Spanish [ɑi], glide faster and to a more closed position than in English.

LL 6.3.03   Compare and contrast:

English		Spanish	
eye	[aɪ]	hay	[ɑi]
knife	[naɪf]	naipe	[nɑi pe]
tight	[taɪt]	taita	[tɑi tɑ]

Remember that if the *i* has a written accent, it is no longer a glide and is pronounced as a separate syllable.

Spanish

LL 6.3.04

caí	[kɑ i]
maíz	[mɑ is]
Caín	[kɑ in]

au

Pronounce *au* as the diphthong [ɑu] similar to the diphthong in the English words *cow, house*. Notice that your jaw closes, gliding upward and backward. When you pronounce the Spanish diphthong, glide faster and farther to a more closed position than in English.

LL 6.3.05 Compare and contrast:

English		Spanish	
out	[aʊt]	auto	[ɑu to]
howl	[haʊl]	jaula	[xɑu lɑ]
couch	[kaʊtʃ]	caucho	[kɑu tʃo]
cow	[kaʊ]	causa	[kɑu sɑ]

LL 6.3.06 Read aloud:

pauta	[pɑu tɑ]
sauna	[sɑu nɑ]
caucho	[kɑu tʃo]
auto	[ɑu to]

The letter

e

Diphthong as you do in English. (For details on singing a pure [e], see "The Italian Vowels e and o" on page 64.)

LL 6.3.07 Compare and contrast:

English [eɪ]		Spanish [e]	
day	[deɪ]	de	[de]
May	[meɪ]	me	[me]
say	[seɪ]	sé	[se]
Kay	[keɪ]	que	[ke]
Fay	[feɪ]	fe	[fe]

LL 6.3.08 Read aloud:

eso	[e so]
era	[e ɾa]
ella	[e ʎa]

Spanish

pero	[pe ɾo]
dice	[di se]
nene	[ne ne]

ey, ei

Pronounce *ey* and *ei* as [ei]. This diphthong is somewhat similar to the English diphthong [eɪ]. As in other Spanish glides, you must raise your jaw faster and close it more than in English.

LL 6.3.09 Compare and contrast:

English [eɪ]		Spanish [ei]	
ray	[reɪ]	reina	[r̄ei na]
pay	[peɪ]	peine	[pei ne]

Note: *ey* only occurs in word-final position.

LL 6.3.10 Read aloud:

rey	[r̄ei]
ley	[lei]
reina	[r̄ei na]
peine	[pei ne]
treinta	[trein ta]
peinado	[pei na ðo]

Remember that if the *i* has a written accent, it is no longer a glide and is pronounced as a separate syllable.

LL 6.3.11

| reí | [r̄e i] |

eu

Pronounce the letter combination *eu* as the diphthong [eu]. Put your mouth in the position for [e]; then quickly glide to the position for [u], rounding your lips tightly. Note that this is not a common sound in Spanish.

LL 6.3.12 Read aloud:

| deudo | [deu ðo] |
| seudo | [seu ðo] |

Spanish

The letter i

Pronounce *i* as [i]. Be sure not to lengthen it; there is no glide, as there usually is in English.

LL 6.3.13   Compare and contrast:

English [iː]		Spanish [i]	
me	[miː]	mi	[mi]
tea	[tiː]	ti	[ti]
see	[siː]	si	[si]
bee	[biː]	vi	[bi]
key	[kiː]	qui	[ki]

LL 6.3.14   Read aloud:

informar	[in for mar]
ira	[i ra]
silla	[si ʎa]
comi	[ko mi]

ia, ie, io, iu

When *i* precedes another vowel pronounce it as the glide [j]. The two vowels form part of the same syllable. They are not separated into two syllables as they are in English.

LL 6.3.15   Compare and contrast:

English		Spanish	
piano	[pi ja no]	piano	[pja no]

Practice the following words. Keep the vowels in the same syllable.

LL 6.3.16

internacional	[in ter na sjo nal]
atención	[a ten sjon]
conferencia	[kon fe ren sja]
desperdicio	[des per ði sjo]
obsequio	[oβ se kjo]
embriaguez	[em brja ɣes]
fiar	[fjar]
piojo	[pjo xo]
criar	[krjar]
piedad	[pje ðað]

Spanish

Note: If an accent mark is written over an *i*, the *i* is no longer pronounced as a glide, and the two vowels are pronounced in separate syllables. (However, be sure not to insert a [j] sound between *í* and the following vowel.)

LL 6.3.17

río	[ri o]
desafío	[de sa fi o]
salía	[sa li a]
tenía	[te ni a]

LL 6.3.18 Read aloud:

odiar	[o ðjaɾ]
historia	[is to ɾja]
criada	[kɾja ða]
cianuro	[sja nu ɾo]
nadie	[na ðje]
diente	[djen te]
alguien	[al gjen]
fiesta	[fjes ta]
miope	[mjo pe]
tardío	[taɾ ði o]
fastidio	[fas ti ðjo]
mafioso	[ma fjo so]
ciudad	[sju ðað]
viuda	[bju ða]

The letter O

Pronounce *o* as [o]. Do not lengthen it or turn it into a diphthong.

LL 6.3.19 Compare and contrast:

English [oʊ]		Spanish [o]	
no	[noʊ]	no	[no]
cocoa	[ko koʊ]	coco	[ko ko]
dose	[doʊs]	dos	[dos]
low	[loʊ]	lo	[lo]

LL 6.3.20 Read aloud:

olla	[o ʎa]
ocaso	[o ka so]
paño	[pa ɲo]
niño	[ni ɲo]

Spanish

oy, oi

Pronounce the letter combination *oy* or *oi* as [oi]. This diphthong is similar to the English *oy* as in *toy, boy*. When you pronounce the Spanish, however, glide faster and close your jaw more.

Pronounce these similar words.

LL 6.3.21   Compare and contrast.

English [ɔi]		Spanish [oi]	
soy	[sɔɪ]	soy	[soi]
boy	[bɔɪ]	voy	[boi]
toy	[tɔɪ]	hoy	[oi]

LL 6.3.22   Read aloud:

voy	[boi]
hoy	[oi]
boina	[boi na]
coincidir	[koin si ðir]

Note: Remember that if an accent mark appears over the *i*, the two vowels are pronounced in separate syllables.

LL 6.3.23

egoísta	[e ɣo is ta]

The letter u

Pronounce *u* as [u]. Although this sound is similar to the vowel in the English word *food*, the English [u] is somewhat longer and is pronounced with a slight glide. When you pronounce the Spanish [u], make sure to keep it short.

LL 6.3.24   Compare and contrast:

English		Spanish	
too	[tu]	tú	[tu]
taboo	[tə bu]	tabú	[ta βu]
Sue	[su]	su	[su]

Notice that many English words that are spelled with a consonant + *u* are pronounced as the consonant + [ju], as in *cute, beautiful, few, mute*. Spanish words never add a [j] between a consonant and a *u*.

Spanish

LL 6.3.25 Compare and contrast:

English [ju]		Spanish [u]	
funeral	[fju nə rəl]	funeral	[fu ne ɾal]
bureaucracy	[bju ɑ krə sɪ]	burocracia	[bu ɾo kɾa sja]
music	[mju zɪk]	música	[mu si kɑ]
cube	[kjub]	cubo	[ku βo]
municipal	[mju nɪ sɪ pəl]	municipal	[mu ni si pal]
occupy	[ɑ kju paɪ]	ocupar	[o ku paɾ]

LL 6.3.26 Read aloud:

una	[u nɑ]
uva	[u βa]
puño	[pu ɲo]
ruta	[r̄u tɑ]

ua

Pronounce *ua* as [wa], *ue* as [we], and *uo* as [wo]. Put your lips and jaw in the position for [u], then quickly move to the position for the vowel that follows. which occurs only in a few words, and the *ui* are pronounced.

LL 6.3.27

suave	[swa βe]
usual	[u swal]
cuerda	[kwer ða]
puesta	[pwes tɑ]
cuota	[kwo tɑ]

ui, uy

Pronounce the combination *uy* or *ui* as [wi]. The first vowel is a glide; the second vowel forms the center of the syllable. When you pronounce this vowel combination, put your lips and jaw in the position for [u]; then quickly move to the position for [i].

LL 6.3.28 Read aloud.

muy	[mwi]
buitre	[bwi tɾe]
huir	[wiɾ]
cuita	[kwi tɑ]

Spanish

The letter

y

When *y* occurs as a single word (meaning *and*) followed by a word that begins with a consonant, pronounce the *y* as [i].

LL 6.3.29

¿Y tú?	[i tu]
cantar y bailar	[kan ta ɾi bai lar]

When *y* is followed by a vowel, pronounce it as [j]. When you pronounce this sound in Spanish, narrow the space between your tongue and the roof of your mouth so that the air hisses slightly.

LL 6.3.30 Read aloud.

yerro	[je r̄o]
yerno	[jeɾ no]
yerba	[jeɾ βa]
cayo	[kɑ jo]
yacer	[jɑ seɾ]
poyo	[po jo]
yaciente	[jɑ sjen te]
yugo	[ju ɣo]
yate	[jɑ te]
yute	[ju te]
yarda	[jaɾ ða]
yuglar	[ju ɣlaɾ]
yunto	[jun to]
yo	[jo]

Spanish Consonants in Detail

b

When *b* begins a word or syllable, it is pronounced [b]. This sound is similar to the English [b], but it is less plosive. However, when *b* occurs between vowels, pronounce it as [β]. This also applies to *b* between vowels in a breath phrase, even if that *b* is in syllable-initial position in a word. Also, remember that when following *s* or *r*, or when in syllable-final position, the Spanish *b* is pronounced as [β]. When b occurs before *r* or *l*, pronounce it as [β].

LL 6.4.01

buzo	[b]	syllable initial
mi buzo	[β]	no longer syllable initial; within the phrase, *b* occurs between vowels

Note: To pronounce [β], pronounce [b] with your lips slightly parted so that air flows through them.

Exercise: Decide how you would pronounce the *b*'s in the following phrases.

LL 6.4.02

mi buen abrigo
bueno y barato
baraja blanca
beso baboso
bulto blando

LL 6.4.03 Read aloud.

syllable initial	[b]	beso	[be so]
		bomba	[bom ba]
		bruto	[bru to]
		brisa	[bri sa]
		bebe	[be βe]
		bono	[bo no]
between vowels	[β]	rábano	[r̄a βa no]
		soñaba	[so ɲa βa]
		cantaba	[kan ta βa]
		hábil	[a βil]
		lobo	[lo βo]
following s	[β]	es bueno	[ez βwe no]
following r	[β]	perturbar	[per tur βar]

Spanish

syllable final	[β]	subjectivo	[suβ xe ti βo]
		obtener	[oβ te neɾ]
		obtuso	[oβ tu so]
before l	[β]	hablar	[a βlaɾ]
before r		sobra	[so βɾa]

C

Pronounce *c* before *a, o,* or *u* as [k].

LL 6.4.04

casar	[ka saɾ]
caña	[ka ɲa]
cama	[ka ma]
comer	[ko meɾ]
cosa	[ko sa]
cono	[ko no]
culto	[kul to]
cuñado	[ku ɲa ðo]
cumplir	[kum pliɾ]

In Latin American Spanish, pronounce *c* before *e* or *i* as [s].

LL 6.4.05

cerca	[seɾ ka]
cerdo	[seɾ ðo]
cera	[se ɾa]
cidra	[si ðɾa]
ciclo	[si klo]
cimar	[si maɾ]

In Castillian Spanish, pronounce *c* before *e* or *i* as [θ].

LL 6.4.06

cerca	[θeɾ ka]

Pronounce *cc* across syllables as [ks]. Remember that the Spanish [k] is not aspirated.

LL 6.4.07

acción	[ak sjon]
ficción	[fik sjon]
acceso	[ak se so]
occidente	[ok si ðen te]

Spanish

Pronounce *ch* as [tʃ]. This is the same sound found in the English word *church*.

LL 6.4.08

charla	[tʃar la]
achacar	[a tʃa kar]
chapo	[tʃa po]
cuchillo	[ku tʃi ʎo]

The Spanish [d] is dental; touch the back of your upper teeth when you pronounce it at the beginning of a syllable.

LL 6.4.09   Read aloud:

dar	[dar]
decir	[de sir]
decena	[de se na]
definir	[de fi nir]
don	[don]
domingo	[do miŋ go]
dulce	[dul se]
dormir	[dor mir]
doblar	[do βlar]
dolor	[do lor]

When *d* occurs between vowels, after *s* or *r*, or in syllable-final position, pronounce *d* as [ð]. When you pronounce this sound in English, as in the word *this*, notice that your tongue is between your teeth. When you pronounce this sound in Spanish, however, place the tip of your tongue on the edge of your upper teeth, but do not thrust it out. Remember that these rules also apply to *d*'s within phrases.

LL 6.4.10

[d]	[ð]
danza	la danza

It's especially important not to use [d] between vowels, because it's dental placement can make it sound like [r], and you will confuse words such as the following:

LL 6.4.11

modo	[mo ðo]	moro	[mo ro]
todo	[to ðo]	toro	[to ro]
mida	[mi ða]	mira	[mi ra]

Spanish

cada	[ka ða]	cara	[ka ɾa]
lodo	[lo ðo]	loro	[lo ɾo]

LL 6.4.12 Read aloud.

todo	[to ðo]
mitad	[mi tað]
poder	[po ðeɾ]
sed	[seð]
duda	[du ða]
red	[r̄eð]
madura	[ma ðu ɾa]
usted	[us teð]
adentro	[a ðen tɾo]
sud	[suð]

LL 6.4.13 Read aloud.

a donde	[a ðon de]
se va de aquí	[se βa ðe a ki]
una duda	[u na ðu ða]
cama doble	[ka ma ðo ble]
casa de arriendo	[ka sa ðe a r̄jen do]
mamá de Pedro	[ma ma ðe pe dɾo]
la droga	[la dɾo ɣa]
pega duro	[pe ɣa ðu ɾo]
Rosa duerme	[r̄o sa ðweɾ me]
Miria dice	[mi ɾja ði se]

LL 6.4.14 Read aloud.

syllable initial	[d]	denso	[den so]
		doctor	[dok toɾ]
		deporte	[de poɾ te]
between vowels	[ð]	dedo	[de ðo]
		pido	[pi ðo]
		adornar	[a ðoɾ naɾ]
following s	[ð]	desde	[dez ðe]
		desdén	[dez ðen]
following r	[ð]	verdad	[beɾ ðað]
syllable final	[ð]	salud	[sa luð]
		Madrid	[ma dɾið]
		virtud	[biɾ tuð]

f

The English and Spanish *f*'s are pronounced alike.

LL 6.4.15

forma	[for ma]
fango	[faŋ go]
fiel	[fjel]
función	[fun sjon]

g

The English and Spanish *g* are pronounced alike, except when the Spanish *g* occurs between vowels or before *e* or *i*: when between vowels, pronounce the Spanish *g* as [ɣ]; when before *e* or *i*, as [x]. Many English speakers pronounce the word *sugar* with this [ɣ].

LL 6.4.16

[g]		[ɣ]		[x]	
gota	[go ta]	la gota	[la ɣo ta]	gira	[xi ɾa]

LL 6.4.17 Read aloud.

before a, o, u	[g]	gamba	[gam ba]
		ganso	[gan so]
		galgo	[gal go]
		golpe	[gol pe]
		golfo	[gol fo]
		goma	[go ma]
		gusano	[gu sa no]
		gusto	[gus to]
		gutural	[gu tu ɾal]
before e, i	[x]	gelatina	[xe la ti na]
		gema	[xe ma]
		gemelo	[xe me lo]
		gimotear	[xi mo te aɾ]
		ingenio	[iŋ xe njo]
between vowels	[ɣ]	soga	[so ɣa]
		llaga	[ʎa ɣa]
		vago	[ba ɣo]
		daga	[da ɣa]
		saga	[sa ɣa]

Spanish

following s	[ɣ]	esgrima	[ez ɣri ma]
		desgastar	[dez ɣas tar]

LL 6.4.18 Read aloud.

juego	[xwe ɣo]
me gusta	[me ɣus ta]
no hago	[no a ɣo]
es gordo	[ez ɣor ðo]
es grande	[ez ɣran de]
desgracia	[dez ɣra sja]
una gota	[u na ɣo ta]
no me da la gana	[no me ða la ɣa na]

gua, gue, güe, gui, güi

When *gua* occurs at the beginning of a word or breath phrase, pronounce it as [gwa]; when it follows a vowel, pronounce it as [ɣwa].

LL 6.4.19

guayaba	[gwa ja βa]
fraguar	[fra ɣwar]
guarnir	[gwar nir]

When *gue* occurs at the beginning of a word or breath phrase, pronounce it as [ge]; when it follows a vowel, pronounce it as [ɣe].

LL 6.4.20

guerrero	[ge r̄e ro]
la guerra	[la ɣe r̄a]

When *güe* occurs at the beginning of a word or breath phrase, pronounce it as [gwe]; when it follows a vowel, pronounce it as [ɣwe].

LL 6.4.21

güepil	[gwe pil]
averigüe	[a βe ri ɣwe]

When *gui* occurs at the beginning of a word or breath phrase, pronounce it as [gi]; when it follows a vowel, pronounce it as [ɣi].

LL 6.4.22

guía	[gi a]
la guija	[la ɣi xa]

Spanish

When *güi* occurs at the beginning of a word or breath phrase, pronounce it as [gwi]; when it follows a vowel, pronounce it as [ɣwi].

h

The *h* in Spanish is silent.

LL 6.4.23

ahogar	[a o ɣaɾ]
haz	[as]
haya	[a ja]
harto	[aɾ to]

j

Pronounce the Spanish *j* as [x]. This sound, similar to the German ach-laut is also similar to the first sound in the English words *Hugh* and *Huron*. Put the back of your tongue near the velum (the soft palate). Feel the air hiss through the small opening.

LL 6.4.24 Read aloud.

justo	[xus to]
juvenil	[xu βe nil]
juzgar	[xuz ɣaɾ]
ajonjolí	[a xon xo li]
arrojar	[a r̄o xaɾ]
bajar	[ba xaɾ]
reja	[r̄e xa]
juego	[xwe ɣo]
jugar	[xu ɣaɾ]
juntar	[xun taɾ]
jóven	[xo βen]
jaula	[xau la]
adjustar	[a xus taɾ]
bajo	[ba xo]

k

The letter *k* only appears in words borrowed from other languages. It has the same basic sound as in English, but is unaspirated. (See "Lack of Aspiration in [p], [t], [k]" on page 313.)

LL 6.4.25

karate	[ka ɾa te]
kilograma	[ki lo gɾa ma]

Spanish

kiosco	[kjos ko]
kilómetro	[ki lo me tɾo]

1

Pronounce the letter *l* as [l], similar to the *l* in the English word *leap*. Keep the blade of your tongue flat; do not lower it. Do not use the English "dark" *l* as in the words hull, hill, fall.

LL 6.4.26   Compare and contrast:

English [ɫ]		Spanish [l]	
mill	[mɪɫ]	mil	[mil]
hill	[hɪɫ]	Gil	[xil]
tall	[tɔɫ]	tal	[tɑl]
call	[kɔɫ]	cal	[kɑl]
all	[ɔɫ]	al	[ɑl]
dell	[dɛɫ]	del	[del]
hotel	[hoʊ tɛɫ]	hotel	[o tel]
mall	[mɔɫ]	mal	[mɑl]

LL 6.4.27   Read aloud.

lava	[lɑ βɑ]
lección	[lek sjon]
multa	[mul tɑ]
soltana	[sol tɑ nɑ]
vil	[bil]
febril	[fe βɾil]

ll

The letter combination *ll* is pronounced in several ways throughout the Spanish-speaking world. The two most acceptable variations are [ʎ] and [j]. The [ʎ] is similar to the pronunciation of the *ll* in the English word *million* (see details on page 316); the [j] is just as widespread, especially in Latin America, and is the sound of the English *y* in the word *yes*.

LL 6.4.28   Read aloud.

valle	[bɑ ʎe]
llamaba	[ʎɑ mɑ βɑ]
callar	[kɑ ʎɑɾ]
llama	[ʎɑ mɑ]
allí	[ɑ ʎi]

fallo	[fa ʎo]
malla	[ma ʎa]
pollo	[po ʎo]
llano	[ʎa no]
llevar	[ʎe βaɾ]
hallar	[a ʎaɾ]
llave	[ʎa βe]
bolsillo	[bol si ʎo]
llamar	[ʎa maɾ]

m

The Spanish *m* is the same as in English.

LL 6.4.29

misa	[mi sa]
amar	[a maɾ]

n

The *n* in most positions is the same as the English *n*, and causes no problems. However, when the *n* occurs before a *bilabial* sound [b], [p], [m], it becomes bilabial like that sound. And when it occurs before a *velar* sound [k], [g], [x], it becomes velar like that sound.

LL 6.4.30

syllable initial	[n]	nudo	[nu ðo]
		inato	[i na to]
before [m],[b],[p]	[m:]	inmutar	[i m:u taɾ]
		un beso	[um: be so]
before [k]	[ŋ]	incautar	[iŋ kau taɾ]
		inclinar	[iŋ kli naɾ]
before g	[ŋ]	inglés	[iŋ gles]
		ingenio	[iŋ xe njo]

Exercise: How would you pronounce the *n*'s in the following words and phrases?

LL 6.4.31

inmejorable
incautar
incantador
comen mejor
denle

Spanish

comen pan
conmemoración
conmigo
contento
toman vino

ñ

Pronounce the Spanish *ñ* as [ɲ], called *enya*. This sound is similar to the *ny* in the English word *canyon*.

LL 6.4.32   Read aloud:

niño	[ni ɲo]
puño	[pu ɲo]
ñapa	[ɲɑ pɑ]
paño	[pɑ ɲo]
reñir	[r̃e ɲir]
baño	[bɑ ɲo]

p

The Spanish *p* is pronounced the same as the English *p* in the words *spill, speak, spank*. There is no aspiration, regardless of where the *p* occurs.

LL 6.4.33   Read aloud:

English [p]	Spanish [p]
paper	papel
Paul	Paul
pessimism	pesimismo

LL 6.4.34   Read aloud:

pena	[pe nɑ]
apelar	[ɑ pe lɑr]
óptimo	[op ti mo]
aptitud	[ɑp ti tuð]

q

The Spanish *q* appears in the letter combination *qu*, which is always pronounced [k]. In Spanish, *qu* only precedes *e* or *i*.

Note: Remember that the Spanish [k] is not aspirated. See "Lack of Aspiration of [p], [t], [k]" on page 313.

Spanish

LL 6.4.35   Read aloud:

que	[ke]
quebrar	[ke βɾaɾ]
quejar	[ke xaɾ]
quechua	[ke tʃwa]
quicio	[ki sjo]
quiebra	[kje βɾa]
quien	[kjen]

Spanish has two *r* sounds. The first sound, ɾ, is called a *flipped r*. When you pronounce it, flip the tip of your tongue against your alveolar ridge once. The sound is similar to the English *t* or *d* between vowels, as in the words *Betty, city, reader, feeder*. Notice that this sound is always spelled with a single *r*.

The second *r* sound, [r̄], is called *trilled r*. There is no comparable sound in English. When you pronounce it, flip the tip of your tongue against your alveolar ridge several times. Notice that this trilled *r* can be spelled either with a single *r* or a double *rr*, depending on the position in the word.

LL 6.4.36

word initial	[r̄]	religión	[r̄e li xjon]
		remo	[r̄e mo]
		rito	[r̄i to]
		resulta	[r̄e sul ta]
syllable initial	[ɾ]	pared	[pa ɾed]
		mira	[mi ɾa]
		virar	[bi ɾaɾ]
		orar	[o ɾaɾ]
		pájaro	[pa xa ɾo]
syllable final	[ɾ] or [r̄]	subir	[su βiɾ]
		teñir	[te ɲiɾ]
		venir	[be niɾ]
		hablar	[a βlaɾ]
after n, s	[r̄]	enredar	[en r̄e ðaɾ]
		Israel	[is r̄a el]
rr	[r̄]	barra	[ba r̄a]
		hierro	[je r̄o]

r

Spanish

348

		cierro	[sje r̄o]
		enterrar	[en te r̄ar]

Exercise: Decide how to pronounce the *r*'s in the following words. Are they flipped *r*'s, trilled *r*'s, or either?

LL 6.4.37

ce__rr__ado
toma__r__
sub__r__ayar
ot__r__o
__r__oto
__r__oba__r__
en__r__oja__r__
en__r__iquece__r__
al__r__ededo__r__
b__r__isa

LL 6.4.38   Contrast the two r's.

[ɾ]		[r̄]	
pero	[pe ɾo]	perro	[pe r̄o]
caro	[ka ɾo]	carro	[ka r̄o]
vara	[ba ɾa]	barro	[ba r̄o]
cero	[se ɾo]	cerro	[se r̄o]
fiero	[fje ɾo]	fierro	[fje r̄o]
amara	[a ma ɾa]	amarra	[a ma r̄a]

Do not confuse *t* and *d* between vowels with [ɾ]. Compare the following pairs of words. They are *not* pronounced alike.

LL 6.4.39

todo	[to ðo]	toro	[to ɾo]
cada	[ka ða]	cara	[ka ɾa]
moto	[mo to]	moro	[mo ɾo]
meta	[me ta]	mera	[me ɾa]
mida	[mi ða]	mira	[mi ɾa]
seda	[se ða]	cera	[se ɾa]

S

The *s* and the *z* in Latin American Spanish and English are pronounced in the same way; the only problem you might have is in deciding which to pronounce in which position.

LL 6.4.40

syllable initial	[s]	sin	[sin]
		sobar	[so βar]
		sur	[sur]
syllable final	[s]	casas	[ka sas]
		asfaltar	[as faltar]
between vowels	[s]	caso	[ka so]
		piso	[pi so]
before voiced consonants	[z]	esbirro	[ez βi r̄o]
		rasgar	[r̄az ɣar]
		desbocar	[dez βo kar]
		isla	[iz la]

Note: In spoken Spanish, *s* is pronounced in different ways depending on the dialect (see page 327). All plurals are pronounced [s]; plurals never have a [z] sound as they do after voiced sounds in English (*boys, chairs, doors*). In singing, however, follow the rules presented above.

Exercise: Decide how to pronounce the *s*'s in the following words or phrases.

LL 6.4.41

mesclar
disgusto
es de
esposo
las vacas
los niños
es mío
está
tienes pecas
tienes becas

LL 6.4.42   Compare and contrast.

[z]	[s]
English	Spanish
president	presidente
present	presente
visit	visitar
rose	rosa
museum	museo

Spanish

t

Pronounce *t* as a dental [t]. To articulate this sound, put the tip of your tongue against the back of your upper teeth. It is never aspirated, as it is before a stressed vowel in English.

LL 6.4.43

ten	[ten]
tinta	[tin ta]
taza	[ta sa]
Atlántico	[at lan ti ko]
ritmo	[rit mo]

LL 6.4.44   Compare and contrast.

[t]	[t]
English	Spanish
two	tu
tea	ti
tan	tan
tuna	tuna
tall	tal

v

The letter *v* follows the same rules as the letter *b*. There is no difference in pronunciation between the two. (You may hear speakers using the [v] for reasons of social prestige, but they are not consistent and the use is confined to a few common words.) The words *tuvo* and *tubo* are pronounced alike. (See the discussion for the letter *b*, page 337.)

LL 6.4.45

syllable initial	[b]	verde	[ber ðe]
		verificar	[be ri fi kar]
following s	[β]	desvanecer	[dez βa ne ser]
following r	[β]	intervalo	[in ter βa lo]
between vowels	[β]	vive	[bi βe]
		cavar	[ka βar]
		la vaina	[la βai na]

w

The letter *w* does not belong to the Spanish alphabet. It occurs only in a few borrowed words. When this letter does appear, it is pronounced the same as the English *w*.

Spanish

LL 6.4.46

| syllable initial | [w] | whisky | [wis ki] |

X

When *x* begins a word, it is usually pronounced [s].

LL 6.4.47

| xenofobia | [se no fo βja] |

When *x* begins a syllable, it is pronounced [ks].

LL 6.4.48

| próximo | [pɾok si mo] |

When *x* ends a syllable (that is, precedes a consonant), it is pronounced [s].

LL 6.4.49

| exquisito | [es ki si to] |

In words of Indian or Central American origin, *x* is pronounced [x].

LL 6.4.50

| México | [me xi ko] |

Note: The sound [x] is often spelled with a *j*, as in the spelling *Méjico*.

Z

The pronunciation of *z* is the feature that most clearly distinguishes the Castillian and Latin American dialects. When singing songs from Spain, use the sound [θ], which is the same as the English *th* in the words *thin, think, thank*. When singing Latin American songs, use the same rules for the letter *s*.

LL 6.4.51

Latin American				Castillian		
syllable initial	[s]	zambuco	[sam bu ko]	[θ]	[θam bu ko]
	[s]	zarzuela	[sar swe la]	[θ]	[θar θwe la]
syllable final	[s]	paz	[pas]	[θ]	[paθ]
	[s]	haz	[as]	[θ]	[aθ]
before a voiced consonant	[z]	paz de	[paz ðe]	[θ]	[paθ ðe]
	[z]	juzgar	[xuz ɣar]	[θ]	[xuθ ɣar]

Exercise: Decide how to pronounce the following *z*'s in both the Latin American and Castillian dialects.

Spanish

352

LL 6.4.52

chor<u>i</u>zo
pla<u>z</u>uela
ra<u>z</u>ón
<u>a</u>zul
influen<u>z</u>a
a<u>z</u>úcar
cerve<u>z</u>a
<u>z</u>abullir
<u>z</u>alamería
re<u>z</u>no

For more information on Castillian Spanish, see "Dialectal Variations" on page 327.